Conceiving of Personality

Yale University Press New Haven and London

Conceiving of Personality

Michael Robbins, M.D.

/II

Designed by Rebecca Gibb.
Set in Joanna type by The Composing Room of Michigan, Inc., Grand Rapids, Michigan.
Printed in the United States of America by Vail-Ballou Press. Binghamton, New York.

Library of Congress Cataloging-in-Publication Data
Robbins, Michael, M.D.
Conceiving of personality / Michael Robbins.
p.   cm.
Includes bibliographical references and index.
ISBN 0-300-06422-5 (alk. paper)
1. Personality.   2. Psychoanalysis.   3. Ethnopsychology.
4. Psychology and philosophy.   I. Title.
BF698.R854   1996
155.2—dc20   95-47043
                                                          CIP

A catalogue record for this book is available from the
British Library.

The paper in this book meets the guidelines for permanence and durability of the Committee on Production Guidelines for Book Longevity of the Council on Library Resources.

10 9 8 7 6 5 4 3 2 1

To the personalities in my life—conceivable and inconceivable—
who presented the challenge that stimulated me to write this book.
And particularly to Barbara and to Seb for the support that
enabled me to complete it.

Contents

Preface

Writing a book is a personal odyssey. I start off believing that I know my destination and can interpret the landmarks that will inform me of my progress. In the course of the journey, I am periodically shocked to discover that I am disoriented, either so lost that I need to re-organize and re-interpret my map and landmarks, or else headed toward a place I never dreamed of. My ultimate destination never fails to surprise me.

As Odysseus attempted to steer a course between Scylla and Charybdis, in the pages to come I will attempt to navigate between the modern or positivist certainty that there is an essence of personality which, if not already discovered, is at least there for the taking, and the postmodern relativism, subjectivism, and contextualism which in its extreme form maintains that any conception of personality is at best an evanescent contrivance and at worst an illusion.

Like that of so many others, my decision to become a psychoanalyst was motivated in large measure by a wish to understand more about the idiosyncrasies of my own personality and those of others who have been profoundly influential in my life. Through that curious combination of fortuitous circumstance and intentionality that governs most of our lives, my professional interest gravitated toward the relationship of psychoanalysis to more seriously disturbed persons—the group I call primitive personalities, subsuming borderline, narcissistic, paranoid, and schizoid, as well as persons diagnosed as schizophrenic. While my belief in the universal importance of some of the broad principles and beliefs on which psychoanalysis is predicated has remained unshaken in the course of these endeavors, I have become increasingly skeptical that the model (others might say models) on which psychoanalysis continues to rely is adequate to account for the personalities of these more seriously disturbed individuals, or that the assumption on which psychoanalysis seems to be based, that all minds and personalities are configured in qualitatively similar ways, is valid. Out of the ashes of my disappointment arose my conceptual phoenix, a pluralistic dialectical approach to personality which I began to formulate in my 1993 book on schizophrenia and which is further elaborated in these pages.

As I became increasingly aware of the diversity of personality within our culture and of the difficulty of representing it adequately on a single continuum of quantitative variation, I also began to realize that this was but one dimension on which personality has been inadequately appreciated and conceptualized. Some of the others include culture, gender, and history itself. It has been chastening to realize how narrow my own perspective has been: that of a relatively normal Caucasian male, immersed in the Western culture of the late twentieth century, particularly its scientific and philosophical conceptual systems. I am reassured to discover that I have plenty of company in this limited way of conceiving, for most persons who have studied personality are themselves embedded in monothetic belief systems, ideologies, or indigenous psychologies based on particulars of their own historical period, cultural origin, gender, personality configuration within the culture, and scientific predilection.

As I pursued my research into some of the relevant fields and literature, I experienced another jolt: my personal change in viewpoint is but a scintilla of a larger intellectual metamorphosis involving many fields—philosophy (postmodernism), history and sociology of people's changing relationship to the world, anthropology of cultural relativism and indigenous psychology, psychology, and psychoanalysis of the hermeneutic, intersubjectively, and socially constructed world, and feminist studies of intersubjectivity, which bridge several of these fields. Many scholars are turning away from a world conceived with a single model and comprised of fixed, objectively knowable fact, truth, and certainty and embracing—at times too enthusiastically, in my opinion—the uncertainty of more relativistic, subjectivistic, and intersubjectivistic, pluralistic, deconstructible conceptions. Perhaps it is a relief to discard the burden of trying to prove one is right and knows it all, and from the vantage point of unprovable relativism simply to critique and deconstruct others' positions. But the "old" modernist and logical positivist school is by no means dead, though it has fewer confirmed disciples than it once had. It flourishes in such areas as the neuroscience of personality with as much vigor, rectitude, and certainty as ever.

From the chastening realization that scholars from a variety of backgrounds and perspectives had encountered common problems, raised similar basic questions, and proposed similar answers came my decision to try to bring together findings and questions from several of these fields, including my own investigations into the intracultural variability of personality (more seriously disturbed personalities), as a single monograph devoted to the problem of conceiving of personality.

The questions I explore in the book include: Is personality phenomenal or epiphenomenal; that is, are we really "more" than the neuro-organic elements to which some scientists feel able to reduce us? On the other hand, in this postmodernist relativistic world in which we live, is constitution an important determinant of personality at all? Are all human beings substantively or qualitatively similar in personality—that is, variable in degree but not in kind along a linear spectrum of normality / deviance—or are there important qualitative differences related to the dimensions of gender, culture, time in history, or intracultural variability? Is any existing psychological theory, particularly the basic theory of psychoanalysis, adequate to comprehend the diversity of personality? Is it possible to develop a single comprehensive theory of personality? Does the concept of normal personality lead or mislead us? Are the gendered aspects of personality products of constitutional differences, cultural influences, or both? How are the personality and cultural background of the theorist of personality related to his or her conceptions? Can we reconcile the notion of personality as a universal essence to be discovered and objectified with the idea of personality as a relativistic social and interpersonal creation?

The book is intended for those whose interest transcends a particular field, whether it is philosophy, history, sociology, political science, the psychologies, gender studies, psychoanalysis, cultural anthropology, or psychological anthropology. As I am a psychoanalyst by trade, I have had to try to educate myself to write creatively about several major fields of knowledge outside my own. Experts from these fields will doubtless perceive deficiencies in my presentation. I can but hope that readers will be able to look beyond these limitations and consider the broader possibility of a collaborative integration of viewpoints that might lead to the creation of a new conception of personality that is more than the sum of its parts.

Conceiving of Personality

CHAPTER 1

Introduction

The enigma of personality, the universal and the idiosyncratic elements that constitute ourselves, the significant people in our daily lives, or those we know only through the media, history, and literature, is an endless source of fascination and curiosity. Sometimes we are convinced we understand ourselves or those with whom we interact, but often we are baffled. Strangers may seem even more incomprehensible—for example, a medieval monk, a member of a fanatical cult, a person from another culture ("the inscrutable Oriental"), a schizophrenic street person, or, closer to home, someone of the other sex who infatuates us, or even our own children.

We all develop commonsensical notions about ourselves and about people in the aggregate, which we cherish and hold tenaciously—for example, the Western concept of the rugged male individualist, man against the cosmos, hyperbolically depicted in motion pictures, both the older Westerns and the more recent superhero genre. We are hardly aware of the narrow and idiosyncratic base from which these stereotypes are derived or of the self-deception we practice when employing them. Our perspectives are unwittingly egocentric, gender-centric, ethnocentric, and history-bound.

It is relatively easy to label historical beliefs about personality, or contemporary ones emanating from another culture, as examples of religious super-stition or folklore and to attempt to transcend such prejudices and biases through what we imagine to be more formalized intellectual studies of per-sonality based on the human sciences. But these, in turn, introduce new ideological elements that are in some respects more insidious, as they acquire the legitimacy afforded to what is current and popular. In the era of modern-ism and logical positivism, from which we may be emerging, it has been generally accepted that all minds and personalities are intrinsically and quali-tatively similar, that the universal truths and realities about personality are "out there" as facts to be discovered with our objectifying minds and tech-niques, and that traditional science and its methodology, and a particular human science, whether it be currently fashionable neuroscience or formerly in-vogue psychoanalysis, is sufficient to do the job. We tend to forget or to minimize the significance of the fact that the particular scientific disciplines on which we rely are part of a Western cultural phenomenon only about three centuries old and that personality has been conceived of as a subject of inquiry within the sciences for only about a century.

The quest for knowledge about the self or person seems complex enough if one believes in the existence of an absolute reality or fact "out there" and in universals that transcend time, culture, and particular intracultural niche, and if one has faith in the potential of reason and empirical scientific methodology, employed with patience and perseverance, to establish consensual certainty about these things. There is still the seemingly endless debate about precisely which view of the way things are might ultimately prove to be the correct one. But suppose we begin to question the basis for our confidence in the scientific viewpoint itself and the human personalities that employ it. Daily, with the wisdom of hindsight, we dismiss beliefs that our forbears, just as intelligent as ourselves, held to just as tenaciously as we now hold to our convictions; we marvel in astonishment at how these erroneous products of flawed perception and reasoning could ever have been promulgated to the naive and gullible masses. With a smug sense of superiority, we invoke the concept of progress and agree that, because knowledge is cumulative and we learn from past mistakes, we have finally found the right answers—or, at least, that we will soon do so.

Moreover, who could possibly obtain an adequate sample of the extraor-dinary range of human diversity among the variety of the world's cultures, within any particular culture, with regard to gender, and over the temporal course of human history? Considering such breadth, one cannot help but question the adequacy of any conceptual schema or system. And this is to say nothing of the personality of the systematizer or conceiver—the mind through which the system evolves. Every theory of personality bears the imprint of its conceivers. Not only is it the construct of a mind or minds, but these minds have a place in history, culture, and society; they are gendered, and they possess idiosyncratic qualities as they represent or deviate from a cultural norm.

Currently popular systems are colored by the ways of perceiving and thinking characteristic of more or less modal or average Caucasian males in twentieth-century Western culture. For this reason, Heelas and Lock (1981) refer to all theories of personality, whether modestly folkloric or pretentiously "scientific," as indigenous psychologies. Indigenous psychologies are rich in specific content and meaning but limited in scope. Unfortunately, disciples of a particular indigenous psychology tend to generalize it ideologically to all humankind and to employ subtle and not so subtle forms of nullification or devaluation of the diversity they cannot otherwise encompass. Unless we can maintain a skeptical relativistic and subjectivistic perspective, the unconscious generalization that usually accompanies subscription to an indigenous psychology leads us directly to the realm of illusion.

But doubt itself, at least particular kinds of doubt, can also be relativistic to a particular time and place, and the doubts I have expressed about the accuracy and sufficiency our existing models of personality are part of a larger shift in epistemological questioning characteristic of many areas of contemporary thinking. Not surprisingly, these are most broadly embraced philosophically in the transition from modernism, as reflected in the doctrine of logical positivism, which until the mid-1980s has undergirded the scientific enterprise with the belief that it possesses the means and the potential to discover the ultimate nature of objective reality, to postmodernism, which makes subjectivity, relativism, and discourse in the construction and deconstruction not of truth, but of meaning (Foucault, 1973, 1979, 1980; Heidegger, 1962; Derrida, 1967, 1978, 1981), into an equivalent system of belief. This shift in thinking and conceiving is reflected in almost every discipline, from political science, historiography and sociology (Mumford, 1956; Nisbet, 1969; Cahoone, 1988; MacIntyre, 1984, 1988; Sandel, 1982); to the natural sciences (relativity and indeterminacy in physics, see Bohr, 1937; Heisenberg, 1958; systems theory in biology, see von Bertalanffy, 1968; Weiss, 1967, 1969, 1977); to mathematics (chaos or complexity theory, see Gleick, 1987); to anthropology or cultural psychology (the universalist-relativist debate; see Heelas and Lock, 1981; Geertz, 1975, 1979; Shweder, 1991); to psychology (Vygotsky, 1978; Luria, 1976; Sampson, 1985, 1988, 1989; Harre, 1981, 1984; Gergen, 1985, 1990, 1991); to gender studies of intersubjectivity (Chodorow, 1978, 1980; Miller, 1976; Keller, 1985; Gilligan, 1982; Benjamin, 1988); and even to psychoanalysis (Lacanians; the interpersonal school, see Sullivan, 1953; Levenson, 1991; the hermeneutic movement, see Schafer, 1976; post-Kohutian intersubjectivists, see Stolorow and Atwood, 1992; social constructivists, see Hoffman, 1983). Science itself is turned on its head by the awareness of the critical roles in perception and cognition played by subjectivity, intersubjectivity (Keller, 1985), indeterminacy, and relativity (Heisenberg, 1958). Suddenly our ways of conceiving of self are fraught with uncertainty. The theory and its creator are in some respects indistinguishable (Popper, 1959, 1987; Kuhn, 1962). As Bruner puts it, "Both science and the humanities have come to be appreciated as artful figments of men's minds, as creations produced by different uses of mind" (1986, p. 44).

Intellectually salutary as it may ultimately be, the postmodern crisis of belief involving disillusionment with concepts of truth, reality, and universality, and the realization of the relativity, perspectivism, indeterminacy, contextuality, subjectivity, and intersubjectivity of our personalities and ways of thinking, has the potential to create new belief systems based on a nihilistic eclecticism and intellectual anarchy. In this religion we are condemned to wander forever in a purgatory of pragmatic gloom. In this ever-shifting narrative cloud of perceived, created, deconstructed, and dissolved meanings and understandings, one idea or system is no better than another except as it might serve dialectically to highlight meanings and problems of the first, thus providing what at that evanescent moment might appear to be a more effective tool. Is there no solidity to rest on? If by virtue of nothing else than our common range of neurobiological inheritance it would appear that there must be something we can turn to and model that is universal.

This book is my attempt to reconcile these seeming polarities of epistemology and conception and to bring psychoanalysis and its associated human sciences more into the mainstream of contemporary intellectual thought. It continues a project I began in a 1993 book on schizophrenia, which took into consideration some of the problems I have outlined, and extends it into a different paradigm for conceiving of personality.

What do I mean by personality, and how do I propose that we go about attempting to conceive of it? The dictionary defines the concept in two ways: as a more or less coherent array of characteristics, traits, or behaviors; and as the quality or state of being a person. It is notable that these definitions, which predate the controversies to which I just alluded, presage the dialectic between objectivity and external reality, and subjectivity and meaning, which occupies many of the pages to come. The first definition leads to efforts to assess or measure what we think of as character. The second definition, which I use as a guide to my inquiry, is more internal and cognizant of the person as subject. It directs our attention to such things as meaning, feeling, and value and their organization into an entity known as self or identity. In either instance, the objectifying of personality as an "it" is in itself a distortion, for this epistemological stance is part of a uniquely Western mode of thinking.

If we assume that subjectivity is the basis of our being and that personality, defined as the meaningful organization and functions of subjectivity, is a concept worthy of study, in what province does that study rightfully belong? I cannot help but share, albeit with some trepidation, the general Western belief that the human sciences provide the most useful conceptual tools for the task. These are equivocal tools, however, for, secure as they may make us feel, the Western human sciences are nothing more than indigenous psychologies (Heelas and Lock, 1981), resting, as we shall see, on philosophically shaky ground.

But this is not the only problem in the effort to conceive of personality. There are several human sciences; is there, then, a "right" and a "wrong" science of personality? If not, can we meaningfully integrate findings from the various scientific disciplines, or must it suffice to make a catalog of ideas from all of them? To begin with, I shall outline the viewpoints of the various human sciences to which I shall return throughout the book. Since the sciences themselves participate in turf disputes over who holds domain over such entities as personality, I shall examine the problems that arise when one attempts to choose a particular scientific viewpoint and tries to coordinate the theories and findings of the various sciences.

From the neurosciences I have drawn upon findings about constitutional differences, particularly those related to gender, to temperament, and to certain pathological conditions.

I have chosen psychoanalysis as the primary viewing point for the study of personality because its focus best fits the internal definition of personality based on meaning, feeling, values, and their organization in a more or less stable and enduring (structured) dynamic system. LeVine says, "psychoanalysis . . . is the only extant psychology that is concerned with the psychological organization of the individual and therefore generates the only theoretical models of personality as a system." In chapters to come, as I examine personality from the vantage point of culture, we may question whether this is so. From a narrower Western cultural perspective, LeVine goes on to write that "American academic psychologists . . . [in contrast] have adopted the position of specialized empirical investigators of response patterns within narrowly defined psychological domains" (1981, p. 63).

Piaget's cognitive psychology is the major alternative psychological system for conceiving of personality. Piaget focussed on normal cognition, a subject psychoanalysis has little to say about beyond such relatively empty generalities as sublimation and ego autonomy, but he hardly alluded to feelings, wishes, and self-deception, subjects Freud focussed on. The fact that Piaget did not consider individual idiosyncrasies, including psychopathology, affect, or interpersonal relationships, makes his theory too specialized and incomplete to deal with either the complexity or the diversity of personality. But Piaget's system is by no means incompatible with classical psychoanalytic theory. And Piaget was the first to introduce a hierarchical systems model into psychology; for this reason his work is of critical importance in relation to the line of thinking I pursue in chapters 13 and 14.

It might seem commonsensical to assume that such organizing concepts as person or self are central to any respectable theoretical model of human psychology, but for psychoanalysis such an idea is of very recent (post–World War II) and probably provincial (Anglo-American) origin. Freud's use of nineteenth-century physics and biology as the model for his youthful discipline accounts for the traditional conceptual preoccupation of psychoanalysis not with people so much as with deconstructive, atomistic analyses of them into mechanical and energic parts.

Important precursors of integrative personality constructs may be found in the work of Hartmann (1950), Fairbairn (1952), Spiegal (1959), Lichtenstein (1961, 1963), and Jacobson (1964). Hartmann was perhaps the first to introduce the term *self* into psychoanalysis; he used it to denote mental representations of the "whole person" as distinct from the "object," a usage Jacobson echoed in her 1964 book *The Self and the Object World*. Fairbairn and Lichtenstein employed the term in a more functional and structural sense, the former to designate the primal dynamic object-seeking and reality-testing unit, the latter to denote idiosyncratic "identity themes" around which individual lives are organized. But it is the relatively recent influence of Winnicott (1958) and Kohut (1971, 1977) that has been decisive in moving psychoanalysis in a more humanistic, person-oriented direction.

Perhaps it is because the personality constructs of contemporary psychoanalytic theory are embryonic that they are limited. Judging from such respected glossaries of psychoanalytic terms as *The Language of Psychoanalysis*, by LaPlanche and Pontalis (1973), and *Psychoanalytic Terms and Concepts*, edited by Moore and Fine (1990) and co-published by the American Psychoanalytic Association, personality is not even formally recognized. Psychoanalysis seems to prefer the concept of character, which the latter publication defines as enduring or habitual patterns of thinking, feeling, and functioning. I prefer not to quibble about definition and assume that the major corpus of psychoanalysis in fact comprises one or more theories of personality.

While research findings from experimental psychology are alluded to throughout the book, particularly in the discussion of gender in chapter 9, other psychological viewpoints on personality, such as behaviorism and psychometrics, are not considered here because they relate to the definition I have chosen not to pursue: that personality is a collection of externally observed characteristics, traits, or behaviors, arranged in linear causal patterns.

I turn rather to the social psychologies of interpersonal and group behavior and to anthropology for analyses and comparisons of personality in different cultures and analysis of the range of personality variation within our own culture. The viewpoints of anthropology, particularly of cultural, primate, and psychological anthropology, are particularly important, though there is a lively debate among anthropologists as to whether the field is truly a separate discipline. Some of its methodology of controlled field observation, interviewing, and experimentation derives from psychology, and some of its selection of data and mode of organizing them is derived from psychoanalysis, a complication explored in chapter 7.

Conceiving of personality involves other problems, including one that is unique: can an entity comprehend its very essence? Can subjectivity be simultaneously the reliable instrument of knowing and the object of knowledge? No doubt the capacity for self-assessment for centrality and deviance is built into the functioning of every vital system because it is essential for the maintenance of homeostasis. But assessing whether and even how some of us are deviant from others is not the same as understanding our basic nature. Human beings are also capable of recognizing the existence of other entities like themselves and hence to study "them" as objects. The neutral position that we can never see ourselves accurately or know for certain just how similar the experience of another human being is to our own is difficult to maintain. We naturally tend to assume, through processes variously referred to as empathic or projective, that the personalities of others are basically very similar to what we conceive to be our own and tend to dismiss those who appear strange, alien, or distant as subhuman—lesser or deviant versions of ourselves.

Even if we put aside the conundrum of whether personality can conceive of itself, we are left with more concrete problems involving the relationship of personality theories to the personalities of their conceivers and to the particular personalities of those they have chosen to study. Most human science theories, especially psychoanalysis, have been abstracted not simply from Western culture but from more or less modal members of that culture. In the instance of psychoanalysis, these modal members are those Horney felicitously referred to as "the neurotic personality of our time" (1937). More specifically, there is the question of to what extent a given theory is simply a projection of the personality idiosyncrasies of its conceiver. These subjects are discussed in chapters 2 and 10.

Chapter 3 consists of a historical review of conceptions of personality, particularly in Western culture, and places psychoanalysis in the context of nineteenth-century European thought. Chapter 4 is a discussion of monistic thinking and models, and the modal constructs that center them. In the human sciences, as I have noted, this takes the form of a no-holds-barred competitive struggle among sciences which might better pool their knowledge of personality. Chapter 5 explores the idea that there are qualitative differences in personality organization that evolve from constitutional differences in central nervous system organization.

Chapter 6, a review of findings about the diversity of personality across cultures and its possible implications, is the first of five chapters that explore the limitation of psychoanalysis as monistic theory. This cultural context sets the stage for chapter 7, which is devoted to limitations of psychoanalysis as an expression of Western culture. Chapter 8 contrasts it with Buddhism, an Eastern counterpart. In chapter 9, I examine the gendered aspect of personality, including the probability that core gender-related differences in identity are constitutionally determined. Although it is generally accepted that culture is a critical determinant of the gendered aspects of personality, I suggest that gendered differences may also serve as substrate for some of the personality differences related to culture. Chapter 10, which examines the spectrum of variability within Western culture from modal personality to the various psychopathologies, raises questions about psychoanalysis' attempt to comprehend them within a single model of personality. Chapter 11 concludes the discussion of monistic thinking in psychoanalysis with an exploration of the psychoanalytic movement and the ideological force that perpetuates it.

In chapter 12 I abstract some common themes from the preceding discussions, particularly the debate between postmodern proponents of theoretical relativism and pluralism, on the one hand, and more traditional universalistic or monistic thinkers, on the other. In the concluding chapters, 13 and 14, I attempt to abstract fundamental principles of a monistic psychoanalytic psychology of personality which might serve as a structural framework for the various dimensions of diversity described in the book, to distinguish such a theory from the multiplicity of particularistic, time- and culture-relative, content-rich indigenous psychologies that might be framed by it, and to outline the conceptual dialectic that needs to occur between them.

CHAPTER 2

Can We Conceive of Ourselves? Three Instances
of Theoretical Conversion

The Omphalopsychites were a medieval group of mystics whose practice involved contemplation of their navels (omphalos), an activity they believed facilitated access to their souls (psyche). Can a human personality comprehend the essence of personality, or even theorize meaningfully about it, or are our efforts more likely to be expressions of our personalities than conceptions of them? Kant (1781) introduced the idea of dual self-consciousness. Remarking on the transcendental role of mind (subjectivity) in constituting the world, he noted the paradox that the subjective mind can make subjectivity itself the object of study. Wittgenstein (1980) noted the contradiction inherent in this position, and Foucault (1973) named the paradox the empirico-transcendental doublet of modern thought. Foucault defined the episteme as the groundwork of knowing and then proceeded to observe that what is unique about our episteme is the idea of a thinkable thought. From this bit of circular reasoning he concluded that one can never know the episteme in which one lives. Because the human sciences "treat as their object what is in fact their condition of possibility" (p. 364), he asserted, they are "warped and twisted forms of reflection" (p. 343).

In a more general context, Kuhn (1962) and Feyerabend (1975) asserted that observations are always theory-laden. Gödel (1962) formulated the incompleteness theorem for formal arithmetical systems, maintaining that they cannot be axiomatized. He claimed that metalanguages and object languages are inherently inseparable and mutually contaminating.

As theorists of personality we bring two special abilities to bear in the effort to transcend Foucault's paradox: a capacity for reflection or self-observation, however imperfect, and a capacity to recognize the existence of other entities like ourselves and hence to study "them" as objects. These must weigh against further obstacles which go beyond philosophical paradox. Personality theories are conceived of by persons who themselves manifest a range of personality types, more or less normal and pathological. It is a fiction that such theorists are neutral observers, objective measuring instruments (Racker, 1957), and that significant personality disturbances are found only among patients, not among clinician-theorists. In the process of theory construction the idiosyncratic personality configuration of the theorist inevitably influences his choice of salient variables as well as how he organizes them.* Furthermore, the theorist is inescapably part of a culture and a historical period in that culture, both of which condition how he thinks. In this chapter I look in some detail at just one of these perplexing variables: the effects of the personality of the theorist, as an intracultural variable, on the theory of personality he conceives. Although it is impossible to definitively separate the personality of the theorist from the ways in which he reflects certain aspects of the culture in which he is embedded, some theoretical controversies within psychoanalysis present provocative natural experiments because the cultural backgrounds of the participants are so very similar that the major variable element becomes the personality differences among the theorists.

Psychoanalytic theories are commonly illustrated by case material, which critics frequently discount by claiming that it is more a reflection of the author's prejudices (his personality) than it is objective data. In a noteworthy plenary presentation to the International Psychoanalytical Association entitled "One Psychoanalysis or Many," Robert Wallerstein (1988) decried the babel of tongues that seems to characterize contemporary psychoanalytic theory. Using excerpts from an analysis to explore the ways in which representatives

---

* Throughout this work the generic masculine pronoun refers to both males and females.

of different psychoanalytic schools organize and understand clinical material, he concluded that many of the differences relate to what he calls "personal metaphor." Since this presentation it has become fashionable to organize panel discussions in which a particular case report is scrutinized by persons of different theoretical persuasions. The result is that there are usually as many constructions as there are panelists. The thing that all the panelists seem most likely to agree about is that the case material in question has been hopelessly contaminated by the personalized ways in which the presenting theorist has selected, organized, and couched the data.

Freud developed his theory from his personal self-analysis, his study of his children, and his analyses of patients from his sociocultural milieu whose illnesses were not sufficiently severe to preclude their participation in his outpatient office practice. Despite our contemporary awareness that quite a few of his classic patients—for example, the Wolf Man—were rather seriously disturbed (Tausk, 1919; Binswanger, 1956; Reichard, 1956), the personalities of Freud himself and of most of his analysands appear to have fallen within a societally defined modal range of mental health. They were, by and large, the "worried well," socially involved and creative individuals, many of whom entered analysis for hygienic reasons, out of curiosity, or as part of their personal study of psychoanalysis. Freud creatively perceived and refracted these data through the lens of his unique personality. It is a remarkable tribute to Freud's genius that most of the shortcomings and limitations of the theory which have thus far come to light appear to have less to do with his personal idiosyncrasies than with the general culture and particular sociohistorical period within which he lived and worked.

Nonetheless, no one seriously disputes that patriarchal, even authoritarian, tendencies played a central role in Freud's own personality and had some bearing on his theory of conflict resolution. He believed that unregulated youthful vitality is a threat to the social fabric of both the family and the larger civilization, and he deemed paternal authority the central constructive force responsible both for perpetuating civilization and for promoting the maturation of the individual. His theory states that intergenerational conflict is resolved through resolution of the Oedipus complex, leading to conformity and inhibition—internal compromise with one's wishes. The process involves "reasonable" identification with authoritarian attitudes and the development of regulatory structures of the psychic apparatus—ego and superego. I shall elaborate this relationship below, with a particular illustration.

I shall highlight the relation of the idiosyncratic personality of the theorist to the nature of his theory by exploring three instances of theoretical conversion. I use the term *conversion* advisedly, because each of these instances bears some resemblance to a religious conversion. The first is Freud's discovery of the centrality of *Thanatos*, the death instinct; the second is Wilhelm Reich's discovery of Orgone energy. Part of the reason I have chosen these two theorists is that Reich's conversion began in the crucible of personal and theoretical conflict with Freud, and Freud's conversion to the death-instinct hypothesis was probably influenced, albeit to a lesser degree, by his conflict with Reich. Close examination of this conflict casts into relief some idiosyncrasies of their respective personalities, the likely relationship of these to their respective theories, and the fine line that divides theory from ideology. The third instance of conversion I shall examine is Heinz Kohut's recantation of orthodox or Freudian drive-conflict-structural theory and his discovery of selfpsychology, as chronicled in "The Two Analyses of Mr. Z" (1979). This article is of particular interest because it contains an indirect acknowledgment by a major figure in the history of psychoanalysis of the way in which a forceful personality can promulgate ideology in the guise of psychoanalytic theory.

It is not my intention in these three illustrations to judge the merits or demerits of the theories at stake or the mental health or illness of the principals. Freud, Reich, and Kohut were learned and sophisticated individuals, and each was at least somewhat aware of the danger of confusing his personal idiosyncrasies with his theoretical contribution. Kohut's awareness is implicit in his retrospective acknowledgment of his own error with regard to the theory of personality that informed his conduct of Mr. Z's first analysis. Freud wrote that "a large part of the mythological view of the world . . . is nothing but psychology projected into the external world. The obscure recognition (the endopsychic perception, as it were) of psychical factors and relations in the unconscious is mirrored . . . in the construction of a supernatural reality" (1901, pp. 258–259). His anticipation of the anthropological conception of indigenous psychology (elaborated in chapter 6) is uncanny, but it seems most unlikely that he intended to include psychoanalysis under the rubric of mythology. Elsewhere, in his discussion of the Schreber case (1911), Freud commented on the striking resemblance between details of Schreber's delusional conceptions and his own theory of libidinal cathexis and paranoia (what he refers to above as "endopsychic process"). He concluded: "It remains for the future to decide whether there is more delusion in my theory than I should like to admit" (1911, p. 79).

Reich was scapegoated and vilified as psychotic at least two decades before his actual psychosis. (Enemies within the psychoanalytic movement, including his estranged wife, Annie, and Otto Fenichel, apparently spread rumors that a 1927 hospitalization for treatment of tuberculosis was actually occasioned by a psychosis.) Decades later he had this to say about his "discovery" of the orgone: "When I first came into contact with the vegetative streamings around 1930 I was confused like everybody else who experiences them. For a while, I wondered whether I was crazy or the world. Intellectually I knew what I was doing, but this was 'outside.' I was confused—'is it me or them?'—like every schizophrenic" (Sharaf, 1971, p. 97).

Biological instinct, mentally represented in the form of wishes, is the motivational underpinning of Freud's theory (the economic viewpoint of his metapsychology). Freud hypothesized that the biological drive for discharge of a vital or libidinal instinct is basically inimical to the perpetuation of civilization, which depends upon intact family structure and the authority of the father. He further postulated that maturation consists of a process of internalization, culminating, with the resolution of the Oedipus complex, in enhancement of the sphere of ego control over instinct as well as the development of the superego (morality). This theory of sexual renunciation and sublimation and of ultimate identification with authority is consistent with what we know of Freud's personality as seen through the eyes of his contemporary biographers Jones and Schur. He appears to have been of obsessive-compulsive temperament, with a variety of somatic complaints, phobias, and anxiety. It is ironic that, although he was responsible, more than any other single person in the twentieth century, for lifting social taboos about sexuality and for publicly affirming its importance in human life, his personal attitudes about sex seemed to mirror the repressive attitudes of his culture and his time. For example, according to Schur (1972), he forbade his fiancée to associate with a friend who "got married before she got married." He seems to have largely renounced sexual gratification by middle age, after an unsatisfactory interlude of coitus interruptus, and to have become increasingly moralistic and pessimistic about the possibility of individual sexual fulfillment. One of his sons revealed some years after Freud's death that they had had a serious falling-out when, as an adolescent, he tried to talk with his father about masturbation and the response was moralistic disapproval. Freud's artistic interests were not expressive but were those of a collector. In his role as leader of the psychoanalytic movement, he was authoritarian—intolerant of dissent and dissenters.

At age sixty-four, in 1920 (around the time Reich joined the psycho-analytic movement), Freud announced a radical reformulation of his theory in a paper misleadingly entitled "Beyond the Pleasure Principle." He postulated a death instinct, "an urge inherent in organic life to restore an earlier state of things which the living entity has been obliged to abandon under the pressure of external disturbing forces; that is, it is a kind of organic elasticity, or to put it another way, the expression of the inertia inherent in organic life" (p. 36). He assigned to this instinct a central role in mental life, writing that "the aim of all life is death" (p. 38), and he turned to it to account for such diverse phenomena as traumatic neuroses, negative therapeutic reactions, the repetitive nature of children's play, and even migratory behavior in birds and animals. With an increasingly grandiose sweep of mind, in some respects similar to the change I shall shortly note in Reich, Freud turned to cellular embryology and proposed that the death instinct might account for recapitulation theory (ontogeny recapitulates phylogeny). From there he moved to cosmology, speculating that "what has left its mark on the development of organisms must be the history of the earth we live in and its relation to the sun" (p. 38).

Max Schur, who was first Freud's personal physician and later a psycho-analytic colleague, had little doubt that the death-instinct concept was a prod-uct of Freud's unique personality, particularly his unconscious self-destructive wishes: "We cannot escape the conclusion that Freud had already arrived at his hypothesis of the 'death instinct' and was using various aspects of 'unpleasur-able' repetitiveness to confirm it" (1972, p. 325). Freud had lived through the gradual dissolution of Viennese culture followed by the Russian Revolution, the Prussian uprising, the cataclysmic world war, and the postwar ascendancy of Communism. Shortly before publication of the paper in question, he had suffered the near-simultaneous losses of his beloved daughter Sophie and his close friend Anton Von Freund. It is possible that he was already experiencing manifestations of the cancer that eventually killed him, which was diagnosed three years later. The death-instinct hypothesis, according to Schur, reflects Freud's understandably pessimistic turn of mind.

Although most psychoanalysts seem to believe that the death-instinct hypothesis differs qualitatively from the major corpus of Freud's work, it is fundamentally an extension of his belief that civilization is humanity's highest achievement and that it is based on the law of the father. He viewed both civilization and the paternal authority on which he concluded it depended as ineluctably at odds with the destructive discharge of individual biological instinct. Freud postulated that instinctual gratification must be renounced via resolution of the Oedipal conflict with the father, leading to repression, sublimation, and endopsychic structuring in the form of ego mastery and superego formation. It is this belief that placed him at odds with Reich.

Freud's distress over the spread of Communism was inflamed by what he considered the temerity of some of his Marxist followers, notably Adler and later Reich, in attempting to incorporate into psychoanalytic theory the Marxist view that aggression, revolution, and the class struggle are natural, even healthy, responses to the suppression of individuality by the authoritarian (capitalist) class. In contrast to Freud, but consonant with Marxist ideology, Reich believed that individual instinctual gratification is the highest goal of personal and social development and that the authoritarian political structures that impede it arise from repressive patriarchal authority in the nuclear family. Reich viewed civilization not as man's highest achievement, but as a regressive product of paternalism.

The ideas of Freud and Reich appear to be mirror opposites that reflect the idiosyncratic personality structure of each man, as well as the prevailing subcultural belief systems. Reich was forty-one years Freud's junior. When he came to psychoanalysis in his early twenties he was also a committed Marxist, active in the Communist party. He, too, was preoccupied with libido, but whereas Freud believed the infant's unbridled libidinal and aggressive expression is the enemy of civilization and of the patriarchal family, Reich maintained that libidinal discharge, orgastic potency, is the basis of mental health, and that civilization, sustained by the patriarchal family, is the enemy of the individual and the cause of orgastic impairment and psychopathology. Reich believed that the repressive authoritarian social structures that characterize civilization are internalized as pathological character structure, or "armor," in the course of individual development. Patriarchal family structure is "a factory for authoritarian ideologies and conservative (character) structures" (1936, p. 72); permissive matriarchal structures are more compatible with the healthy development of personality. Reich emphasized the importance of the free expression of affect and described how somatization, or what he called bodily armoring, prevented it. While he is sometimes maligned for advocating unbridled licentiousness (as was Freud when he originally asserted the importance of sexuality), in fact his concept of the genital character is of a responsible, caring, mature person who is emotionally open to profound experiences of pain as well as pleasure.

The elements of Reich's theory are similar to those of Freud, but the mix is very different, with emphasis on the pathogenic role, not of biological instinct, but of civilization and authoritarian repression, so that the significance of the Oedipus complex is more or less reversed. Reich's ideas bear considerable resemblance to Freud's early theory of actual neurosis. And just as Reich was really no advocate of total self-gratification, neither was he completely opposed to civilization—only to the authoritarian form in which it was constituted at the time. He envisioned a different (matriarchal) and more permissive social form of organization.

One cannot simply dismiss Reich's ideas as being without merit, as most orthodox analysts have done. In fact, in retrospect some of his ideas seem to presage a contemporary paradigm shift in psychoanalysis itself, generally attributed to the so-called object relations school, from a biologically based model of a mental apparatus to one that emphasizes a separate self molded by its good-enough or pathogenic childhood relationships with caregivers. Reich's emphasis on affect and on somatization, his central focus on character and personality rather than on symptom, and his observations on the traumatic and abusive perversions of authority in families, with their pathogenic consequences, have all become accepted elements of contemporary psychoanalysis. His meticulous description of character typologies and their defensive and adaptive functions remains a major source of information on the subject.

Not that I mean to imply that Reich was "normal" and Freud was not. From my own researches culminating in an unpublished manuscript, and Sharaf's (1983) excellent biography, it appears that Reich's own personality was a mix of impulsive, rebellious, authoritarian, and masochistic features. His sex life was not only full but also unrestricted by social convention, right up to the time of his death at age sixty. Indeed, according to one of his wives, he was lost without a woman. He had four legal or common-law wives and countless affairs. His sexual activity seems in no way to have impaired his productivity and creativity, for in addition to his research and prolific writing he played several musical instruments, composed, painted extensively, and had a considerable and practical interest in architecture and design which he carried to fruition in the construction of his Maine headquarters, called Orgonon. Although his view of man's fate was optimistic in contrast to Freud's, in his personal life Reich's rebelliousness and authoritarianism masked a more subtle and pervasive masochism. His life might be thought of as an illustration of Freud's repetition compulsion and death wish, for he engaged in cycles of provocation and rebellion against the ideology and authority under which he placed himself, both political (ranging from Communism to socialism, fascism, and ultimately the U.S. Food and Drug Administration) and professional (the psychoanalytic movement). In each instance he eventually asserted the conviction that he was the sole and ultimate arbiter of truth, and he did so in a way that invited persecution and expulsion. At the end he was left in isolation with a cult of more or less blindly devoted followers, in a role much like that of the kind of autocratic patriarch he so despised. The persecution he had invited culminated when he was investigated by the FDA, at the height of McCarthyism, prosecuted, convicted, and imprisoned, in a manner that in retrospect seems a terrible miscarriage of justice.

It is not difficult to imagine how conflict might have arisen between these two men. Reich himself acknowledged his "father fixation" on Freud (1967, p. 213), although elsewhere he boasted he was free of Oedipal conflict. Loosely speaking, each man was preoccupied with issues of love and hate in familial relations between father and son. In his earlier theoretical work, Freud asserted that the wish for unbridled libidinal gratification was a characteristic of youth, which had to be tamed by progressive internalization of the authority of the father, and his later death-instinct hypothesis was his assertion that man destroys himself. In his practice as titular patriarch of psychoanalysis, he maintained a tight authority over his followers and a conservative, husbanding attitude toward what he considered to be his basic contributions to psychoanalytic theory. He was more concerned with propagation of the movement he had spawned than with encouragement of creativity among his followers. His reaction to original and deviant ideas was extreme and personalized.

Reich, in contrast, felt that paternal authority was the first cause of self-destructiveness and repression. Although he agreed with Freud that, in the short run, these self-destructive and repressive elements might be lysed by a psychoanalysis, he believed that the real pathogenic culprit was authority, as embodied in the patriarchal family and in all autocratic forms of government. In the long run, he argued, these must be overthrown and abolished. In this position he was inconsistent, for he viewed himself as an exception. Although he saw authority and aggression as pathological forces, like all revolutionaries he also felt entitled to expropriate and normalize the exercise of these forces in the service of his own beliefs. Both Freud and Reich were intransigent personalities, unable to accept criticism constructively. Each was accustomed to issuing it to others, and both tended to cut out of their lives individuals who disagreed with them. Freud remained a giant and triumphed repeatedly over pretenders to his authority, whereas Reich repeatedly tilted with giants and always seemed to lose.

The ultimate conflict between the two men was politically about Marxism, psychologically about masochism, and interpersonally about intergenerational power. Freud's pessimistic construction was based on his belief that masochism is a primary biological phenomenon (death instinct); Reich's seemingly more optimistic one was based on the thesis that masochism is a defensive and adaptive response to familial and societal authoritarianism and repression. In 1927 Freud published The Future of an Illusion. The illusion in question is the belief that authority generates hostility, and the truth, as Freud saw it, is that the relevant dialectic is internal, related to the death instinct. This paper seems, among other things, to have been a response to the younger psychoanalysts, including Reich, who were attempting to incorporate Marxist philosophy into psychoanalytic theory. Freud's 1930 monograph, Civilization and Its Discontents, was the culmination of his efforts to demonstrate that the authority of the father and its structuralized internal precipitates are a normal and necessary civilizing force in the struggle between individual instinct and society. Reich submitted a paper, "The Masochistic Character," for the 1932 volume of the Internat. Zeitschrift für Psychoanalyse. It is a rather mild statement to which no analyst nowadays could conceivably take offense, that actual trauma and the resultant pathological identifications of the victim play a significant role in masochistic disturbances, along with a catalogue of some of the multiple adaptive and defensive functions masochistic attitudes may serve. In fact, it is probably more in line with contemporary psychoanalytic beliefs than Freud's death-instinct hypothesis.

Today's theories of stress, of the interpersonal and intersubjective, and of good-enough, empathic parenting versus traumatic, unempathic parenting are outgrowths of yesterday's Marxist influence on psychoanalysis. This unconscious linkage may have much to do with why psychoanalysis has remained so resistant to concepts of pathogenesis. In any case, Freud and some of his colleagues were deeply offended by Reich's article. In his official biography of Freud, Jones claims that the reason for the rift was the article's assertion: "The death instinct is a product of the capitalistic system" (1953, 8:166). This is entirely inaccurate. According to Reich (1933), Freud accepted the article on the condition that Reich write a preface acknowledging that it was written "in the service of the Communist party" (p. 209). Eventually the paper was published with an ad hominem rejoinder by Sigfried Bernfeld, speaking for Freud, which identified Reich as a Marxist.

I cannot pretend to do justice to the conflict between these two men in so short a space; certainly Freud's concerns about Reich's use of a more active technique played a part. As for Reich's sexual practices and his mental health, both of which were subjects of rumor, ethical standards for psychoanalysts in those days were nothing like what they are today, and his sexual practices seem not to have been especially deviant from more or less accepted norms of the time for other analysts. His mental health was not really an issue until many years later. In any case, the psychoanalytic hierarchy put increasing pressure on Reich to renounce his Communist and socialist ties. In 1933 Freud denied Reich's wish to have the official psychoanalytic press publish his book *Character Analysis*. Finally, in 1934, Reich's name was quietly and surreptitiously deleted from the official roster of the International Psycho-Analytical Association.

Ironies abound. Despite Reich's disclaimers, his conflict with Freud appears to have been blatantly Oedipal in nature. The psychoanalytic movement spearheaded by Freud during the period between the world wars, with its relative intolerance for dissension and its tendency to confuse teaching with inculcation of dogma or ideology, was probably a good illustration of Reich's hypothesis about the destructive influence of paternal authority. On the other hand, the life of Reich himself is an excellent illustration of Freud's conceptions of the repetition compulsion and the death instinct. In any case, the personalities of both men so drove their theories and professional interactions around theoretical matters that the dispute between them rapidly went from being personal to irreconcilably ideological.

Reich shared with other psychoanalysts a deep aversion to fascism, and as war approached he moved first to Norway, then to Denmark, and finally to New York City. In what we might now call a midlife crisis, Reich ceased being a rebellious follower in movements controlled by other authorities and became a charismatic leader of his own movement, the ultimate arbiter of reality and truth—the very kind of autocratic patriarch he despised. But he did so in a manner that brought him into conflict with still higher authorities, those in government itself, and rendered him increasingly difficult for even his most devoted followers and intimates to live with. He gradually evolved a theory, not only of human behavior, but of the functioning of the cosmos. It is notable, in light of his previous emphasis on the pathogenic role of social, cultural, and interpersonal forces, that his ultimate theory is both concrete and biological.

First he became convinced that the spontaneous bodily movements characteristic of orgasm were expressions of what he called orgone energy. He decided, contrary to generally accepted neurobiological theory, that the autonomic nervous system is the seat of conflicts underlying psychopathology. The sympathetic nervous system, he asserted, is the locus of pleasure, whereas the parasympathetic nervous system produces anxiety and musculoskeletal inhibition or armoring. His theory of orgone energy was initially electrical, and he studied it with a galvanometer. He discovered in the bodily armoring a malignant form of energy he named DOR (deadly orgone), the antithesis of orgone energy. In a sense he had concretely reinvented the life and death instincts he so objected to in Freud's work. As the scope of his theories gradually enlarged beyond human personality, he discovered orgone energy throughout the universe and studied it by means of an electroscope (a device for measuring static electricity). He concluded that DOR energy is responsible for a variety of ills, from neurotic inhibition to cancer, drought, malignant cloud formations, and alien spacecraft (UFOs). In his work he employed microscopes, telescopes, and, eventually, shortly after World War II, a device called a Cloudbuster, which looks like nothing so much as a wartime antiaircraft gun. Under the microscope he was able to identify orgones, mass-free pulsating vesicles, and bions (pulsating blobs of energy with an electrical charge which stained gram-positive). He further refined bion particles to what he called PA bions, components of healthy tissue which emitted orgone energy, and T-bacilli, which he extracted from diseased tissue. In the mid-1940s he claimed that he had succeeded in generating life from energy by extracting the water from boiled soil, freezing it, then filtering it.

In the late 1940s and early 1950s Reich became manifestly paranoid, though most of his beliefs were shared by the disciples with whom he surrounded himself. Once again he was somewhat prescient insofar as his interests turned to preservation of the natural environment. He launched a program he called CORE (Cosmic Orgone Engineering), invented the Cloudbuster, and commenced a series of operations designed to control the weather, reverse worldwide desert conditions, and do battle with alien spacecraft. He began to drink heavily and became pathologically jealous of his wife, Ilse.

In 1951 he conducted his fateful Oranur experiment using radioactive material and discovered that NR (nuclear radiation) plus OR produces DOR. He reported that the experiment generated high levels of radiation at Orgonon (factors such as cloud-drift from concurrent atomic experiments in the Southwest and possible radon emissions from the large granite formations that comprised his residence and the surrounding mountain area were not considered). Shortly thereafter he had a heart attack. His paranoid thinking increased, as well as strife with both intimates and followers.

Reich had also developed what he called an Accumulator, designed to concentrate orgone energy, and used it medically to cure a variety of conditions ranging from sexual dysfunction to schizophrenia to cancer. As his theory became increasingly biological and concrete, he scoffed at psychoanalysis, saying, "with hypotheses, with such things as the 'id' . . . one cannot change blood corpuscles or destroy cancer tumors; with orgone energy one can" (1933, p. 304). He published numerous books, and his work gained him a considerable following. He had never bothered to obtain a medical license when he emigrated to the United States, and when consumer groups and advocates began to protest about his alleged medical quackery the FDA, then in its infancy, decided to pursue him as a test case. It spent large sums of money and substantial effort to obtain evidence that Reich was practicing medicine without a license. Finally, in 1955, one of his followers was caught transporting an Accumulator across state lines, and legal action was instituted. The FDA actually burned Reich's published books.

In 1953 Reich published a two-part work called *The Emotional Plague of*

Mankind; one of the parts was called *The Murder of Christ.* In it he described Christ's persecution in much the same terms he used elsewhere in describing his own. In a rage against the FDA, he launched OROP-EP (Orgone Operation Emotional Plague) and threatened to use the Cloudbuster to unleash floods and a plague on the eastern United States. He interpreted planes flying overhead as messages of support from President Eisenhower. He refused to fight the charges against him in any constructive way, however, even spurning help offered by the American Civil Liberties Union, and he was eventually tried and sent to a federal penitentiary, where he died of a heart attack at age sixty. His ideas live on however, among a devoted core of followers, mostly located in New York City.

Personality idiosyncrasy and its contribution to theory become progressively easier to visualize as each of these men, Freud and Reich, experienced an increasing sense of personal mission in later life and carried his thinking to an extreme position. It may seem that the differences between Reich and Freud were related to culture rather than personality (Marxism versus an enlightened form of imperialism). But the culture in which they lived was very similar, and I believe that personality was the major differentiating variable.

The final illustration of theoretical conversion, that of Heinz Kohut, is similar to Reich's in that both Reich's beliefs (paradoxically, his earlier ones more than his later ones) and Kohut's new psychology of the self involve clearly articulated breaks with Freud's belief that personality develops out of the crucible of conflict between biological, instinctual motivation and civilization in the form of patriarchal authority. As Kirschner stated, there was a paradigm shift in psychoanalysis, and "increasingly, in these post-Freudian theories, the primary imperative of reality is no longer considered to be instinctual renunciation, but rather separation and individuation" (1992, p. 164). Whereas Reich was preoccupied with the stultifying effects of authority on emotional and, in particular, sexual expressiveness, Kohut focussed on the role of caregiver empathy or lack thereof on cohesion of the self and its goals.

As I mentioned earlier, Kohut's recantation of his previous belief may not be unparalleled in psychoanalysis, but it is certainly unusual. Freud (1887–1904) repudiated his seduction hypothesis in favor of elaboration of the pathogenic role of fantasy. But this recantation, unlike Kohut's, was not in the process of revolutionary change in a belief system. Had Freud continued to develop the seduction hypothesis, a trauma theory that emphasized the pathological potentiality of relationships and specifically the child's actual relationship with his or her father, he would have had to deal with the fundamental incompatibility of his two motivational hypotheses, one based on biology and instinct, the other on interpersonal relations with caregivers.

Mr. Z was in his early twenties when he first consulted Kohut because of difficulties with intimacy and limited satisfaction in his work. Kohut, who had recently graduated from his own psychoanalytic training, proceeded to analyze him for four years. Kohut interpreted Mr. Z's "narcissistic" demands of him in the transference as efforts to maintain control over his mother and as defenses against Oedipal strivings and related castration anxieties. (Retrospectively, he informed us that this was what he had been taught to do during his own analytic training.) While Mr. Z remained skeptical of the validity of Kohut's interpretations, he did become more autonomous and better able to relate to women. During the termination phase, Mr. Z, whose dreams rarely contained human imagery, dreamed the first of three such dreams: he was fearfully barring the door of his house against his father who had come bearing gifts. In fact Mr. Z's parents were separated from the time he was a year and a half old until he was five. During that time Mr. Z regularly slept in the same bed with his mother.

Despite the achievement of a separation from his mother and improvement in his work life, Mr. Z's capacity for pleasure remained limited and his heterosexual relationships shallow. As a consequence he sought Kohut's help a second time ten years later, when he was in his mid-thirties. By this time Kohut had consciously repudiated the classical psychoanalytic theory he had been taught. As the second analysis unfolded, Kohut realized that he had projected these classical interpretations onto Mr. Z's material in the first analysis and that "My theoretical convictions . . . [those] of a classical analyst . . . had become for the patient a replica of the mother's hidden psychosis . . . which he had accepted in reality . . . [with] an attitude of compliance" (1979, p. 16). Early in the second analysis Mr. Z had the second in the sequence of human-image dreams, about a richly dressed man, whose air of strength and relaxation inspired confidence. This time Kohut was more accepting of Mr. Z's "narcissistic" demands, and new material emerged about his mother's controlling and infantilizing attitudes, and the attributions of meaning she forced onto Mr. Z. As Mr. Z struggled to be freer of his mother he dreamed a third human-figure dream. In this one, his mother stood with her back to him, and he experienced an uncanny feeling about her unseen and presumably incomprehensible aspect. As termination of his treatment approached, associations to the first termination arose, including a review of the first of the human-figure dreams. This was now re-interpreted to reflect Mr. Z's infantile longings for his father and his overstimulation when father re-entered his son's life when Mr. Z was five. Subsequently, and for the first time, he grieved his father's death. Apparently there was no investigation of why such a dream had appeared during the termination of what Kohut believed was a compliant, false-self analysis in which the two of them had re-enacted Mr. Z's childhood enslavement by his mother. When the second analysis ended Mr. Z had still not formed a satisfying relationship, although his work life had continued to improve. Some years following termination, Kohut learned that Mr. Z had married and become a father.

In retrospect, after rejecting the framework of classical psychoanalysis, Kohut was convinced that his conduct in Mr. Z's first analysis had been biased. Another way to look at it is that factors of his personality had influenced his theoretical thinking. Actually, he seems to have been quite convinced of the accuracy of his constructions during both analyses, and much of the data of the report comprise abstractions that are hard to distinguish from formulations. There is a paucity of historical and clinical material in Kohut's report and a lack of attention in both analyses to object-relations elements.

In the conclusion of his report Kohut presented a Fairbairn-like diagrammatic view of Mr. Z's personality, split vertically (dissociation) and horizontally (repression), each compartment consisting of a bit of ego or self, a bit of object, and a linking affect. Kohut described two dissociated configurations: an arrogant, aggressive, grandiose self merged with a normally idealized object (mother); and a devalued, masochistic self in relation to a defensively idealized object. These do not readily fit Kohut's theoretical descriptions of the archaic bipolar selfobject configurations that enter into narcissistic transferences (Robbins, 1982). On the basis of the evidence of the report, it seems equally plausible that Kohut's personality influenced his theoretical formulations in Mr. Z's second analysis.

My intent is not to question the value of either of Mr. Z's analyses, for there is evidence that he benefited from both. Nor do I mean to question the validity of either theory, classical or self-psychological. Rather, my purpose is to suggest that personality—Kohut's personality—in particular a tendency to be convinced of the correctness of whatever his current belief system might be, seems to have played a large part in each of the very different constructions that determined his understanding and his modes of intervention in the two analyses. In fact, Kohut's self-psychology, presumably a corrective to the dogmatism of classical theory, has ironically reified an egotistical conceit, which further muddies the waters of conceiving of personality. By elevating the analyst's empathy to the status of a dependable epistemological tool, Kohut elevated enlightened subjectivity to the status of a way of knowing and asserted that the mind of the analyst is capable of truly comprehending the essence of any other human being. The range and diversity of personality enumerated in these pages will suggest that this is a dangerous fallacy.

To paraphrase Freud's caution about the potential relationship of personality idiosyncrasy to personality theory: in the effort to conceive of itself, personality is likely to express illusions and to mistake them for its essence. Such a sobering conclusion might tempt us to turn to modernism and logical positivism in the search for objectivity and to a reductionistic analysis of bits of quantifiable data and their linear connections, which purports to be "scientific." The danger is that the personality idiosyncrasies of the theorist will not only inform his theoretical construction but drive it so that it becomes a stifling ideology, perhaps even the scripture of a movement.

The discovery of the individual person and his mind, the other polarity of personality conceptions (which I refer to as self-centric), appears to have occurred in the pre-Socratic Athens of the sixth and fifth centuries B.C. and is attributed to such figures as Heraclitus and Empedocles (Simon, 1978). The pre-Socratics conceived of a mind characterized by abstraction and organization, and of two modes of thinking, mythological and physiological.

The self-centric conception of the person and of mind was elaborated in some detail by Plato, in fourth-century Athens. The extent to which it appears to presage elements of Freud's theory is striking (Dodds, 1964; Simon, 1978). Plato separated *psyche*, which has been defined as mind or soul, and appears to encompass elements of self, from *soma*, body. He believed that the psyche, which is private and internal, is situated in the brain. It is characterized by consciousness, in the form of thought, decision, and morality, and is the initiator of action, the mover of the person. It has organization, structure, and energy. The structure of the psyche is tripartite and hierarchical in its humanness, ranging from the most human part, *logistikon*, or reason, to the spirited or passionate portion, *thumoeedes*, which includes courage and anger, to the most animal or appetitive part, *epithumeikon*, which Plato believed houses thoughts of incest and murder. The structures come into conflict in an anthropomorphic struggle for control of the human soul. Mind as a whole is fueled by the energy of *eros*.

The other element in ancient Greek writings—especially those of Hippocrates in the fifth and fourth centuries B.C.—that is germane to themes to be developed in subsequent chapters is the preoccupation of a culture with pathology of the mind or personality. Each culture, and hence the models of the person created within its confines, views personality in relation to explicit or implicit conceptions of normal or modal personality. Furthermore, Hippocrates related personality deviations to the body, specifically the brain and the humors.

Coincidentally, in around the sixth century B.C., Siddhartha, the Buddha, was systematizing a sociocentric view of personality consistent with the Eastern culture of his time. He looked upon the conscious preoccupation with things, including a self reified as a concrete entity and the active organization of life around the satisfactions of individual personhood, as an illusion (*sem*) to be dissolved. Suzuki characterized the Buddhist quest for "the point of absolute subjectivity" (1960, p. 25). These conceptions are elaborated in chapters 6 and 8.

A Brief History of Conceptions of the Person

Foucault's (1973) observation that the self cannot meaningfully be considered apart from the larger sociohistorical fabric of its time will serve as the theme for this highly selective discussion, which is limited to the development of ideas of the person in Western civilization. Evidence from Western civilization should suffice to substantiate Foucault's point. Discussion of personality in other cultures may be found in chapters 6 and 8.

As of so many aspects of Western culture, the roots of our contemporary concepts of personality can be found in ancient Greece, both in the period of the Homeric epics, around the seventh century B.C., and in the pre-Socratic and Socratic eras, extending roughly from the sixth through the fourth centuries B.C. (Simon, 1978; Snell, 1982). In the Homeric view, the individual person is not clearly differentiated from the human aggregate. Individuality as we know it does not exist. There are no terms for self or for gender distinctions. Mind (psyche), body, thought, and feeling are not clearly differentiated, nor are structure and function. There is little sense of subjectivity—no interior mind. Forces that in this era would be conceptualized as internal are attributed to external agency—fate or the gods. This is one pole—I call it sociocentric—of a dichotomous conception of personality to which I shall return throughout the book.

During the medieval period, comprising the millenium between the collapse of the Roman empire during the fifth century A.D., and the Renaissance, which began around 1500, Saint Augustine (397) was one of the first to articulate the view of person held by the Catholic church, the dominant civilizing force and social organization of the time (Taylor, 1988; Cushman, 1990). The person has an inner life, he wrote, involving a constitutional predisposition to evil (original sin) and bestial impulses, as well as a conscience whose purpose it is to expunge the sinful part of mind. The personal norm demanded by the church was one of selfless participation in the harmonious life of the church-defined community. Exploration of personality at that time consisted of confession and inquisition. In the fifteenth-century treatise *Malleus Maleficarum*, deviation was defined in supernatural terms, as demonic possession. People were cogs in the wheel, defined according to their larger social contexts (domain or fiefdom, church) and indistinguishable from them. Individual human life was of little importance, for value resided in the larger community and its purpose (MacIntyre, 1984, 1988).

Around the millenium, Western Europe began to undergo an intellectual awakening known as Scholasticism (Knowles, 1962; Morris, 1972), a development that flourished particularly during the twelfth and thirteenth centuries. Attention was once again paid to the questions about personality, about the human soul and its relation to behavior, that had preoccupied the ancient Greeks. Saint Thomas Aquinas, one of the major figures of Scholasticism, elaborated the ancient Greek preoccupation with the similarities and differences among soul, mind, and body. Changes in personal customs regarding food, table manners, and household arrangements, including development of individual seating and utensils, and enhancement of personal privacy, suggest a renewed focus on the individual at the conclusion of the Middle Ages (Tuan, 1982). Nonetheless, I know of no substantial evidence to suggest that conceptions of the person and his relation to society altered dramatically during this period.

The age of modernism coincides roughly with the end of the medieval period and the Reformation and secularization (fifteenth and sixteenth centuries) as part of the Industrial Revolution. Cities were spawned, centered around industry and peopled by immigrants. The integrity of centuries-old feudal domains and communities was disrupted, and the central control of the church weakened. As ancient sociocentric bonds were disrupted, decontextualized and isolated individual selves became central units of initiative and meaning. Freed from traditional social constraints, the individual began to strive for rights and for expression. New and more democratic forms of government were required to supplement and to replace the traditional social structures. In short, the individual began to emerge as a more central focal point in the social order, able to choose his personal values and goals (Nisbet, 1969; Sandel, 1982; MacIntyre, 1984, 1988; Sampson, 1985, 1988). Shakespeare's psychological dramas illustrate some of these developments during the seventeenth century. He remarks in *Julius Caesar*: "The fault, dear Brutus, is not in our stars but in ourselves."

The secular mode of thinking that characterized the modern age of enlightenment, of which science is emblematic (Whitehead, 1967), gradually supplanted religion as a belief system and remains to this day so dominant that we tend to forget that science is a Western cultural phenomenon only about three centuries old. Science has retained a significant ideational tie to its religious, pre-Copernican predecessors—namely, a kind of totalitarian tendency to generalize, to search for truth, and to articulate monistic, omniscient, universalistic ideological systems. Other characteristics of the scientific mode of thinking include dualistic logic (Descartes' *Meditations*, 1641); the related belief in objective empiricism and a real world of measurable facts; logical positivist ideas that the universe is governed by a process of linear, dynamic, causal trajectories, and that construction and reduction or deconstruction are reversible, analyzable, and measurable processes. The future is believed to be contained in the present.

The work of da Vinci and Vesalius legitimized the physical body and mental faculties as objects of scientific inquiry. Religious and supernatural understandings of deviations from modal personality began to give way to more systematic study of the insane. A remarkable convergence of developments during the seventeenth century led to the beginnings of quantitative conceptions of normality and deviance and provided a framework for much subsequent thinking about personality. Kepler and Galileo discovered measurement around 1600, and the advent of statistics made possible scientific studies of people. Graunt began to collect vital statistics in 1662, and during the late 1600s Bernoulli and the astronomer Halley (1693) developed the concepts of probability, chance, and deviation. In 1733 de Moivre conceived of the normal distribution curve. During the nineteenth century these ideas were refined by Laplace, Poisson, and Gauss. A Belgian, Quetelet, was the first to apply these ideas to human measurement, in 1835. He introduced the concept of average. Stimulated by Darwin's (1859) focus on the evolution of individual differences, Weber and Fechner in Germany began the experimental study of psychophysiology during the late nineteenth century.

Personality has been conceived of as a subject of scientific inquiry for only about a century (Foucault, 1979, 1980). The work of Galton (1869, 1883) on individual differences in intelligence and social deviance in the latter half of the nineteenth century heralded development of the human sciences, and the separate threads of statistical study of human characteristics and of normal and deviant personality became interwoven. In 1890 Cattell first employed the terms "individual differences" and "mental test." In 1896 Binet introduced his test of intelligence. As the science of psychology developed, Rorschach (1921), Murray (1935), and others began to develop instruments for assessing personality deviance.

As I have noted, theories of personality characteristic of the more recent modern age are colored by ways of perceiving and thinking characteristic of more or less modal or average Caucasian males in twentieth-century Western culture. The traditional Western conception of personality is predicated on the idea that all minds are intrinsically and qualitatively similar, though they may vary on a quantitative continuum such as normality-deviance or maturity-immaturity. Universal truths about personality are "out there" to be discovered by the conscious rational mind, using Cartesian dualistic modes of thought involving subject and object, fantasy and reality, mind and body, and a polar system of values (good and bad). The rational dualistic stance assumes a normal state of separation and alienation between the observer and the phenomena under consideration, which are considered to be objects. The Western conception values individual autonomy and the striving for objectivity and mastery that accompanies it. The observer-theoretician engages in a struggle with aspects of the phenomenological world, in the hope and expectation of ultimately being capable of comprehending and controlling it. Shweder (1991) described the goal of such a thought process as man's objective rational comprehension and ultimate control over "mindless nature devoid of subjectivity" (p. 53).

Western logical positivist conceptions of self include psychoanalysis, to which I return throughout the book, and Piaget's epistemology, which exemplifies rational Cartesian thought and the related belief in real truth and universal structure. Piaget believed that both the self and the world possess absolute properties in time, space, and material substantiality, and are potentially knowable by a maturing, less solipsistic, and increasingly rational and objective self. His beliefs are reflected in work on friendship (Selman and Jacquette, 1977), race (Alejandro-Wright, 1985; Spencer, 1984), social rules (Turiel, Edwards, and Kohlberg, 1978), and moral reasoning (Kohlberg, 1969).

Such conceptions are historo-centric, ethnocentric, and gender-centric, to say nothing of being egocentric. Johannes Herder, in the eighteenth century, was one of the first to observe that judging members of other cultures by our standards is a form of arrogance (Berlin, 1976). Although, as I have mentioned, Heelas and Lock (1981) refer to all theories of personality, whether modestly folkloric or pretentiously "scientific," as indigenous psychologies, Western male bias continues to infiltrate conceptions of personality (see chapters 7 and 9). Choi, Kim, and Choi (1993) point out that "Psychology became naturalized in the land of individualism. Its basic foundations became intertwined with the basic assumptions of individualism" (p. 193). Keller (1985) notes the gender bias inherent in the scientific model of thinking.

Psychoanalysis is also a child of the modern age, and it should hardly be surprising that its theories, for the most part, are Western, indigenous psychologies of the individual person. It emerged at the end of the Victorian era, when the self was conceived of as divided. The Victorian self was at the same time rational—capable of viewing the world objectively, of capturing, controlling, and measuring it—and subjective—possessed of hidden aggressive, sexual, imaginative, and conflicted inner content (Lowe, 1982; Baumeister, 1986; Trilling, 1971).

The theories of Freud and Melanie Klein articulate, in a nineteenth-century scientific language based on concepts from the Industrial Revolution and the age of the machine, individual human strivings against the forces of a monarchical, theologically oriented society for more individual expression. Freud's preoccupation with deconstructive, atomistic analyses of each person into mechanical and energic parts that seem more real and more valuable than the organic whole sometimes makes it appear that the person or self is epiphenomenal. However, Freud's concept of *das Ich* may have had a personal connotation which was lost when the translator's zeal to ensconce psychoanalysis as a "legitimate" science of the mind led to its homuncular rendering as "ego" rather than the more obvious "I," or self. Regardless of whether the person was formally conceptualized in psychoanalytic theory, he is the center of initiative and action. Personality is modeled after an amalgam of older theological conceptions of evil and sinfulness and the newer concepts of the machine, an organization of discrete parts whose purpose is to harness and regulate the discharge of powerful and potentially dangerous quantities of energy. While the development of the individual self is the normative goal of the theory, the established order and its designated social structures—particularly the patriarchal family, in the case of Freud, and the mother, in the case of Klein—retain unquestioned rectitude and authority. Freud and Klein recognize the presence and validity of innate sexual and aggressive drives and fantasies, yet the individual expression of sexual impulses (in the case of Freud) and of rage (in the case of Klein) is considered destructive to the fabric of civilization. The goal of personal maturation through intrapsychic conflict, both moral and pragmatic, is to form regulatory and inhibitory identifications with authority figures, which perpetuate the existing social order. The paradox of Freud's theory is that it respectfully attends to and validates the individual mind and sexuality, so that Freud is known as the liberator of society from sexual repression, even as an advocate of licentiousness, at the same time that the theory retains the old theological view of human constitutional bestiality.

But not all psychoanalysts regarded existing society and culture as good and the unbridled individual quest for expression as destructive or evil. Social revolution, including Marxism and the world wars over fascism, has led to the ascendancy of government based on the Anglo-American Protestant tradition of individualism and has been accompanied by a paradigm shift in psychoanalysis, reflected in ideas about the primacy of the self (Kirschner, 1992). Influenced by Marxism, Wilhelm Reich, Erich Fromm, and Karen Horney maintained that the Freudian model is a blueprint of social autocracy and even dictatorship. Along with Fairbairn, who was reared in the British tradition of respect for the individual person, these analysts viewed the person as inherently good. Reich placed primary value on the very sexual impulses Freud felt were dangerous, and Fairbairn valued the innate goodness of the infant and the primary wholeness of its person over Freud's emphasis on the father and Klein's on the mother. In contrast to Freud's idea that basic human biological nature is a threat to order, authority, and civilization, Reich proposed that it is the authoritarian aspects of society, beginning with the family, that are repressive and destructive to the individual and to a more enlightened social organization. Fairbairn, Winnicott, Bowlby, and Kohut all conceived of the individual as beginning life in a kind of Edenic state of harmony from which he is coldly cast out by parents, and thereby afflicted with the struggle between good and evil. Fairbairn even couched his views in a theological metaphor, remarking that the child chooses to internalize the sense of badness, for it is preferable to be a sinner in a world governed by God than to be a good person struggling to survive in a world controlled by the devil. Kohut conceived of the infant as a "tragic man," struggling for personal meaning and purpose, in contrast to Freud's infant, who is engaged in guilty inner conflict over sexual expression. These conceptions are products of their creators' historical time and place in the Western culture of individualism (Kirschner, 1992; Lasch, 1995; Elshtain, 1995).

Now we are in the midst of the intellectual paradigm shift from modernism, reflected in the doctrine of logical positivism and in the belief of traditional science that it has the means and the potential to discover truth in the form of the ultimate nature of objective reality, to postmodernism. This new way of looking places equivalent value on subjectivity, relationship, relativism, and discourse in the construction and deconstruction not of truth, but of meaning (Foucault, 1993; Heidegger, 1962; Derrida, 1967). Once again, but with greater sophistication, representatives of many disciplines have returned to larger systemic, relativistic, contextualized modes of thought (Cahoone, 1988; MacIntyre, 1984, 1988; Sandel, 1982). This movement has influenced every intellectual sphere:

- political science, historiography, and sociology (Mumford, 1956; Nisbet, 1969; Cahoone, 1988; MacIntyre, 1984, 1988; Sandel, 1982);
- the natural sciences (relativity and indeterminacy in physics [Heisenberg, 1958]; systems theory in biology; see chapter 13);
- mathematics (chaos or complexity theory; also see chapter 13);
- anthropology or cultural psychology and the universalist-relativist debate (Heelas and Lock, 1981; Geertz, 1975, 1979; Shweder, 1991; see chapter 6);
- psychology (Vygotsky, 1978; Luria, 1976; Sampson, 1985, 1988; Harre, 1981, 1984; Gergen, 1973, 1990);
- gender studies of intersubjectivity (Miller, 1976; Keller, 1985; Gilligan, 1982; Benjamin, 1988 (see chapter 9); and

- psychoanalysis: Lacan; the interpersonal school (Sullivan, 1953; Levenson, 1985, 1991); the hermeneutic movement (Schafer, 1976); the feminist and post-Kohutian intersubjectivists (Stolorow and Atwood, 1992); the social constructivists (Hoffman, 1991).

Science itself is no longer an unassailable bastion of certainty as we become awareness of the critical roles in perception and cognition of subjectivity, intersubjectivity (Keller, 1985), indeterminacy and relativity (Heisenberg, 1958). The theory and its creator are in some respects indistinguishable (Popper, 1959, 1987; Kuhn, 1962). As Bruner puts it, "Both science and the humanities have come to be appreciated as artful figments of men's minds, as creations produced by different uses of mind" (1986, p. 44).

Before I attempt to draw conclusions from this brief historical survey, it is important to note the limitations of the data here presented, especially the formidable methodological obstacles to obtaining truly meaningful information about historical conceptions of the person. In chapter 2 I examined the question of whether people can conceive of themselves in a meaningful fashion, and throughout the remainder of this book I examine a variety of general obstacles related to the unique perspective of the observer, the limited data available to any person or group, and the effects of the observer's unique personality. When it comes to surveying personality throughout history, however, these problems are compounded. Lack of access to the people we wish to study, except through their writings and artifacts, forces us to rely on historical documents written for other purposes, many from perspectives we cannot hope to comprehend.

With these caveats in mind, what is there to say about personality from a historical perspective? Much of the data indicate that people have always reflected about human nature, about questions of mind, meaning, and identity, but that these reflections fit differentially into two broad conceptions of person. Moreover, there is suggestive evidence that, in Western civilization alone, the psychological organization of the person has undergone qualitative alterations over historical time. The first of these conceptions, which I call sociocentric, may be traced to Homeric Greece. Greek mythology reflects an absence of subjectivity, psychological-mindedness, a sense of individuality, and of an interior mental life. In lieu of these things there is a relatively undifferentiated distribution of elements we would now look upon as person-constituting among the interpersonal, social, natural, and supernatural environments. The data for this trend, however, comprise myth and legend, which were probably not intended as veridical accounts of real persons and their behavior to begin with. (The relation of mythology to members of a culture is a subject I explore in chapters 6 and 14.) It is possible that the Homeric legends are more expressions of a collective cultural unconscious than descriptions of how people actually thought, felt, and behaved in ancient times. Sociocentric identity is established primarily through structured linkages with the social and natural environment. In the second conception, which I call self-centric, the person is basically conceived of as a separate individual, whose purpose, meaning, and regulation come from within. Self-centrism also has roots in antiquity but was not significantly elaborated until the age of enlightenment and the modern era.

CHAPTER 4

Monistic Thinking and Modal Constructs

Theoretical monism is the conviction of the explanatory sufficiency of a single system. It leads to universalistic generalization and reductive impoverishment and oversimplification of experience, and its quality is totalitarian or ideological. Monistic or monothetic thinking seems to be integral to the human mind. The very attributes that contribute to the success of a theorist and his model— tendencies toward organization and coherence, abstraction and simplification—also predispose toward monistic thinking. It follows that the clearest and most powerful theories are most likely to become monistic systems, overgeneralized as universal explanations. It is a relatively rare individual, at least in Western culture, who can, Escher-like, simultaneously and flexibly entertain more than one basic viewpoint, perspective, and model of thinking about a class of phenomena.

Monism is encountered both in action and in thought or conception, and, of course, in the gray area between the two. In action, at the most basic level, monism is the law of the jungle, social Darwinism, the struggle for survival and for dominance. It may be expressed by individuals who are so completely self-centered and egotistical in their behavior that they are unable to treat others as separate persons with separate rights; by elitist groups that practice discrimination, peacefully or violently; and by ethnic groups and cultures whose behavior toward members of other cultures is similarly devaluing. In its most destructive guise monistic beliefs inform the international politics of imperialism, colonialism, world domination, and even genocide, as well as the national politics of totalitarianism and dictatorship. Paradoxically, monistic action and thought imply dualistic thinking, as well. In order to conceive of an entity so valued that it can be said to be the only one, it is necessary to have a null frame of reference, a no-thing, a devalued thing, an abnormal or deviant or defective thing with which to contrast it. For example, revolution is a characteristic of monistic systems, whether in the ideational or the political sphere; uprisings by socially disenfranchised, devalued, persecuted, or simply unrepresented groups, leading (if they are successful) to their usurpation of power and domination, from which new position of equilibrium the entire cycle begins again. This cyclical process is commonly mistaken for progress or evolution.

At the level of thought, monism is a single-minded attitude about the correctness and sufficiency of a belief system, in this instance about the nature of human personality. In other words, monism implies value judgment, often self-righteousness. Hayles remarks, "To see the oppression that global theories have too often reinforced or enabled, it is enough to remember how a few European cultures have been equated with mankind; how mankind has been equated with humankind; how humankind has been equated with intelligent consciousness" (1990, p. 213). What is destructive about monistic thinking is not the quest for underlying structures and abiding or universal truths but the belief in their attainability and the egocentric tendency of authors of conceptual systems and their adherents to overgeneralize them and to believe they have achieved comprehensiveness, sufficiency, and totality. Because the human mind is prone to self-deception, as observers from both East (Buddha) and West (Freud) have noted, and none of us likes to think of ourself as rigid, single-minded, and inflexible, monistic thinking is particularly opaque to recognition and refractory to alteration. Monists typically convince themselves that they are, in fact, broad-minded and appreciative of persons and ways of thinking that are "different." The striking distinction between psychoanalysis as a theory of mental liberation and psychoanalysis as an ideological movement, which I explore in chapter 11, is a case in point.

Monothetic modes of thought, and the related failure to appreciate diversity and difference in personality, manifest themselves in many forms, including that of indigenous or local theories which pose as universal psychologies but are based on a personality considered modal for a particular culture (chapter 7), intracultural stereotypes about modal personality that ignore differences or construe them as abnormality or deviance (chapter 10), gender-biased theories (for example, phallocentric, chapter 9), overvaluation of Western science or of a particular human science (chapters 3, 6, 7), and insistence upon the explanatory sufficiency of a single model within a given science (chapter 10). Although the ensuing discussion will touch on some of these areas, it will focus primarily on monistic thinking in the sciences, both intersystemic, in their relations with one another, and intrasystemic (see also chapter 10).

The particular form of monistic thinking in which we—I who write this book and most of you who read it—are fundamentally and inextricably embedded is that of modern, male-biased Western culture. In chapter 3 I argued for a historical perspective, on the ground that the typical personality may actually change over time, and with it the way in which reflective persons think about personality. Personality itself, as well as the way in which we think about it, is embedded in the particulars of both time and place or culture (Harre, 1981, 1984; Choi, Kim, and Choi, 1993). Shweder writes of the "unilateral degrading of other people's supposed truths about nature and the world" (1991, p. 49) which pervades Western conceptions of members of other cultures. Their minds are viewed as less mature, and their theories of mind are dismissed "as though they were supernatural, rhetorical, imaginary, or fantastic" (p. 50). This indigenous Western bias has, for the most part, been unconscious or unintentional (Whiting and Child, 1953; Whiting, 1959; Spiro, 1965, 1982, 1984, 1986). Efforts to observe persons of other cultures and to conceive of personality in less biased, more relativistic terms are recent (LeVine, 1973).

Monistic thinking has pervaded gender-related conceptions of personality, as well. The world and the persons in it tend to be regarded, whether in folklore or in more pretentious philosophy and science, through male eyes (see chapter 9).

Some of the most egregious expressions of monistic thinking with regard to personality are to be found in science and among its practitioners. The term *science* is derived from the root *sciens*, meaning knowledge, and the equation is one that most of us tend to accept. In chapter 3 I wrote of how science is not absolute revealed truth but is a rather systematic expression of the modern, post-industrial, Western mind with very particular parameters (Whitehead, 1967). Science, when viewed not simply as one way of knowing and one form of knowledge but as a superior form of knowledge—perhaps the only true knowledge—free of the subjectivity, imprecision, emotionality, self-interest, and bias which presumably contaminate ordinary modes of thought, becomes oxymoronic insofar as it expresses a monistic belief system in the guise of a means of gaining knowledge and truth. Keller (1985) points out that the elements of dualism, alienation, objectification, negation and devaluation, abstraction, and domination and control which characterize science are also particular features of the Western male mind. She goes so far as to speculate that different and equally legitimate forms of "science" might be predicated on what some now believe to be typically female modes of personality and thought, including emotionally based, contextually dependent personalization of perception and cognition and a sense of the interrelatedness of the personal and interpersonal worlds.

The perspective of traditional science is limited, not simply because it is embedded in the specifics of modern time and Western culture, but also because it is a system formulated according to monistic principles or postulates designed to give it universal explanatory powers. These include reversible linear causal dynamics of construction and predictability, on the one hand, and analytic reduction and deconstruction, on the other. Reductionism, a cornerstone of monistic thinking, is based on the implicit promise of eliminating the bewildering complexity of life and finding in its place elemental solutions to problems (Occam's razor). Implicit in this way of thinking is an overvaluation of science in relation to other systems of thought, an intersystemic value and reality hierarchy based on reductionism among the sciences themselves, and a similar (intrasystemic) tendency toward single, all-encompassing theories within each particular science. The overvaluation of science in relation to other modes of thought, a usurpation of the role formerly assigned to religion, is a relatively recent phenomenon, one I consider elsewhere in this book, especially chapters 6 and 8, in reference to systems of other cultures.

Intersystemic monism in science consists of a value hierarchy in which "higher order" human sciences and their findings are covertly devalued and believed to be ultimately dispensable once the phenomenology (or, more accurately, the epiphenomenology) with which they deal is reduced to the explanatory concepts of more basic "lower-order" sciences, usually (but, as we shall see, not always) ones dealing in concrete particles specifiable and analyzable in terms of mass, space, and time. Quantification—the reduction of human phenomena to atomistic elements and then to numbers—is the epitome and the logical conclusion of this approach.

Each of the human sciences (neuroscience, individual psychology and psychoanalysis, interpersonal psychology, social psychology, and cultural anthropology) tends to function more or less as a totalitarian system, as though it were sufficient to account for all the phenomenology of personality. Relations among the sciences are characterized by a kind of social Darwinism. Each one either ignores the existence of others or else attempts to extend its explanatory powers in such a way as to obviate the need for them or reductively to subsume them. The most striking contemporary example is to be found in the current incarnation of the ages-old mind-body debate, the relationship (or lack thereof) between the neurosciences and the psychological sciences. The question in this relationship, which is seldom addressed by either party, is whether material scientific ways of thinking about mind and personality can be reconciled with psychological ones; if so, how, and if not, what then? We tend to equate science with the idea of progress, but with regard to understanding personality there has been more oscillation in dominance between what the bygone era called moral and we now call psychological models of the person, on the one hand, and physical models, which are currently the province of neuroscience. As the pendulum swings between these viewpoints, one "movement" gains acceptance and momentum and is mined myopically and exhaustively until disillusion eventually supervenes, then that one loses favor and is replaced by an equally extreme incarnation of the other viewpoint.

While it is safe to assume that all but the most fanatical or socially isolated neuroscientists live their lives outside their laboratories based upon the premise that their personalities are psychologically meaningful, and that their emotions and relationships possess intrinsic significance, nonetheless, in their activities as scientists most refuse to recognize the significance of these elements as a "real" causal system and, therefore, a legitimate entity for separate study by specific psychological sciences. Instead, they maintain that mind and meaning, normal and pathological, are epiphenomena that are best reduced to their concrete essence as physically dimensioned entities. Some neuroscientists are quite blunt about their concrete, materialistic beliefs. In his 1993 book *The Astonishing Hypothesis: The Scientific Search for the Soul*, Sir Francis Crick, co-discoverer of the structure of DNA, unabashedly asserts, "'You,' your joys and your sorrows, your memories and your ambitions, your sense of identity and free will, are in fact *no more than* the behavior of a vast assembly of nerve cells and their associated molecules" (p. 3, italics mine). A more subtle example of such thinking is a statement by Joseph Coyle, chief of the joint Harvard Medical School departments of psychiatry, quoted in the *Boston Globe* (Bass, 1994): "Our increasing understanding of the brain is abolishing the historic dichotomy between mind and body." The general editor of a psychiatric monograph series states in his introduction that "psychiatry is moving, still relatively slowly, but irresistably, from a more philosophical, contemplative orientation to that of an empirical science. . . . Biological psychiatry provided psychiatry not only with a basic new science and new treatment modalities, but also with the tools, the methodology, and the mentality to operate within the confines of an empirical science, *the only framework in which a medical discipline can survive*" (Van Praag, 1992, p. v; italics mine). Findings from twin adoption studies are beginning to suggest that genetic variations in the nervous system characterize a variety of pathological conditions hitherto thought to be psychological, such as anxiety and obsessive compulsive neurosis (Pardes et al., 1989), and it is likely that they characterize normal personality variants, as well. Because all mental activity, both normal and pathological, has an organic substrate, it is but a small step to conclude that personality itself is nothing more than its organic constituents, a position Eisenberg (1986) trenchantly characterizes as "mindless."

As I have intimated, such reductionist attacks by some neuroscientists on the validity of the concept of mind are not simply products of personal egocentrism, but are inherent in the traditional structure of science, including the philosophy of logical positivism and its specific derivative, scientific materialism (Huxley, 1898; Whitehead, 1967). Such doctrines not only hold that thoughts and feelings are epiphenomena without intrinsic meaning, by-products of an organic essence, the smoke produced by the fire; they also provide a reversible linear causal logic of construction and reduction with which to operationalize this belief. It follows from such reasoning that those who regard mind and meaning as existential entities with causal substance are engaging in an illusion, like the primitive tribes who might attribute corporeal essence and intrinsic nature to human images on a movie screen. In this view disciplines such as psychology and psychoanalysis, which seek to make causal sense of the phenomena of mind, are nothing more than primitive forms of thinking. The phenomenology of personality and the psychological disciplines that study it are destined to be consumed and digested in the process of discovering intrinsic reality, leaving behind metabolic end-products recognizable only to those with training in the neurosciences.

The naked antagonism of materialistic monistic thinkers toward psychology is usually disguised by civilized rationalization and platitudes. The stress model of illness, generally attributed to Cannon (1935) and Selye (1950), is a particularly insidious example of monistic thinking because it is expressed as though it were an appreciation of psychological forces. Its application to schizophrenia, the stress-diathesis model (Zubin and Spring, 1977; Marsella and Snyder, 1981; Gottesman and Shields, 1982; Kringlen, 1987), holds that a biological diathesis produces enduring traits or vulnerabilities that become activated if and when predisposing factors in the environment reach a critical (stressful) threshold. However, in its original usage (Selye, 1956), the term *stress* referred to a physical event in the brain, not a psychological one. According to the principle of neural plasticity, the stressed brain is altered by quantitative material forces, which are described in a way no different from the way one would portray bacteria, viruses, toxins, or physical injury. The independent reality and causal significance of psychic factors of meaning and feeling which make events or even thoughts stressful for one individual and not for another are not appreciated. The patient is conceived of as a psychologically unremarkable host who is responding to the physical stress of an environmental event such as the death of a relative, job loss, a move—that is, a generic human stressor that requires no intervening systemic appreciation of unique configurations of mind. After all, observing the same sporting event may make one person ecstatic, another gloomy, a third angry, and may trigger a heart attack in a fourth. My point is not to criticize stress models per se, for they are necessary and useful so long as they are accurately represented not as psychological models but as neuroscientific ones, but to call attention to the way they are misused to give lip service to the importance of mind and the psychological disciplines that attempt to comprehend its workings while in fact reducing meaning to what can be encompassed by an organic theory.

Intersystemic monism masquerades in other disguises as well. Most clinicians of personality and its vicissitudes appear to be pluralists and to respect the findings of other sciences, at least in their daily clinical work. They readily employ the insights of any field that seems of immediate value in a particular case situation. These pragmatists tend to mix psychodynamics, psychopharmacology, neuroscience, and family dynamics in a kind of stew, as though these could be related in a linear causal sequence, without regard to whether the individual elements are conceptually compatible. However useful it may seem, such a practice is more akin to technology than to science, and the result is a monothetic pseudo-system that gives the illusion of flexibility and ecumenicism. I call this commonplace form of monism naive interactionism.

The naive interactionist form of monistic thinking is found in more formalized scientific guises as well. One extreme is a theory called upward and downward causation, which holds that the forces conceptualized at one system level, usually a lower one, such as neuroscience, may act in a linear causal fashion within a system conceptualized at a different level, usually higher, such as behavior and thinking (Sperry, 1969; Campbell, 1974). Although the fallacy of upward causation—the belief that analysis at an organic systemic level is sufficient (not merely necessary) to account for phenomena of mind and meaning—is now better appreciated than it once was, similar reasoning characterizes the use of concepts of downward causation and transduction (Delbrück, 1970; Weiner, 1970) to account for the observed fact of neural plasticity; namely, that experience, including pathogenic environmental "stress" and psychological therapies, appears to modify the central nervous system structurally.

It may seem ironic that Freud, who will be remembered for his unparalleled efforts to create a separate psychological model of mind and personality, appears to have espoused a materialistic monist position early in his career (Jones, 1953). This is somewhat less surprising if one considers his training as a neuroscientist and his wish that psychoanalysis be recognized as a "legitimate" science. For example, in his *Project for a Scientific Psychology* (1895) Freud wrote: "The intention is to furnish a psychology that shall be a natural science: that is, to represent psychical processes as quantitatively determinate states of specifiable material particles" (p. 295). While Freud eventually came to hold different views, he never abandoned his neuroscientific reductionist position. In 1914 he suggested, "it is special substances and chemical processes which perform the operations of . . . special psychical forces" (p. 78). Again, in his discussion of the life and death instincts, he stated: "The deficiencies in our description would probably vanish if we were already in a position to replace the psychological terms by physiological or chemical ones. . . . We may expect it [biology] to give us the most surprising information and we cannot guess what answers it will return in a few dozen years to the questions we have put to it. They may be of a kind which will blow away the whole of our artificial structure of hypothesis" (1920, p. 60).

I do not wish to imply that materialistic monistic thinking is characteristic of all neuroscientists or is an exclusive failing of neuroscientists. Some renowned biologists and physicists have been pluralists with regard to their respect for the psychological sciences of meaning (Heisenberg, 1958; Weiss, 1977; MacLean, 1990), and Freud was not the only psychoanalyst to espouse an organic reductionistic point of view. Such a position is occasionally encountered even among contemporary psychoanalysts. Schwartz argues, "feelings too are ultimately neurobiological 'things'" (1988, p. 366) and proposes that neuroscience and psychoanalysis should share a common conceptual language. And Willick asserts that schizophrenia is an organic illness whose mental manifestations are relatively meaningless. He claims that negative symptoms "are most likely caused by a primary biological disturbance. . . . Other symptoms do appear to be a consequence of regression brought about by the illness disrupting the mental organization . . . reactions to or attempts to deal with the trauma of the dimly perceived but poorly understood organic deficiencies" (1990, pp. 1067–1068).

Moreover, psychoanalysts are guilty of other forms of intersystemic monism. Just as neuroscientists often fail to appreciate the reality of the psychological world, so psychoanalysts have often seemed content to ignore that there is an organic substrate to all personality configurations, normal and abnormal, and that knowledge of the varieties of neurobiological organization might be critical to articulating psychoanalytic theory. With equal acerbity Eisenberg (1986) has characterized this position as "brainless." Psychoanalysts have often reasoned reductionistically, as well, thinking nothing of "analyzing" social, political, national, and international phenomena, and even individual conditions such as autism, which, according to mounting evidence, appears to be constitutionally determined. The relationship of psychoanalysis to interpersonal psychology, family-systems psychology, and sciences (such as sociology and cultural anthropology) that study larger social and cultural entities frequently reflects monistic bias. Psychoanalysis has tended to interpret the data of these fields as though they were all in the mind, implicitly suggesting that separate disciplines with their own methodologies and theoretical structures are not necessary.

Monistic thinking as an intrasystemic problem, within the theoretical confines of each of the human sciences, manifests itself as a tendency toward universalistic, all-encompassing theories, ones billed as not only necessary but sufficient for the entire science. Because such intellectual autocracy is oppressive to the truly curious mind, it tends to foster periodic scientific revolutions, after which the status quo may be reinstated in a new guise. A current example is the tendency of some feminist theorists to replace Freud's monistic model of gender, in which females are viewed as nothing more than defective males, with a model that denies innate differences and asserts that if women were not culturally oppressed they might best men at their own game, so to speak; or else with a model which grants that the female mind is different, with capacities for empathic, intersubjective relationships that males are said to lack, but elevates this difference to a position of normalcy, implying that males are not different so much as deficient.

Judging from the evolution of physics and biology, tendencies toward monistic intrasystemic models may be commonplace in the early history of a science. Physics, for example, abandoned a monistic position early in the century and embraced an eclectic use of models based on principles of relativity and uncertainty. Biologists followed suit not long thereafter and turned to general systems theory. In the course of its evolution, an individual science is likely to begin modestly, as a single theory, and then to manifest an inflexible, resistant attitude toward the development of multiple models, even when the classical model seems inadequate to the task of accounting for all observable phenomena. In chapters 7 and 10 I elaborate how, rationalizations to the contrary notwithstanding, psychoanalysis remains basically a monistic theoretical system.

The kind of pseudo-pluralism or naive interactionism I have described in interscientific relations is also found in the relations among different theoretical models within a particular human science. Especially during case discussions or at difficult points during an individual treatment, psychoanalysts may mix classical concepts, self psychological concepts, a bit of Winnicott, and a bit of Klein, as though these shared a common theoretical base. The anthropologist is confronted with analogous problems when exposed to a bewildering cultural variety, and may borrow ideas from representatives of the various camps Shweder (1991) describes—universalism, evolutionism, and relativism. In other words, under the illusion of appreciating diversity we may treat different theoretical systems as though they were part of a single system, overlooking critical distinctions between phenomenological levels and the organizing concepts used to account for them. Pragmatically useful as this hybridized form of thinking may sometimes be, it must be seen for what it is, a form of applied science or technology that overlooks crucial conceptual and organizational distinctions among theoretical models.

Possibly the only human science in which there is an active debate about the merits of monistic and pluralistic hypotheses is anthropology. The monistic hypothesis is known variously as universalism and structuralism. It has roots in the work of Benedict (1934, 1946), Mead (1939), Gorer (1943), Kluckhohn (1953), Osgood (1964), and Lévi-Strauss (1949, 1963, 1966; see Gehrie, 1978). Kluckhohn, for example, proposed that we search for "universal categories of culture and personality . . . invariant points of reference supplied by the biological, psychological and sociosituational 'givens' of human life" (1953, pp. 521–522). The ongoing debate over the universality of the Oedipus complex illustrates not only the controversy within anthropology but also the extent to which, as a field, it is incompletely differentiated from psychoanalysis. The pluralistic position within anthropology is generally attributed to Geertz (local knowledge; 1975, 1979) and Heelas and Lock (indigenous psychology; 1981) and is supported by Shweder (1991) and Spiro (1984). Geertz, perhaps the most outspoken of the relativists, prefers that anthropology be consciously (not naively) indigenous, oriented from the native point of view. However, he also recognizes that universalism and pluralism are not necessarily mutually exclusive positions. Shweder points out that indigenous psychologies retain a kind of contextual lawfulness: "The fact that there is no one uniform objective reality (constraint, foundation, godhead, truth, standard) does not mean there are no objective realities . . . at all. The death of monotheism should not be confused with the death of god(s). Ontological atheism or subjectivism is not the only route to relativism. Polytheism or the idea of multiple objective worlds is the alternative" (1991, p. 29).

Modal personality constructs serve as conceptual anchors for monistic theories of personality. Such theories represent personality in terms of normality and deviance on a linear quantitative scale. Modality is an important concept in all systems; the related functions of the establishment and maintenance of centrality or normalcy and the recognition and regulation of deviance are critical to the homeostasis of any vital system (see chapter 13 on systems theory). The concept of modal personality is based on the concept of population, and populations are generally considered to be qualitatively homogeneous entities with regard to the characteristics being measured. Modal constructs are associated with the assumption that variance represents not difference but deviance, which is measurably distributed on a linear scale. Hence the application of modal constructs carries with it a subtly disguised value system in which polychromatic complexity, quality, or difference is sacrificed for the simplicity of a monochromatic scale.

The theoretical model of personality I consider of greatest potential value—psychoanalysis—is basically a monistic theory. It is constructed around the concept of a modal personality, and it tends to reify as a universal standard the neurotic or mildly disturbed male typical of nineteenth- and twentieth-century Western culture. Personalities that diverge from the mode, if they are noted at all, tend to be conceived of not as qualitatively different but as a null category, a hole or void, lacking or defective, immature or pathological. Examples of nullification or nonsignification include dismissing schizophrenia as a lack of neurotic organization or conceiving of the female as an anatomically and psychologically defective male. Homosexuality has until recently been thought to result from deficiencies in normal psychosexual development. Boyer (1962) applied a Western personality scale monistically and classified Apache shamans as psychotic. Additional examples of nullification by pseudo-empathy, that is, by the observer assuming that the subject is qualitatively similar, are cited in chapter 10 on more seriously disturbed personalities.

Modal personality constructs and a monistic frame of reference make psychoanalysis an indigenous psychology, unable to appreciate qualitative culture-related differences in personality (see chapter 7). They are responsible for the inability of psychoanalysis to conceive of qualitative intracultural diversity of personality as well (chapter 10) and for its failure, until very recently, to conceive of female psychology adequately (chapter 9).

We of Western male-dominated culture may be unknowing victims as well as perpetrators of monistic thinking based on modal personality constructs. Eastern observers may conclude (chapter 6) that persons who demonstrate self-aggrandizing, aggressive, competitive behavior and who value individualism above values of the group, who might be not only considered normal but valued in Western culture, are pathological. And some feminist authors, as I describe in chapter 9, have attempted to restructure modal personality in such a fashion as to cast male personality as immature or deviant.

Monistic and reductionistic thinking is an artifact of the personal embeddedness of the creator of a model in the particulars of time, gender, and culture. Many of its limitations are more or less apparent from the preceding discussion. Reductionistic efforts have generally proven unsuccessful; even within the organic sciences, the hoped-for reduction of chemistry to physics now seems unlikely. Convictions of the sufficiency of a single conceptual system are based on overvaluation of linear causal thinking—fallacious beliefs that construction and creation are linear and atomistic and that analysis (deconstruction) and synthesis (construction) are equivalent in the sense of being causally reversible. One of the best known expressions of this idea, Laplace's contention that it should be possible to predict the entire future of the universe from a thorough analytic knowledge of all of its parts, has been thoroughly discredited by chaos theory (chapter 13). Such convictions do not take into account that nature consists of complex nonlinear, non-equilibrating dynamic systems that are related by a process of hierarchical transformation, creative synthesis, or recursive iteration.

The use of modal constructs as a starting point for personality theory has numerous drawbacks. First, it is based on the assumption that it is possible to define a population of qualitatively similar personalities to which a linear scale can be applied. This seems implausible, even within a particular culture at a given time in history. It is an even less tenable hypothesis cross-culturally and seems hardly plausible when one views the shifting norms of personality over time, as cultures evolve. Those who build personality theories around modal personality risk failing to note and appreciate diversity, or else equating it with abnormality.

Challenges to the monistic overgeneralization of reductionistic modes of thinking come from all fields of knowledge. From science see, for example, the summary of a symposium on systems theory by Koestler and Smythies (1969), chapter 6 on culture and anthropology, and chapter 13 on systems theory and chaos theory. The biologist-philosopher Paul Weiss (1977) says succinctly and elegantly: "The study of parts—analytical information about parts—paid off magnificently as long as we indulged primarily in learning more and more about less and less, relying on the ingrained conviction that from the parts of that diminutival knowledge we would be able to reconstruct, 'synthesize' (at least in our mind) the typically patterned order of the phenomenon that we had deliberately disordered in our analytical procedure as if we could resurrect the phoenix from its ashes" (p. 24). More concretely, the physicist Niels Bohr (1937) notes that the linear reductionistic study of life, taken to its extreme, literally destroys its subject.

From the vantage point of philosophy Bertrand Russell (1945) notes that values are outside the realm of science. In his 1926 Lowell lectures Whitehead notes that because science is devoted to measurement it is inherently materialistic, and science is incapable of representing quality or value (1967). Nozick (1981) points out that logical positivist and scientific materialist accounts of the human being are not only philosophically and scientifically unsound, but also morally bankrupt. "In devaluing people, the reductionist violates the principle that everything is to be treated as having the value it has. Reductionism is not simply a theoretical mistake, it is a moral failing" (p. 631). In the process of analysis or deconstruction something essential is lost. Toulmin (1970) imagines the paradoxical state of affairs when materialistic reductionism is complete and the neuroscientists gleefully wish to take credit for their discovery. The Buddhist D. T. Suzuki (1960), commenting from an Eastern perspective about the problems inherent in applying the dualistic, objectifying analytic stance of science to human beings, observes that scientific analysis literally kills the object and then attempts to reconstruct its vitality from the dissected parts. By denying the diversity, complexity, and richness of the phenomenal world, reductionists devalue the meaning and value of human life and experience. The same may be said of reductionistic attempts on the part of one science to consume the phenomenology and legitimacy of another. However essential it may be to our thinking, the process of analysis which is so typical of science is inherently nihilistic and therefore potentially dangerous.

Of course there is nothing inherently wrong with mining any single model of personality, even a reductionistic one, until its full potential has been realized. The problem arises in the omniscient illusion that so often accompanies immersion in a monistic system; the unfortunate synergism between a powerful model, the model-user's embeddedness in his or her culture, gender, and period of history, and his or her natural human egotism. A monist is a frog that overestimates its size and underestimates the dimensions of its puddle. Monistic thinking may also be thought of as a form of systemic pathology, a cognitive-energic aberration. In the intersystemic realm, this means that the curiosity of investigators operating within a given scientific discipline does not remain confined to the particular system under consideration, where it might legitimately and exhaustively express itself studying all human phenomena from the perspective of that system, but instead degenerates into a combination of greed and sloppy thinking about the boundaries between systems and their concepts, leading to misinformed and disrespectful efforts to consume and destroy adjacent higher order systems. In the instance of neuroscientific and psychological systems, both are necessary but neither is sufficient. Each may legitimately lay investigative claim to the entire range of human behavior and thought, but neither is sufficient to comprehend personality in its entirety.

If we reject the naive monistic position that there is but a single model for all personality, centered around a knowable modal personality type, we might instead adopt Geertz's (1975, 1979) and Heelas and Lock's (1981) position of extreme relativism and conclude that there must be a multiplicity of independent theories, each centered around modal personality constructs. Or we might take a different direction and attempt to distinguish the structure that underlies all systems and the process of their transformation, from time-and place-bound specifics of content, meaning, and value, which uniquely characterizes each one.

CHAPTER 5

Constitution-Bound: The Neurobiological Basis
of Personality

When attempting to conceptualize unfamiliar phenomena I sometimes scan familiar imagery to find a match. The relationship of a foundation to the superstructure of a building is analogous to the relationship between the biological and mental systems of personality. A foundation is necessary and limiting but not sufficient or totally determinative. But this imagery is in certain respects inaccurate and misleading. The neurobiological substrate appears to be organized, activated, and reconstituted in relation to life experience. For this reason, although we may envision the neurobiological element as having an antecedent quality with regard to mind or as being somehow more basic, unlike a foundation, it is neither cast in concrete nor topographically situated beneath mind.

The neurobiological element unfolds or evolves over time in a reciprocal exchange with the environment, limited by such variables as critical period, neural plasticity, organization, and activation. Evidence has accumulated in support of the hypothesis of neural plasticity (Vital-Durand, 1975), the continuing adaptive structural modification of the nervous system throughout life as a result of experience. At the cellular level Kandel (1978, 1979) and Carew et al. (1981) have demonstrated microscopic changes in single neurons of the marine snail *Aplysia* during and after learning of a conditioned aversive response; they have suggested that this may be a simple neurological model for the changes evoked by psychotherapy. Kandel says, "It is only insofar as our words produce changes in each other's brains that psychotherapeutic intervention produces change in a patient's mind" (1979, p. 1037; see also Levin and Vuckovich, 1987). Diamond (1988) reports animal experiments which demonstrate that experience can influence the thickness of the cerebral cortex. Davis and Fernald (1990) have demonstrated that following socially induced changes in the dominance/submission status of male cichlid fish there are alterations in hypothalamic neuronal size. And Kolb's (1987) hypothesis that post-traumatic stress disorders are mediated by neuronal changes appears to have been confirmed by Ornitz and Pynoos (1989), who have demonstrated in traumatized children inhibition of the startle response, which is a brain stem mediated reflex.

The complex interactive deterministic process involving the nervous system, experience, and time, evolution, or development, may be viewed in more than one way. From a strictly neuroscientific perspective all of the elements, including experience, may be viewed as physical. From a multiple-systems perspective, however, experiential events operate within separate systematic conceptual frameworks and require distinctive theoretical language. In any case, it is reasonably certain that the deterministic process is not one of simple linear causality but is field-interactive and involves systems in transformation. Hence the limitation of a construction metaphor of foundation and superstructure and the need for a more complex postmodernist perspective.

The reader whose background is in the social sciences will readily appreciate the conceptual limitations of the neuroscientist, in particular the fallacy of underlying concrete structure associated with reductionistic thinking. But he is less likely to be aware that the enthusiasm of the postmodern hermeneuticist who scorns concepts of reality, truth, and structure to be discovered in favor of a radical subjectivity and contextual relativism, carries with it equivalent dangers.

Constitution sets the limits within which personality can unfold, although these continue to evolve throughout the life span in concert with experience, and in ways that have not been completely determined at birth. In this flexible, interactive sense, constitution is a determinant both of specific qualitative variants of personality and of general invariants common to all humankind. Since the constitutional basis for human personality in general is both self-evident and difficult to demonstrate, I shall concentrate on some evidence for the former proposition, that of qualitatively specific constitutional determination. I shall present three sets of data suggestive of specific biology-personality relationships, related to gender differences, homosexuality, and schizophrenia. Considerable anecdotal evidence and a few genetic studies also suggest that there is a constitutional basis for temperamental differences of all kinds. Pardes et al. (1989), for example, note that the incidence of anxiety disorders is nine times greater in first-degree relatives of patients than in the general population, and that there is a 31 percent concordance for such disorders among monozygotic (MZ) twins.

The first set of data relates to organic-constitutional gender differences. It may be the brain and not, as Freud believed, the genitals that is the major gender-differentiating body part. More specifically, it appears to be the neuroendocrine aspects of brain. Hormonal effects are of two types: organizing (or structuring) and activating (or motivating). Hormones organize the sex-specific differentiation of the central nervous system in utero and in the neonate, in patterned ways and at so-called critical periods of development, which themselves differ for each gender (MacLusky and Naftolin, 1981; Jacklin, Maccoby, and Doering, 1983). At conception sex is determined by the presence of the second X chromosome, which produces ovarian tissue, or by the XY combination, which produces testicular tissue. Testicular tissue, in turn, produces fetal testosterone and Mullerian duct inhibiting hormone. The undifferentiated fetus is proto-female, a finding more consistent with Fairbairn's (1952) theory than with Freud's belief that females are aborted or defective males. In the genotypically male fetus testosterone secretion stimulates masculine organization and differentiation, and Mullerian duct hormone suppresses the development of feminine characteristics. In the genotypically female fetus testosterone is not secreted, and feminization proceeds unimpeded. The masculinizing activational pathway has been studied in rats, and there is no reason to believe that it is fundamentally different in humans. This involves the conversion of fetal testosterone to estrogen. The female fetus is not masculinized by the high levels of maternal estrogen found in neonatal rats because of the presence of a specific fetal protein (McEwen, 1983, 1991; Meaney, 1989; Meaney, Stewart, Poulin et al., 1983).

It is in three areas of the brain that permanent structural sexually differentiating changes are hormonally induced. These areas, the cortex, the amygdala, and the hypothalamus, particularly the anterior portion, each contain sexually dimorphic interstitial nuclei—that is, nuclei that are differentially responsive to testosterone (Swaab and Fliers, 1985; Fuxe et al., 1988; Seeman and Lang, 1990; Kopala and Clark, 1990). These structural differentiations include larger groupings of nuclei INAH-2 & 3, SDN-POA, and BNST in the male brain and midline structures that are larger (surface area of the midsagittal anterior commissure and massa intermedia) and differently shaped (a bulbous shaped splenium, or midsagittal section of the corpus callosum) in the female brain (Gorski, 1991).

Studies of rats indicate that sexual differentiation of the brain is accompanied by the development of a wide range of behaviors and functions, including ones whose social significance goes beyond what is ordinarily associated with sexual and reproductive activity. These include specific sexual posturing and behavior, aggressive behavior, taste preferences, food-intake patterns, body weight and weight-distribution, urination posturing, playfulness, and other social behaviors; territoriality, cognitive learning attitudes, maternal behaviors, and patterns of peptidase secretion (Phoenix, Goy, Gerall, et al., 1959; Goy and Goldfoot, 1974; Meaney, 1989; Beatty, 1979; Gorski, 1991). The rough peer play that characterizes males and appears to be the developmental route to adult male dominance patterns commences in juvenile relationships among peers, prior to the pubertal activational effects of testosterone. The fact that such patterns appear to be universal in males of many species suggests that they are organizational or neurostructural in origin (Meaney, 1989). The amygdala appears to be the locus of this response (Meaney, Dodge, and Beatty, 1981; Meaney and McEwen, 1986; Meaney, 1989; Maccoby, 1990).

Organizational changes in the brain are not confined to the intrauterine and neonatal stages of life. Witelson's human studies (1976) of pre- and postpubescent males and females suggest that the process of hemispheric specialization continues through adolescence, and is completed earlier in males, whereas the female brain retains plasticity until later in development. Like the finding that the fetal brain is intrinsically female, this is at odds with Freud's belief that female superego development tends to arrest at an early age as a result of failure to experience and resolve a normal Oedipus complex.

The second category of hormonal effects is activational or motivational. Complex feedback loops are involved. The sexually differentiated areas of the brain, including the hypothalamus and amygdala, regulate hormonal secretion and are differentially responsive to it.

The hypothalamus depends on the amygdala for its connection to the cortex and to the sensory-perceptual world. The amygdala is believed to be responsible for both the establishment of stimulus-response learning patterns and their evocation in response to subsequent stimulation (MacLean, 1990). From this we may infer that intactness of the amygdala is crucial to the continuity of learned control over emotionality. Amygdalectomy in male primates diminishes aggressiveness, whereas in females it enhances aggressive behavior (Haber, 1981). In terms of the learning function of the amygdala, this suggests that inhibition of aggressiveness and assertion may be a socially learned behavior, so that amygdalectomy, conceived of as a form of unlearning, leaves the female less submissive and the male less aggressive.

In rodent species hypothalamic control of progesterone secretion regulates aggressiveness in females. In humans estrogen is thought to be protective against affect disturbance and psychosis (Sherwin, 1988; Seeman and Lang, 1990; Kopala and Clark, 1990). Lowered estrogen levels, found in the late luteal phase of the menstrual cycle, postpartum, and in menopause, seem to have some relationship to emotional disturbance.

The literature relating androgens (especially testosterone) and aggression is difficult to interpret. Experiments with neonatal female mice and rhesus monkeys given testosterone, and "natural" experiments with female human infants who for reasons of individual pathology or maternal exposure have sustained elevated testosterone levels, show that as these females grow they continue to be more aggressive than normal female controls (Leventhal and Brodie, 1981; Bronson and Desjardins, 1968; Joselyn, 1973; Rose, Haladay, and Bernstein, 1971). Studies of primates by Rose, Haladay, and Bernstein (1971) and Mazur (1976) reveal a bidirectional correlation between testosterone levels and social status. For example, subsequent to conflict resolution and social status change within the group, newly dominant male rhesus monkeys show elevated testosterone levels, whereas those demoted to subordinate status show diminution. In adult male primates including humans, however, there is no simple correlation between testosterone levels and aggressive behavior (Leventhal and Brodie, 1981). Aggressive adult males do not always have elevated testosterone levels, and the administration of testosterone to adult females does not necessarily make them more aggressive. As mentioned earlier, social learning patterns, structured through the amygdala, appear to play an important role and have the potential to override the activational effects of testosterone.

The combination of hormonally induced organizational and activational effects on the brain with interpersonally activated modifications that are consistent with the principle of neural plasticity results in clear-cut differences in brain function between males and females. The new neuroimaging technology is beginning to demonstrate the nature of these differences. PET (positron emission tomography) scanning of metabolic activity (Gur et al., 1985) reveals that males have a higher level of metabolism in the temporal-limbic system and cerebellum and a lower level in the cingulate gyrus. Small differences in hemispheric functioning were found during performance of typical "male" skills (spatial, mechanical, and motor) and "female" skills (abstract, verbal, mental flexibility). An interesting finding in this study relates to stereotypes about crossover or empathy: men were much more likely to possess "female" brain characteristics than vice versa. Shaywitz, Shaywitz, Pugh, et al. (1995) presented phonological tasks (involving rhyming of unfamiliar words) to males and females and found that the males processed them exclusively in the left frontal gyrus, whereas the females employed more diffuse neural systems including both frontal gyri. These findings further reinforce the widespread belief that there are differences between typical male and female patterns of thinking, although it must be emphasized that, taken by themselves, they do not allow us to distinguish constitutional effects from environmental ones.

What can we conclude from these studies? There is evidence to support the hypothesis that such gender-stereotypical traits as masculine motivation to master the external environment and feminine social relatedness and adaptability are not simply expressions of differential cultural forces. In the male there are the aggressive, environmental-manipulative aspects of constitution, and in the female those constitutional elements suggestive of primary adaptability or relatedness, not only the neurobiology related to conception and pregnancy, but the postpartum lactation responses to sensations and perceptions of the infant. In the female, one striking finding suggests a constitutionally heightened sensitivity to biologically unrelated others, as first observed by McClintock (1971) and anecdotally confirmed by many others, women who live primarily in close or intimate proximity to other women tend to attune their menstrual cycles to one another.

Turning attention to homosexuality, while it is not possible to distinguish homosexuals from heterosexuals on the basis of neuroanatomy, some evidence has accumulated in support of a genetic component in both male and female homosexuality. Studies of monozygotic twins reveal an almost 50 percent concordance (Bailey and Pillard, 1991; Bailey, Pillard, Neale, and Ageyei, 1993; Buhrich, Bailey, and Martin, 1991). Friedman and Downey (1993) note in homosexuals findings suggestive of a hormone-related organizational disturbance in fetal androgen metabolism. Nuclear changes in the hypothalamic area have also been observed. The mid-saggital area of the anterior commissure appears to be larger in homosexual males than in females, and smallest in heterosexual males. Interstitial nucleus INAH-3 in the anterior hypothalamus also appears to be larger in heterosexual than homosexual males, and smallest in females (Swaab and Hoffman, 1990; LeVay, 1991; Allen and Gorski, 1992). Findings of enlargement of the suprachiasmatic nucleus in homosexual males have been reported but remain controversial. Of course, homosexual brain structure may also be a consequence of homosexual mental states. Once again, we might postulate an interactive matrix, including innate neurobiological elements.

The final instance of constitutional substrate I consider is schizophrenia. It may seem inappropriate to use what is generally looked upon as an illness as a model for relating constitution and personality. However, fully a century of research has failed to yield evidence of a definitive lesion underlying schizophrenia, and it is time to consider replacing concepts of illness and lesion with concepts of difference and diversity in the structure and functioning of the brain. Also, while there is suggestive evidence, mostly genetic but also anatomic, physiological, metabolic, and endocrine, for an organic substrate in schizophrenia, it is not as convincing as the evidence of a neurobiological substrate for gendered differences in personality, which also relate to patterning of the brain and are not conceived of as illness at all. Modeling schizophrenia and other serious personality disturbances as difference rather than illness—that is, abandoning a linear scale in which schizophrenia is deviant from modal personality—is part of my broader conception of personality.

I shall not review the organic data about schizophrenia in detail (see

Robbins, 1993). The presence of a genetic factor in many if not all cases of schizophrenia now seems established, although genetic factors appear to account for considerably less than half the variance. Gottesman and Shields (1982) and Kringlen (1987) have summarized twin concordance studies for schizophrenia, which have yielded the most conclusive evidence in favor of the genetic hypothesis. They report that concordance for schizophrenia among dizygotic twins ranges from 7 to 19 percent, averaging 10 percent, and monozygotic concordance ranges from 15 to 42 percent, averaging 30 percent. Thus monozygotic concordance is three times dizygotic concordance, and 35 to 60 times the lifetime risk for schizophrenia in the general population. Kendler (1992) has summarized eleven major twin studies in which monozygotic concordance ranges from 31 to 78 percent. Torrey (1992) has conducted his own survey of these studies, and he estimates monozygotic concordance at 28 percent and dizygotic concordance at 6 percent.

Many of the studies of differences in schizophrenia brain patterning have concentrated on the left temporal-limbic area because it is part of the dominant hemisphere in most patients and hence part of the language center. It contains the planum temporale, which is language-specialized. There have been reports of atrophy of these areas based on postmortem studies and noninvasive imaging techniques. Stevens (1982) reports increased gliosis in the basal limbic system of schizophrenics, even those who have never been medicated. Left temporal hypermetabolism, consistent with so-called positive symptoms, has been noted by Gur et al. (1985) and Andreasen (1988). Tamminga et al. (1992) report hypometabolism in the hippocampus and anterior cingulate gyrus of actively psychotic, drug-free schizophrenics with deficit and nondeficit symptomatology. They note that the deficit group manifested hypometabolism in frontal, parietal, and thalamic areas, as well.

Psychophysiological studies by Broff and Geyer (1978), Adler, Pachtman, et al. (1982), Liberman et al. (1984), and Holzman (1987) suggest functional alterations consistent with a sensory gating defect related to the temporal-limbic area. Broff and Geyer note an exaggerated acoustic startle response in schizophrenics. Holzman (1987) and Liberman (1984) report that the skin conductance orientation response to innocuous environmental stimuli (SCOR), which is an indicator of "gating" or modulation of incoming stimuli, is absent in 40 to 50 percent of schizophrenics, in contrast to only 5 to 10 percent of controls. It is more frequently absent in the most withdrawn and disorganized patients. The SCORs of those schizophrenics who do respond tend to be abnormally high. Kopala and Clark (1991) report olfactory agnosia in approximately half of all schizophrenics; olfaction is also a function of the temporal-limbic part of the brain. Holzman reports diminution in the variation and latency of the early components of stimulus-evoked brain potentials (ERP), which suggest impaired modulation and inhibition of stimulus input. McCarley and associates (1991) report that in 85 to 95 percent of unmedicated schizophrenic patients there is diminution of a characteristic EEG spike following a cognitive stimulus that requires the patient to make some alteration in his world-view. MRI studies of these same patients show significant tissue loss in the dominant posterior superior temporal area, which includes the limbic system structures: the extent of tissue loss seems to be correlated with severity of the patient's thought disorder.

Atrophy and hypometabolism, which have been noted in the frontal lobes of schizophrenics, may also be linked to the abnormalities of the limbic system, which appears to inform the more rational, judgmental, planful frontal lobes of the emotional significance of events through afferent striatal connections and to modulate the visceral, emotional, and sensory-perceptual information transmitted to it. Weinberger (1988) speculates that prefrontal hypometabolism might be secondary to disrupted limbic system input.

Few of these changes have been sufficiently replicated to be considered definitive. Moreover, the norms have not been established for many of the variables, hence their distribution in a normal population and in patients with other diagnoses is not well known. Organic changes that have been found to distinguish large groups of schizophrenics from controls with statistical significance are usually not sufficiently deviant in any particular patient to be classified as abnormal by an investigator assessing the patient without knowing that he or she has been diagnosed as schizophrenic. Most of the presumed abnormalities, like ventricular enlargement, are neither universal in schizophrenia nor specific to it. In fact, most schizophrenics fall within the normal range on such variables.

As is the case with homosexuality and gender differences, whether the neurobiological differences that have been reported in schizophrenics are primary manifestations of constitution, are secondary to environmental changes, or are interactive is not known. For example, cerebral atrophy might be secondary to the mental attitudes (the reluctance to think and to feel) that characterize negative-symptom schizophrenics as well as to the stimulus-impoverished environments in which some institutionalized people live. The effects of the neuroleptic medication most of these people have chronically received is also difficult to assess, as most of these medications are known to be neurotoxic (potential causes of such conditions as tardive dyskinesia).

In summary, there is a constitutional substrate of personality, consisting both of universal elements common to all of us, and specific configurations which distinguish us from one another. There is evidence for broad classes of constitutional difference that are not simply individual idiosyncrasies or pathological lesions. While the specific configurations of brain noted in research studies conducted on adults may be products of life experience, at least in the instances of gender, homosexuality, and schizophrenia, neurobiological differences appear to have been present from birth and probably before. These differences are subtle and diffuse, noticeable only as statistical averages when comparing large groups, so that it is not possible to definitively distinguish single male from female brains, homosexual from heterosexual brains, or schizophrenic from "normal" brains. It is probable that these categories relate in some way to the development of qualitatively diverse personality typologies.

CHAPTER 6

Ethnocentrism: Culture, Local Knowledge,
and Universal Truth

The brain, the culture, and the disciplines that study them comprise the outer limits or bookends, so to speak, of the human person. The leap from the human brain to human culture, and from neuroscience to anthropology, is immense, and the task of conceiving of it and of modeling just how one might get from one to the other occupies a substantial portion of this book.

The diversity associated with major differences among cultures is arguably the single most important of the dimensions that are not adequately conceived of in existing theoretical conceptions of personality. However we choose to understand it, culture-related diversity is readily apparent to the casual observer compared to personality diversity related to history (chapter 3), gender (chapter 9), and the normal and pathological variants that characterize a particular culture (chapter 10). The effects of culture on conceptions of personality are apparent at several reciprocally interactive levels, ranging from the personalities of the theorists who construe the data, to their models of modal personality, personality deviation, and gender (Harre, 1981, 1984; Choi, Kim, and Choi, 1993).

It is important at the outset to note that science itself is embedded in Western culture and that in choosing it as a model for viewing culture we are already making a cultural commitment, for its fruits are necessarily hybrids of insight about human beings generally with re-presentations of Western cultural bias. Of course this is no more true of science than of any epistemology, and Geertz (1979) cogently refers to the result of all such systems as "local knowledge." The theories of personality that emerge under such circumstances, as I have mentioned, are what Heelas and Lock (1981) call indigenous psychologies.

I should like to review some of our knowledge of the relationship of culture and personality, as well as some aspects of anthropology, the human science in whose domain of study it principally falls. It is difficult to separate anthropology from psychoanalysis, as the two have enjoyed a kind of love-hate relationship in the study of non-Western personality, even though their methodologies differ—field observation in the case of anthropology, assisted intensive personal introspection in the case of psychoanalysis. Ever since publication of Freud's *Totem and Taboo* in 1913 psychoanalysts have been neither modest nor cautious about applying the theory to members of other cultures. At times anthropologists have embraced the psychoanalytic viewpoint uncritically as a frame of reference for observing and interviewing, and then for organizing their data, while at other times they have rejected psychoanalysis as too bound to Western culture to be of use. These uneasy bedfellows, psychoanalysis and anthropology, have made a fruitful union in some respects. In others they have simply repeated at an intellectual level the imperialistic, colonialistic history of the world, mistaking culturally relativistic understandings about persons and relationships for universal verities and imposing stigmatizing and devaluing interpretations on members of other cultures in the guise of scientific understanding. In this chapter I focus primarily on the issue of culture-related similarities and differences in personality from the vantage point of anthropology. The cultural embeddedness of psychoanalysis and its monistic limitations as an indigenous psychology is the subject of chapter 7.

As early as 1871 Tylor (1958) defined the mind of members of non-Western cultures as primitive: childlike, erroneous, and unable to differentiate internal from external. Levy-Bruhl wrote that "primitive mentality considers and at the same time feels all beings and objects to be homogeneous, that is, he regards them all as participating either in the same essential nature, or in the same ensemble of qualities" (1965, p. 19). There is no doubt that the complexities of entire cultures (Australian aborigines, Melanesians, Somali, Indians, and Native Americans, to name but a few) have been overlooked by Western researchers, who have contented themselves with labeling them immature, primitive, deficient, or lacking (Whiting and Child, 1953; Whiting, 1959; Spiro, 1965, 1982; Devereaux, 1956). Roheim (1945, 1950), who is characterized as "a thorough-going universalistic psychoanalytic reductionist" (Spain, 1992, p. 6), was perhaps the most zealous of these naive monistic thinkers.

The monistic tendency of culture-personality theorists and their models, and the related tendency to equate deviations from Western modal personality with primitivism, have not gone unnoticed and unprotested within anthropology. Johannes Herder, in the eighteenth century, was one of the first to decry ethnocentrism, proclaiming that judging members of other cultures by our standards is a form of arrogance (Berlin, 1976). In late nineteenth-century Germany, Steinthal and Lazarus (Danziger, 1983) established the *Journal of Ethnopsychology and Linguistics*, a precursor of the contemporary discipline of cultural psychology. This work was continued in the first half of the twentieth century by Wundt (1916), in his investigations of *volkerpsychologie*, or folk-psychology, by Hallowell (1939), and then by Kardiner (1939, 1945), Linton (1936, 1945), and Whiting and Child (1953). Toward the end of this century a new anthropological discipline known as cultural psychology has emerged, expressly devoted to understanding this critical dimension of personality.

Currently there is a debate within anthropology between the universalists, who postulate innate deep structures undergirding diversity, and the relativists, who espouse not only the necessity for but the sufficiency of local or indigenous hypotheses. Shweder (1984) calls these the scientific and romantic schools, respectively. The universalist camp includes Benedict (1934, 1946), Mead (1935, 1939, 1953), Gorer (1943), Kluckhohn (1953), Osgood (1964), and Lévi-Strauss (1949, 1963, 1966) (see Gehrie, 1978). The goal of universalism, as of other monistic theories, is to delve beneath appearance and phenomenology by a process of reductionism, in search of underlying order. Kluckhohn (1953) proposed that we search for "universal categories of culture and personality . . . invariant points of reference supplied by the biological, psychological and sociosituational 'givens' of human life" (pp. 521–522).

In 1991 Shweder articulated some of the problems of universalist hypotheses, including tendencies toward overgeneralization (denial of differences) and restriction of data. He concluded: "The path travelled by the universalist is rarely the one that leads to ethnographic illumination; only occasionally does it lead to a powerful, context-rich universal generalization. However, when it does it should not be scorned" (p. 117). Spiro (1984, 1986) suggests that deep structures and superficial patterns may co-exist, each requiring separate attention and formulation. In this debate each camp suspects the other of a form of illusion or mythologizing; the universalists hold that the apparent diversity of the relativists is actually superficial or epiphenomenal, whereas the relativists hold that the belief in universals involves projection or overgeneralization of local beliefs.

It would be a mistake to conclude that monothetic thinking about culture and personality is a monopoly of Western observers. Other cultures have views of the West that are similar in form if not content. For example, some of the self-attributes Westerners look upon as normal and desirable, which cause a person to stand out from others and sometimes to function in opposition to or struggle with the social world—for example, aggressiveness, competitiveness, the striving for equality and even upward mobility and superiority—tend to be devalued by Eastern observers. Persons with such characteristics may be regarded as immature or even pathological, insufficiently attuned to and aware of their place in the natural and social worlds. Buddhists maintain that such people are pursuing an illusion (of self), an ailment they call *sem*.

How can we account for these culturally very different ways of looking at personality? Countless observers from a variety of fields have loosely grouped these under the rubrics "Eastern" and "Western." These admittedly ambiguous terms seem to refer most reliably to skin pigment (Caucasian / dark-skinned). They are certainly not synonymous with geography, at least as we know it today, for Native Americans (Shweder and Bourne, 1982; Miller, 1984); Eskimos (Briggs, 1970) and at least one African tribe, the Gusii (LeVine, 1990) appear to conform to descriptions of Eastern culture. But the different perspectives may have been related to a prehistoric geography prior to the hypothesized migration across the Siberian-Alaskan land bridge.

Neki (1976) seems to have been among the first to propose that there might actually be qualitatively different psychic systems that characterize these groupings. The highly abstract outline that follows is presented for heuristic purposes, with full awareness that most dichotomies, particularly those involving complex phenomena, are drawn at the expense of oversimplification.

The Western concept of personal maturity is that of an independent, autonomous self. The self is dualistically conceived of as separate, even alienated, from society and culture and in opposition to them, whether in Freud's sense of the core biological self as the enemy of culture, Reich's sense of authoritarian culture as the enemy of self-actualization, or the contemporary object-relations sense of self in apposition, if not necessarily opposition, to the object. Western culture values a certain degree of personal antagonism toward others (rebelliousness, competitiveness). Self-discipline and inhibition, however socially necessary (for example, Freud's ideas about instinctual renunciation and sublimation), are considered equivalent to personal sacrifice—an infringement of rights and privileges—and tend to elicit anger and aggressiveness. Aspirations to better one's social circumstances are culturally desirable. From his individuated and separated position the Western person is believed to be capable of abstract, objective, and objectifying (literally, making objects of) thinking about the world. Insofar as objectification tends to be dehumanizing, the result is loss of distinction between the inanimate and animate worlds. In its extreme form such analytical thinking has traditionally been called science. From this position the Western person can potentially render absolute and universal judgments; determine fact, truth, and reality; and by virtue of these capabilities exercise free or unencumbered choices. As a consequence he believes himself capable of comprehending the inner workings of his environment and gaining actual dominance, power and control over it. Because the Westerner conceives of himself as a unique individual, he takes the workings of his mind very seriously and literally and tends to believe in free will. His valuation of each of his thoughts and feelings, wishes and desires, and his objectifying preoccupation and attunement to them are quite different from the attitude of the Easterner. The anthropologist Clifford Geertz has put it succinctly: "The Western conception of the person as a bounded, unique, more or less integrated motivational and cognitive universe, a dynamic center of awareness, emotion, judgment, and action organized into a distinctive whole and set contrastively against other such wholes and against a social and natural background, is, however incorrigible it may seem to us, a rather peculiar idea within the context of the world's cultures" (1975, p. 48). D. T. Suzuki, a prominent Buddhist speaking from the Eastern perspective, summarizes: "The Western mind is: analytical, discriminative, differential, inductive, individualistic, intellectual, objective, scientific, generalizing, conceptual, schematic, impersonal, legalistic, organizing, power-wielding, self-assertive, disposed to impose its will on others" (1960, p. 5). In summary, typical Western personality is self-centric.

What of the self in Eastern cultures? First we must ask, is there such a thing, in the Western sense of the term? Of course self-referential concepts, terms that denote the corporeal self and the individual thinking and acting human person, are pragmatically necessary and are found in all languages. Nonetheless, the concept of self may have nowhere near the organizing centrality or richness in Eastern cultures that it has in Western ones. If the term is used for purposes of comparison and communication between Easterners and Westerners the illusion of understanding may mask an underlying confusion.*

Elements organized in the Western mind under the rubric "self" are either not highly articulated in the Easterner to begin with or are conceived of as parts of a larger social-environmental-historical unity, which holds an analogous place in the construction of a sense of identity. The focus is on this larger identity rather than on the person, who comprises a part. From the Western vantage point these central organizing units would more aptly be termed non-self: family, social group, culture, nature, or religion. Kakar (1985), Roland (1988), and Ramanujan (1992) have written about the person in Indian culture. Kakar remarks that whereas the Western psyche is individual, the Eastern psyche is undifferentiated from relationships with others and with the universe; to denote it he coined the term *dividual*. Ramanujan (1992) refers to Indian culture as a "field society" in which kinship bonds play an integral role determining identity and behavior. Shweder and Bourne (1982) and Miller (1984) asked Native American subjects and a control group of Americans to describe an acquaintance. The Americans tended to employ egocentric or context-free traits, whereas the Native Americans used descriptors that were sociocentric or other-related. In Eastern cultures identity is organized around holistic, interdependent, interconnected, interactive, and contextual lines, not around personal autonomy. In Japanese the term for self is *jibun*. *Bun* refers to

* See Caudill and Weinstein (1961), Lebra (1976), Doi (1973), and Rohlen (1974) for studies of the Japanese; Geertz's study of the Balinesians (1975); Read's work on the Gahuku-Gama of New Guinea (1955); Selby's studies of the Zapotecs of Mexico (1974, 1975); studies of Indian culture by Dumont (1970), Lannoy (1971), Roland (1980, 1982, 1988), Kakar (1971, 1979, 1982, 1985, 1990), Johnson (1993); and Levy's 1973 work on Tahitians.

portion or share, and *jibun* means that the person is part of a larger social entity (Lebra, 1976). In Korean a group-collective pronoun, *woori*, is used (Choi, Kim, and Choi, 1993). In summary, Eastern personality is typically socio-centric.

The elements that make for self as it is defined in Western cultures, particularly organization of experience and action around concepts such as drives, appetites, or emotions, are consciously eschewed as illusory among Buddhists (*annatta, niratma*) and Hindus (*atman*). Buddhism does employ the term *self*, but in a different sense. Suzuki, for example, says that "The Self is the point of absolute subjectivity," and he adds, "the Self is to be taken hold of from within, and not from the outside" (1960, p. 25). Erich Fromm, one of the few Western psychoanalysts, until late in the twentieth century, to give serious intellectual consideration to Buddhism, says that "the aim [of Buddhist meditation] becomes that of overcoming alienation, and of the subject-object split in perceiving the world" (1960, pp. 135–136). Such ideas suggest that the Buddhist conception of a self, which is preoccupied with the process of experiencing and with the content of experience freed of active efforts at organization, cannot be embraced in Western thinking under the rubric of either self or non-self. Yet the commonplace Western dismissal of Eastern religions as encouraging regressive states of boundary-less instability and passivity is ethnocentric and incorrect. Just as the Westerner has developed particular skills and abilities in organizing experience around notions of self, others, and objects, so the practiced Buddhist has achieved a self-discipline and stability of personality which enables him to experience his existence in the world in a rich and nuanced way without imposing a categorical mental organization. This achievement is beyond the reach of the average Westerner.

For these reasons it seems more meaningful to utilize the concept of identity rather than self when making comparisons between East and West. With regard to the centrality of social organization in the establishment and maintenance of personal identity, Ruth Benedict says: "Westerners are likely to feel it is a sign of strength to rebel against conventions and seize happiness in spite of obstacles. . . . [To the Japanese] strength of character . . . is shown in conforming not in rebelling" (1946, p. 207). In Eastern cultures the social forces and organizations that bind persons together provide each person with a sense of identity, stability, and coherence analogous to the way intrapsychic structures and integrating linkages, including the capacity to tolerate conflict and ambivalence, are hypothesized to bind the Western psyche together. Lebra says of the Japanese, "Both the pride and the shame of the individual are shared by his group" (1976, p. 36). According to Benedict (1946), a Japanese expression for mental confusion is "neither older brother nor younger brother." Another indication that social organization serves a function among Easterners analogous to that of intrapsychic organization among Westerners is that Japanese personality is not characterized by enduring traits as is Western personality. A Japanese individual may manifest very different, even seemingly contradictory personality traits and values in each of a variety of spheres of duty or obligation, as though, to Western eyes, it was not the same "person" functioning in each one (Benedict, 1946). A Western observer might find this confusing and impute a sense of personal incoherence or fragmentation. Benedict explains, "In most cultures individuals respect themselves in proportion as they attain some virtue . . . [or] set up as a life goal some objective. . . . The Japanese follow more particularistic codes" (1946, p. 212). And, "In Japan 'respecting yourself' is always to show yourself the careful player. It does not mean, as it does in English usage, consciously conforming to a worthy standard of conduct" (p. 219).

One of the most important of the socially binding linkages that comprise identity among members of Eastern cultures is a complex system of obligation and debt, defined in hereditary caste terms. Ho (1993) characterizes Eastern cultures as "obligation-preoccupied," in contrast with Western cultures, which are "rights-preoccupied." Among the Japanese there are many situationally specific nuances of lifelong obligation, with such names as giri, jin, and gimu, which organize the interpersonal and social worlds in fixed ways that may seem abnormal to Westerners accustomed to the pursuit of equality and social mobility. Among the Japanese even suicide is deemed, under certain circumstances, a normal response in repayment or discharge of a debt or obligation (Hsieh and Spence, 1981). In Eastern cultures familial, natural, cultural, and religious concepts are more highly articulated, including concepts of affiliation or adaptation and obligation involving highly structured hierarchical relationships. Individual life, well-being, and death are all less important than in the West, for people are looked upon as parts or cogs in relation to other people and to larger natural and social wholes on which value is placed. The person is not differentiated from his station or role in the culture. As a consequence social equality is not a goal, and obligations and rights are naturally apportioned differentially than in the West (Bourne, 1991). At the same time the resulting part-relatedness does not have the dehumanizing connotation it would have in the Western world. In other words, there is not the polarization or opposition between individual and society that there is in Western culture, so that among Easterners self-discipline and self-deprivation are not necessarily looked upon as self-abnegation and do not seem to generate frustration as they do in Westerners. As identity is socially structured, these vicissitudes of self-discipline are also much more finely articulated.

Japanese psychoanalysts have made some significant attempts to adapt psychoanalytic theory to their sociocentric culture. In 1931 Kosawa presented a paper to Freud in which he proposed the term *Ajase*, derived from a Japanese folktale, to denote the ambivalent dependency of infants on their mothers (Okonogi, 1979). Takeo Doi (1973) proposed that the Japanese concept *amae* may have the centrality which accrues to *self* in Western culture. Caudill (1962) writes of the fundamental organizing nature of *amaeru*, which he defines as the desire to be loved passively. Popp and Taketomo (1993) define *amae* as sharing a mode of interaction in which particular restraints applicable to relating have been suspended; this is consistent with a definition of identity that transcends the individual. Among Koreans, *cheong* denotes a binding attachment among family members and in close-knit groups which circulates freely and is not located within any particular individual (Choi, Kim, and Choi, 1993). According to Neki (1976) the words for dependency in Hindi translate as "bond" or "kinship." In these cultures shame (a social emotion) is far more prevalent than guilt (an individual emotion) (Johnson, 1993). Benedict says, "True shame cultures rely on external sanctions for good behavior, not, as true guilt cultures do, on an internalized conviction of sin" (1946, p. 223).

An Eastern person thinks of himself not only as inextricably and harmoniously interdependent with others but also as being vitally continuous with the natural world, past and present. Kakar notes the paucity of references to the individual body in Indian culture, for the social body or body politic more than the corporeal body is related to selfhood.

Emotional awareness, motivation, introspection, and a sense of personal history are all more or less absent in Easterners, for these are organizers of a separate and reified self-sense. Direct expression of affect, especially anger, is inhibited (Tsui and Schultz, 1985; Leong, 1986). "Self-aggrandizing" behavior tends to be frowned upon, and the preferred selfless state is known in Japanese as *enyro*. The Japanese have a saying, "The nail that sticks up gets hammered down." In this culture where persons are parts of larger wholes, communication is largely nonverbal—empathic and gestural. Roland (1988) quotes another Japanese saying: "Nothing important is ever to be communicated verbally." Among Asians it is considered normal to somatize and even to be self-denigrating.

The selflessness that characterizes the behavior of the typical Easterner is associated with a mode of thinking that is more situational or contextual than that of the Westerner. This makes it appear concrete to superficial Western scrutiny. Another way to say this is that, for the Japanese, context-dependency assures an appropriate fit, whereas abstraction leads to responses that are less rich and specifically articulated. Because such Eastern thinking is not readily conducive to objectification and abstraction (Bourne, 1991) it is not surprising that these cultures have been slow to respond to Western science (Levy, 1973).

We should beware of the judgmental conclusion that members of Eastern cultures are less capable of self-observation, rational thought, objectivity, and abstraction than their Western counterparts, reached by observers such as Pavenstedt (1965), however. Epstein's (1990) comments about the mental sophistication characteristic of Buddhist meditation and Bourne's (1991) study of the Oriya Indians, utilizing psychological testing, suggest that this is not at all the case; rather, the capacity for abstraction is not ordinarily called upon in the context-dependent culture in which they live. Closer to home, we need only look for evidence to the technological accomplishments of contemporary Asian cultures, and the disproportionate numbers of Asian students at the top of their respective American university classes in the sciences and technology. Since personal regulation in Eastern cultures is sociocentric or collective, interpersonal-intersubjective and not primarily intrapsychic, the mature adult may seem to be a selfless cog in a larger social or cosmic wheel, and by Western standards unusually dependent rather than separate, autonomous, and self-regulating. Yet Eastern dependency or symbiosis should not be thought of in the Western sense of immaturity or pathology of the capacity for differentiation and integration. The dependent and selfless individual may have a strong reality sense and ability to reason, as well as the capacity for

sophisticated observation of the workings of his mind and, within the boundaries of his society and culture, be a highly adaptive, successful, even creative
individual. Surya (1969) points out that, in Indian culture, the capacity to
sustain satisfactory interdependent relationships with family and co-workers
is a criterion of maturity, and that self-reliance and autonomy tend to be
frowned upon as pathological. In lieu of the special sensitivity to nuances of
his inner experience and feeling that characterizes the Westerner, the Easterner
may be much more refined in his awareness of how his thoughts and behavior
may contribute to a larger natural and social harmony and may be capable of
kinds of perceptive attunement and skill in areas of aesthetics, logic, and
human relations which exceed or at least are very different from those of the
average Westerner (Nakane, 1970; Lebra, 1976). In other words, there are
qualitatively distinctive forms of subjectivity, self-centric and sociocentric.

A group of psychologists led by Witkin (Witkin, Dyk, Faterson, Goodenough, and Karp, 1962; Witkin and Berry, 1975; Witkin and Goodenough,
1976; Berry, 1992) have developed a universalist theory of personality derived from systems theory, based on the concept of differentiation, which they
use in a traditional linear quantitative research paradigm to relate measurable
differences in cultures to the personalities of their members in a content-free
and nonjudgmental way. They hypothesized that personalities and the cultural
organizations in which they live and function can each be distinguished
according to their degree of differentiation or complexity. They designed
several perceptual and spatial tests to measure a cognitive variable they call
field-dependence. In a series of experiments they found that field-dependence
is inversely related to psychological differentiation as measured by indices of a
person's separateness and autonomy from others, dependence on them, social
conformity, self-definition (as contrasted to being defined by the context in
which he or she lives and functions), and intellectualization. Then they ranked
cultures in terms of their social complexity, from hunter-gatherer (least),
through agrarian, to modern industrial (most), and assessed the field-dependence of representative members of each. They concluded that the complexity
of a culture and the field-dependence of its individual members are inversely
related, a finding which is not surprising considering the contextuality of
Eastern personality and the individuality of Western personality. Because
Witkin and his associates operate from within a classical linear and statistical
experimental paradigm in which complexity or differentiation, whether cul-

tural or individual, is conceived of as a one-dimensional variable, their theory has not been applied to the study of the qualitative differences between Eastern and Western culture organization such as I have described. Nonetheless, their findings are consistent with the observation of LeVine, comparing the personalities of African Gusii and Americans, that "all peoples depend more on institutional devices for some ego functions and operate more self-reliantly in other areas" (1990, p. 471). Johnson also states, "in Japanese and most other Asian cultures, identity formation is consolidated at the interface of relationships to self and others. Since persons are more decentered in these cultures, the connections (identifications) with others remain more conscious and substantiated. Failure to make and continue these connections puts Asian children (and, eventually, adults) at more risk in terms of identity crises than their Western counterparts" (1993, p. 120). Hofstede (1983) has measured a dichotomizing variable he calls individualism-collectivism, which differentiates personalities characteristic of sixty-six countries.

Just as personality and identity are conceived of very differently in Eastern and Western cultures, so is psychopathology, or the question of what is culturally modal and what is deviant. In fact, in some respects Eastern and Western views in this matter are polar opposites. Certain intrapsychic configurations and the observed behaviors related to them, which are normal in Eastern cultures, are considered pathological from a Western psychoanalytic view, including the persistence into adulthood of functional and intrapsychic dependent states (that is, reliance on the interpersonal, familial, and social environment for self-regulation); a sense of identity which is undifferentiated from one's family and ancestors, from social networks, and from nature or the cosmos; a kind of introspection focussed on what to the Westerner are externals rather than on affective and bodily self-states; and acceptance of states of interpersonal inequality and even servitude and denigration. According to Eastern standards, pathology is defined not so much in terms of individual intrapsychic distress, which tends to be taken more for granted as a norm, as in terms of disordered or dis-harmonious relations to the familial, social, spiritual, and natural worlds. Nonconformist personal characteristics which make an individual stand out from others, such as aggressiveness, competitiveness, dominance, and self-aggrandizement, which may be virtues among Westerners, are looked upon by Easterners as causes of suffering, and an individual who insists on personal equality and aggressively challenges authority may be seen as disturbed and socially disruptive. The Western person who is separated from family and prefers to function autonomously and rationally, placing his self-interest above that of family and social group, may be perceived as schizoid and detached. The self-centeredness we take for granted in Western culture and the Cartesian distinction between self and other that is so basic to a mature conception of the Western mind are thought of in Buddhism to be illusions and indications of immaturity.

The most obvious conclusion of this analysis is that the way personality is constituted and identity is attained, and the relationship between the person and his culturally constituted group of others, differs qualitatively from one culture to another. It seems likely that broad differences in cultures constitute one set of forces that shape personality and are responsible for qualititative differences in its organization. Furthermore, evidence strongly supports the hypothesis of a dichotomy of culture-personality organizations; a broad distinction between personality typologies in Eastern (sociocentric) and Western (self-centric) cultures. Some of the important maturational lines and achievements of Eastern cultures, which involve specialized attunements to the interpersonal and social world, seem inconceivable in existing Western psychoanalytic models of personality, and, by analogy, the development of an autonomous and separate self is inconceivable in Eastern models. I use the term "inconceivable" advisedly, to refer to limitations of the indigenous psychology of one culture, Eastern or Western to comprehend persons from another. However successful Eastern and Western observers may be in learning about one another's values and ways of looking at the world, persons of one culture seem unable truly to empathize with persons from another. This suggests that the personality differences to which I refer are not part of a thought continuum but are qualitative. In support of this proposition Berry and Kim write of "the incommensurability of the values of different cultures and societies" (1993, p. 153), and Sampson, elaborating a similar distinction between what he calls self-contained as contrasted with ensembled individualism, similarly asserts, "One is not dealing with two opposing tendencies that can balance each other, but [with] two incommensurate systems of belief and understanding. . . . Once we enter the framework of the former, we have already defined our terms in ways that contradict their very essence within the framework of the latter" (1988, p. 21).

It seems natural and appropriate to be suspicious of generalizations and of the concept of natural dichotomies, and these should be no exception. After all, dichotomizing seems to represent a tendency of mind, particularly of the Western self-centric mind, toward monistic-dualistic thinking. Trimble (1991) refers to the loose thinking involved in making generalizations about culture and personality as "ethnic gloss." Johnson (1993) points out that within Eastern cultures there are differences as well as similarities between Indians and Japanese, one of the most obvious being the greater freedom among Indians to express interpersonal aggression, at least under some circumstances. In this particular instance, however, it is possible that we may in fact be dealing with a natural (biological) difference or dichotomy—the constitutional gendering discussed in chapter 5. That is, just as culture creates personality, so personality may create culture. The possible relationship between core gender-related differences in personality and the dichotomy between self-centric and sociocentric cultures is explored in chapter 9.

Perhaps our traditional models for conceiving of personality are inadequate for the task of encompassing culture-related diversity. Is it possible to conceive of a new model capable of embracing both self-centric and sociocentric personality, or is such an effort nothing more than monistic thinking in another guise? Is there no recourse but a potentially infinite pluralism of unrelated models of personality? As we contemplate how to answer these vexing questions we encounter a profound and potentially insuperable roadblock: given the personality parameters, limitations, and biases our cultural embeddedness has imposed on all of us, who is in a position to answer them?

CHAPTER 7

Psychoanalysis as an Indigenous Psychology

I set as my task in writing this book to attempt a broad conception of personality, defined as the study of subjective identity, meaning, and value. In my
judgment, psychoanalysis is the most comprehensive and powerful model of
personality available to accomplish this; yet it is also profoundly limited by
being a linear monistic theory based on a modal personality. As a result of its
contextual embeddedness, psychoanalysis expresses an inherent contradiction: it is at the same time both the unconscious bearer and represener of
contemporary cultural beliefs and perspectives about the person and the consciously designated analyst of these beliefs and perspectives. For this reason
psychoanalysis has been characterized by a confusing, at times maddening,
mixture of dogmatism and intellectual openness and vitality. This limitation
neither distinguishes psychoanalysis from the other human sciences nor
makes it unscientific, for science itself is monistic in the sense of being an
indigenous Western way of thinking.

This chapter continues the exploration of the limitations of psychoanalysis as a theory of personality that began in chapters 2 and 3. In chapter 2 I
explored the relationship between egocentrism and theory construction as it
limits psychoanalysis. In chapter 3 psychoanalysis was situated with regard to

its relative place in the history of Western culture. The extraordinary popular acclaim accorded the new discipline of psychoanalysis in the first half of the twentieth century reflected the historical ascendancy of individualism or ego-centrism in Western culture and met the associated need for a culturally acceptable way to look at the person.

Psychoanalytic theory is based on a modal personality configuration Freud considered universal—that is, not bound by time, place, or culture. In the next bloc of four chapters I shall demonstrate that psychoanalysis is an indigenous psychology because of the myopic centering of its theory around a personality structure arbitrarily defined as modal in twentieth-century Western culture. In chapter 8 psychoanalysis is contrasted with Buddhism, an indigenous psychology whose centrality in Eastern culture parallels that of psychoanalysis in the West. Chapter 9 explores the implications of the fact that the classic modal personality of psychoanalytic theory is male. Chapter 10 consists of a detailed explication of the limitations of the model of personality on which the fundamental theoretical propositions of psychoanalysis are based when it comes to conceiving of intracultural diversity of personality. And chapter 11 examines the ideological aspect of the psychoanalytic movement. These chapters pave the way for a concluding discussion of the strengths of psychoanalysis and its potential to transcend these monistic limitations.

With the benefit of historical hindsight it seems likely that the so-called neurotic personality of Freud's theory was, at the most, modal for the culture of his time. As a result, it is a safe assumption that, when it comes to the cultural and historical dimensions of personality, the theory is at best an admixture of universal and indigenous elements. The population from which the theory was derived included Freud himself—that is, his self-analysis, as detailed primarily in the *Interpretation of Dreams* (1900), the study of his own children (a source that is slighted in historical accounts of the origin of psychoanalysis probably because Freud himself made but passing reference to it), and his analyses of patients from his social-cultural milieu. For the most part, as I noted earlier, his patients were the "worried well," able to ask his help in his office for their symptoms while at the same time leading constructive and even creative lives in society. Many of them entered analysis out of personal curiosity or as part of their study of psychoanalysis. In other words, despite the fact that a few of his classic patients—for example, the Rat Man and the Wolf Man—were rather seriously disturbed (Tausk, 1919; Binswanger, 1956; Reichard, 1956), the personalities of Freud himself and most of his analysands *appear* to have fallen within a modal range of mental health for the culture of his time, although we have no way of knowing whether the population from whom the theory was derived truly reflects a normal sample of the social-cultural population from which they were culled.

Newer psychoanalytic theories suffer from similar limitations with regard to the population from which they are derived, for most analysts tend to work with upper-middle-class patients from Western cultures who are able to function reasonably productively, often in the mental health field, and can make office visits and pay private fees. As a consequence of this limited perspective, Kohut's self psychology, for example, is based on the dubious premise that the mature self of the therapist is qualitatively similar to any other self that has achieved at least the rudiments of coherence and therefore is capable of understanding and empathizing with it.

Psychoanalytic theory thus comprises a set of underlying principles about culturally modal (contemporary Western male) personality which are believed to be universally applicable. To use the term I introduced in earlier chapters, it is a self-centric psychology, as contrasted with the sociocentric one characteristic of Eastern cultures. The basic organizational and conceptual field of psychoanalysis comprises the individual person and the workings of his or her mind (Greenberg and Mitchell, 1983). Choi, Kim, and Choi, writing from a Korean perspective, note: "Psychology became naturalized in the land of individualism. Its basic foundations became intertwined with the basic assumptions of individualism" (1993, p. 193).

Psychoanalysis is a self-centric psychology in three senses. First, it is solipsistic insofar as the conceptual field is exclusively limited to the mind of the subject. The individual personality is defined exclusively in intrapsychic terms. This is a natural outgrowth of the embeddedness of psychoanalysis in the biological science of individual persons. Freud's theory of personality begins with an individual person generating wishes, which are psychic phenomena at the boundary between mind, and instincts which characterize the biological body. These wishes undergo maturation according to phylogenetically determined psychosexual stages. Even in newer psychoanalytic theories that eschew Freud's so-called economic theory of biological motivation in favor of ones based on emotion, affect, the need to relate to another, or self-cohesion, self-contained individuality is inherent in the system.

Second, Freud chose to elucidate the fantasy aspect of experience rather than pursue an understanding of the nature and meaning of human inter-relatedness and interpersonal experience, particularly the elements of seduction and trauma, which his early clinical experience had brought to his attention. Both the bio-centeredness and the fantasy-centeredness on the individual person are self-centric and consistent with Western dualistic thinking about the person in apposition to "external" reality and to objects.

Although psychoanalysis is a solipsistic theory of intrapsychic life, paradoxically, the self as an organizing entity is not fully appreciated by the classical theory, most likely because the nineteenth-century reductionist models based on the physical science of Newton and Helmholtz that influenced Freud's thinking attribute more substantive reality and causality to what appears to be hidden than to what is readily visible. They consider concepts of person or self as epiphenomenal and place more substantial value on the atomistic mechanical and energic parts derived from deconstructive analysis.

The third sense in which psychoanalysis is a self-centric psychology is in its emphasis on the person or subject as distinct from the animate and inanimate external world, and even from his own body, so that he is capable of an attitude of objectification or de-animation. Identity is defined in apposition or opposition to others. From this idea arises such corollaries as the concepts of the external conflict of self with other persons and with society, of intrapsychic conflict between distinctive elements of self, of a part of the mind dynamically hidden by and from another part, and of the person more or less objectively observing parts of himself. These are inherent in Freud's theory of biological instinct, which, in addition to its source and aim, comprises a component of otherness, of the object of tension discharge. In the models of Freud and Melanie Klein, other persons initially are phylogenetic figments, subsidiary aspects of the instinct necessary for energy discharge; subsequently they are forces mitigating for the development of internal regulatory capacities. Their individual selves are comprehended only insofar as they facilitate or impede the appetitive and developmental needs and wishes of the subject. Interpersonal relations and social networks are secondary activities the person engages in and are not considered a primary aspect of identity, except, in some of the newer object relations theories,* in states of immaturity and certain pathological conditions. In contrast, in sociocentric psychologies, as we have seen, the person's subjective sense of identity is intertwined with his or her relations with others and with the natural world.

It is a paradox of Freud's model that while its respectful attention to the individual and his mind is unparalleled in history, it is predicated on the assumption that the person—in this case both the infant, with his biologically based wishes, and his mother—represents a danger to civilization. Neither one is inherently part of the social fabric, as is the case in sociocentric cultures. Viewed from a different perspective, the psychoanalytic subject does not take the viewpoints of others seriously except insofar as they are a threat to his own. Psychological maturity as well as the achievements of civilization and culture are based on instinctual renunciation and internalization of paternal authority via resolution of the Oedipus complex. This postulated innate antagonism among humans helps to explain why it has taken so long for empathic concepts to gain a foothold within psychoanalytic theory.

The subject of analysis is presumed to have achieved a reasonably sophisticated state of psychic integration and differentiation from other persons so that he can function independently of them. The mental apparatus is believed to unfold epigenetically along a single developmental pathway, toward a maturational end point of stable, self-contained individuality, and the capacity to function autonomously, separate from "objects." The conflict of wish (for Freud) or phantasy (for Klein) with the intrapsychically represented aspects of the environment is the crucible in which this development occurs. This conflict is conceived of as the inevitable consequence of efforts to reconcile the biological wish to discharge energies on or with others—vital, passionate, and destructive—with reality in the form of the law of the father, which constitutes civilization. This conflict leads to instinctual renunciation, psychosexual maturation, and psychostructural maturation, including internalization of paternal authority (superego formation) via resolution of the Oedipus complex

* Fairbairn and Kohut conceive of other persons as undifferentiated sustaining or frustrating and potentially disorganizing aspects of the self. Some of the newer psychoanalytic interpersonal, intersubjective, and constructivist theories may appear to be exceptions, but I shall argue that thus far they are theories of therapy, or what was once known as "technique," not theories of the person (Gill, 1994).

(Freud, 1913, 1927). For Klein these developments are preceded by an earlier healing of primal splitting in which internalization of conflict and re-direction of rage lead to the ambivalence of the depressive position. For Kohut the motive force for separate development is optimal frustration of efforts to be merged with the object, which leads to what he calls transmuting internalization of an independent motivational system of ambitions and ideals. In each of these models, "objects" or the functions they serve for the subject (reality testing, conflict resolution, self-regulation, motivation, and adaptation) are progressively internalized until they become aspects of a separate individual mind.

The mature mind in self-centric personalities is internal and classically comprises three structures. The first is the primary unconscious part, an unciv-ilized biological heritage that sets each person forever apart from others—*das Es*, the it or id, as it eventually came to be known. Prior to his death-instinct hypothesis Freud conceived of the id as vital or libidinal. Later, as events in his personal life and the horrors of world war led him to develop a sense of pessimism, he emphasized the power of entropy or destruction, which he named *Thanatos*, or the death instinct, and which Klein took as the motivational cornerstone of her theory. During civilizing development the id is diminished by what has become conscious and under ego control and is augmented by subsequent repressed wishes. The other structures comprise the external world as it has been taken in during the resolution of obligatory infantile dependency, including the rational, reality-perceiving self, which combines innate capabilities with selective identifications with others, and the superego, an accretion of civilization or paternal authority which is the "heir" to the Oedipus complex and becomes the source of civilizing guilt feeling.

Freud charted this self-centric theoretical course when he elected to eluci-date the fantasy aspect of experience in a setting (the couch of the analytic consulting room) at once alienating to self (that is, fostering self-analysis) and to other. Rather than design a treatment in the interpersonal or social setting, emphasizing the person's relationships, or a treatment supportive of action or behavior, emphasizing the unity of self, Freud focused on the individual patient, put the analyst in the role of observer-interpreter, and attempted to create a split between the experiencing and observing parts of the patient. Had Freud elected to pursue interpersonal elements—for example, the elements of seduction and trauma which his early clinical experience brought to his attention—and to support the "victims" of such treatment, he might have ventured outside of his consulting room into the families, clinics, and social institutions of Vienna.

The Western conception of mind not only pervades the psychoanalytic theory of development, normalcy, and pathology, but in crucial ways also informs the technique of the analyst as therapist and as scientific observer. It provides the undergirding and legitimation for viewing the analyst as an independent, autonomous being capable of objective observations, perceptions of unvarnished reality and truth, and neutral judgments—e.g., as an analyzing instrument rather than a subjectively inextricable participant in a relationship.

While psychoanalysis has moved beyond and away from Freud in many respects, its self-centric model has not really changed. The remedial efforts of some who have been most vocal in their criticism of the so-called classical psychoanalytic model with its emphasis on instinct rather than relationship have actually reiterated self-centric conceptions in new guises, particularly beneath the umbrella concept of object relations theory, which is misleading insofar as it implies a more sociocentric conception. Many analysts, both classical and "object relations" in orientation, insist that psychoanalysis does conceive of the relations of the person to others. Those who believe that Freud had an "object relations theory" point out that he conceived of "the object" as an integral aspect of the instinct, but this view tends to reduce the riches and complexity of other humans to dessicated stereotypes, and their influence to generic universal forces: objects of desire, vehicles for tension-discharge, or representatives of civilizing and inhibiting patriarchal authority, to be assimilated generically as identification, conscience, and reality principle. Although persons who show a preference for object relations theories in their work probably tend to approach patients with more of an interpersonal perspective than classical analysts use, I believe that close analysis of object relations theories per se will reveal that, like the classical model, they are self-centric in principle.

Although Klein is generally looked upon as an originator of object relations theory, her ideas about objects are very similar to those of Freud. Both have a phylogenetic conception of objects and object relations. That is, the object is a subsidiary aspect of a bio-constitutional process, primarily instinct or drive. The drive has a source, an aim, and an object on whom the tension is discharged and from whom gratification is obtained. From Freud's hypothesis of the death instinct and from the crucible of World War II and the Holocaust, Melanie Klein derived her belief that human nature is inherently evil. She conceived of an innate antagonism or split between life-destroying and life-affirming parts of the mind or self. The infant in her theory is almost entirely solipsistic, and its phylogenetically conceived of object appears to be little more than a figment of its inherently rageful and envious phantasies via processes of splitting and projective identification. Klein also postulated an innate alienation between the self and the external world (paranoid position) and between aspects of the self (schizoid position). As the infant learns to struggle with his rage, and to experience feelings of guilt and depression as his rage threatens to destroy his love-objects, he gradually acquires the civilizing, objectifying capabilities to see the self and others more realistically, to heal the split in the self, and to achieve a position of intrapsychic sufficiency and personal autonomy, including ambivalent relations with whole "objects."

W. R. D. Fairbairn, a member of the British Psychoanalytic Society around the same time as Klein, is responsible for the current popularity of the term *object relations theory* (Fairbairn, 1952; Robbins, 1992b). Fairbairn's system, like Klein's, is an effort to explore the schizoid and paranoid elements of personality. What is different is Fairbairn's conceptual emphasis on the self. In fact, Fairbairn was probably the first to propose a psychology of the self, although he never received his due for this achievement. The theories of Fairbairn and of Kohut (1971, 1977) share common ingredients. Both reject concepts of biological drive. Both are organized around a supraordinate concept of self which has no parallel in the classical theory (Robbins, 1980, 1992b), and neither allots a normal role in development and adult personality to intrapsychic conflict and defense. Fairbairn's use of the term *object* is different from Freud's and Klein's insofar as, first and foremost, it denotes the other from whom the infant is initially psychologically undifferentiated. As in the classical theory, however, this other has no substance apart from the psyche of the subject self. As development progresses, object relations comes to have another meaning, referring to what Fairbairn calls the endopsychic (read intrapsychic) struggle of dynamic forces derived from frustrating aspects of the primal relationship which have been internalized (repressed and split). In this respect his use of "object relations" is similar to Klein's. Separation and alienation from others are basic to Fairbairn's theory; neonatal life is like the exodus from the Garden of Eden. As a result of early unsatisfactory experiences with caretakers, we are all schizoid, more or less. The "parts" of the maturing psyche are pathological products of fission or disintegration rather than constructive products of differentiation and integration. Fairbairn's theory of maturation is based upon the Western assumption of a separated and individuated self.

Kohut approached theory-making with what would appear to be an interpersonal perspective, an appreciation of the dyadic relationship rather than individual biology as the prime mover. Like the theories of his predecessors, however, Kohut's (1971, 1977) psychology of the self turns out to be self-centric, expressive of Western biases about mind and society. Motivation comprises the teleological urge to develop a cohesive self. Others are important only insofar as they are useful in the self's efforts to cohere and to remain cohesive. They are reduced to the servile status of monochromatic facilitators of or impediments to the subject's development. The irony of the self-centered nature of Kohut's theory is its failure to account for the psychological development of the wonderfully other-attuned and empathic individuals to whom he assigns the responsibility for promoting the healthy development of his patients as infants or pathological adults. These parents and analysts seem like another species, requiring a separate theory which it never occurred to him to develop.

Margaret Mahler's career as a child analyst made her especially sensitive to the mother-infant dyad. She also tried to address the self-centric theory of psychoanalysis using objective observations of the dyad rather than subjective reports from traditional individual adult analyses (1975). However, Mahler was also unable to free herself from her Western cultural heritage. She, too, perceived personal autonomy, self-sufficiency, and the capacity for objectivity as the outcomes of normal development. In her theory of separation and individuation, continuing states of dependency are considered pathological, and the caregiving person who assists or impedes growth is once again perceived as a one-dimensional object.

In all these psychoanalytic theories, dependent and symbiotic structures (that is, an identity sense that is intertwined with three-dimensional others) are viewed as features of early life and immaturity to be outgrown, or of persistent pathology. Lines of development such as psychosexual maturation via conflict and internalization of intrapsychic structure, narcissistic maturation, or separation-individuation are considered normal. Group and social formations are more or less taken for granted but are not given much weight with regard to the basic organization of adult personality and the maintenance of adult identity.

During the late 1980s and early 1990s a new field of psychoanalytic investigation which answers to various names including interpersonal, hermeneutic, intersubjective, or social-constructivist began to emerge. This psychology is based on the concept of object relationship rather than individual self. Sullivan (1953) and Levenson (1985) introduced the notion of an interpersonal field. Stolorow and Atwood introduced the concept of intersubjectivity (Atwood and Stolorow, 1984; and Stolorow and Atwood, 1992), and concepts of intersubjectivity have also arisen from the women's movement. Hoffman (1983, 1987, 1991) has elaborated the model known as social constructivism. For the most part, however, these ideas have not been articulated into true theories of personality and have been utilized more as perspectives or orientations to the clinical treatment situation. Gill's (1994) explication of this subject is particularly illuminating. He makes a distinction between psychoanalysis as a theory of personality which is intrapsychic (within one body), and psychoanalysis as a therapeutic discipline, or what he calls a situation, which takes the form of an interactive interpersonal dialogue. His assertion that psychoanalytic theory is intrapsychic or one-body is not a repudiation of so-called object relations theory, nor is his conceptualization of a psychoanalytic situation an expression of his allegiance to an object relations perspective. Gill explains that while some psychoanalytic theories emphasize constitution and biology (one-person psychologies) and some emphasize relationships with other persons (two-person psychologies), all psychoanalytic theories are intrapsychic. His conception of a clinical dialogue between two actual persons (the field to which interpersonalists and social constructivists refer, which he calls the psychoanalytic situation) does not qualify in his eyes as a psychoanalytic theory.

I have presented evidence that psychoanalysis is an indigenous psychology, a self-centric theory, modeled after Western conceptions of personality, and selectively attuned to individual-intrapsychic aspects of the person. Beginning with Freud, psychoanalysts have tended to think of the theory as universally applicable, and as sufficiently powerful and comprehensive to account for all that seems strange and unfamiliar about personality, regardless of culture of origin. Freud can hardly be faulted for exploring the boundaries and limits of his new discipline. Among his numerous universalistic pronouncements are *Totem and Taboo* (1913), in which he postulated a universal hypothesis about the origins of the patriarchal family and of culture, commencing in prehistory with the primal murder of the father by hís sons, who lusted after their mother; papers on Leonardo da Vinci (1910), Michelangelo (1914c), and Moses (1939) in which he applied the model to historical figures; and various ventures into political science (for example, 1933). It was a deceptively easy step from his universalistic assumption about personality and culture to the application of psychoanalytic theory, as though it were a normative yardstick, to members of other cultures. In this process such concepts as drive theory, psychosexual developmental stages, intrapsychic conflict and its resolution (specifically the Oedipus complex of the nuclear Western family), and a modal separate, independent self have been applied in more or less subtly judgmental ways, and cultures in which these do not seem to figure prominently have been labeled immature or primitive.

There continues to be a lively debate about the accuracy of Freud's assertion that the Oedipus complex is universal and hence innate, beginning with Kroeber's (1920) critique, and Malinowski's (1927, 1928) conclusion that no Oedipus complex was evident among the Trobriand Islanders. Marxist analysts like Reich and Horney (1937) maintain that the Oedipus complex, far from being universal, is an artifact of Western capitalistic domination and exploitation. Kardiner (1939) reported that there is no Oedipal conflict among the Marquesas Islanders. Devereaux drew upon the assertions of Kroeber and Malinowski that the Oedipus complex is not culturally universal, and in his own psychoanalytic study of Native Americans concluded that classical theory overemphasizes Oedipal phenomena. Spiro (1982) claims that re-analysis of Malinowski's data indicates that Trobrianders *do* experience an Oedipus complex. Johnson (1992) analyzed folk tales from every region in the world and every level of social complexity, including nonstratified societies in which Marxist and neo-Marxist theorists maintain that there should be no Oedipus complex, and gathered more than one hundred examples of stories with Oedipal themes. Obeyesekere (1990) and Cohler (1993) consider the Oedipus controversy in larger terms. They contend that all cultures regulate the sexual behavior of their members, but the way in which each culture goes about it—that is, the particular conflictual familial-social configuration responsible for internalizing limits and controls—is indigenous and specific to each one.

The tendency to apply psychoanalysis monistically in a way that is dismissive of personality differences in other cultures is not simply a historical curiosity. Elaborating on Mitchell's (1957) assertion that all Indian personalities are orally and pre-Oedipally fixated as a consequence of excessive maternal gratification of infants, Silvan (1981) postulates a combination of excessive infantile gratification and stimulation combined with a constraint on expression of aggression. The problem is encountered in psychoanalytic considerations of Native American cultures, as well. Boyer (1962, 1979) asserts that Apache religious leaders, or shamans, are psychotic individuals; that Apache mothers, as a group, suffer from pathological ambivalence; and that fathers tend to be absent. Proceeding from the assumption that this combination is pathogenic he concludes that Apache adults are immature and suffer from structural failures of integration and differentiation. He ends his 1979 book with the emphatic assertion that he has "demonstrated beyond question that the psychoanalytic developmental schema within the framework of ego psychology . . . are as valid for these Apaches as they have been repeatedly shown to be for individuals of varying Western origins. . . . I believe that this conclusion will prove to be generally applicable" (p. 171).

Psychoanalytic ethnocentrism also assumes much more subtle guises than these. Erikson expressed obvious sympathy for the Native Americans he studied and a wish to avoid simplistic and devaluing conclusions when he noted: "The discovery of primitive child-training systems makes it clear that primitive societies are neither infantile stages of mankind nor arrested deviations from the proud progressive norms which we represent: they are a complete form of mature human living" (1950, p. 112). Nonetheless, he betrayed his bias when he asserted that "neurosis is an individual state in which irrational trends are irreconcilably split off from a relatively advanced rationality; while primitivity is a state of human organization in which pre-rational thinking is integrated with whatever rationality is made possible by the technology" (p. 184). Pavenstedt, a sensitive and sympathetic observer of Japanese culture, wonders "whether in this culture, where for generations the importance of the family superseded the importance of the individual, an individual ever reaches the degree of differentiation that is desirable in Western culture" (1965, p. 425). Her conclusion that the typical Japanese personality is immature in the sense of lacking complexity rather than being different from Western personality was examined in chapter 6 and found to be incorrect.

Okimoto and Settlage (1993) set out to design a psychoanalytically informed experiment to contrast Japanese and American infant development. They chose to study separation responses in Japanese and Caucasian infant-mother dyads, utilizing Mahler's theory of separation-individuation as a framework to construct their experiment and interpret the results. Their use of Mahler's theoretical model has major consequences. With it, they reached the unexceptionable conclusion that Japanese infants react more intensively and with greater disturbance to separation experiences. While Okimoto and Settlage recognized that such separation reactions are products of the closer and more prolonged symbiotic bond between mother and infant in Japanese culture, the theory of Mahler that they used to interpret these phenomena is predicated on the modal Western conception of maturation: separation, individuation, and autonomy. Had there been a developmental theory that emphasized some of the attainments in areas of complex interpersonal attunements, discriminations, and behaviors, such as those Benedict (1946), Johnson (1992), and Freeman (1993) describe as characteristic of Japanese, and were an experiment designed which tested American and Japanese toddlers of similar age on some of the social achievements which are expectable at that age in Japanese culture, for example, behavior in highly structured social situations demanding ritualized nuances of social conformity and a highly sensitized social attunement, the experimenter would likely reach the opposite conclusion—that it is the American infants who are more "disturbed" or "immature."

In other words, as I noted in chapter 6, a Western analyst is likely to believe that the seemingly prolonged states of dependency, selflessness, lack of personal assertiveness and ambition, and willing acceptance of conditions of personal inequality often encountered among members of Eastern cultures are indications of widespread immaturity or pathology and that the Buddhist quest for *annatta*, an ego-less state of "no self," is an immature or pathological loss of boundaries. This was the conclusion reached by Freud (1930) when he described the "oceanic feeling," and by other analysts, both before (Ferenczi, 1913; Jones, 1913, 1923) and after (Federn, 1928; Lewin, 1950).

Horney (1937) was one of the first analysts to express concern about the importance of maintaining a culturally relativistic view of personality. She observed that "Freud's disregard of cultural factors . . . leads to false general-izations" (pp. 20–21) and that "there is no such thing as a normal psychology, which holds for all mankind" (p. 19). Long before Boyer's (1962) psycho-analytic pathologizing of Apache shamans, Horney remarked of the very same tribal group: "One would run a great risk in calling an Indian [Native American] boy psychotic because he told us that he had visions in which he believed" (1937, p. 14). She pointed out that, from the perspective of the Native American, the Westerner who failed to hallucinate under certain circum-stances could just as well be deemed pathological. "It is advisable to call [an apparent peculiarity in a member of another culture] a neurosis only if it deviates from the pattern common to the particular culture" (p. 29). Erikson notes that "different cultures make extensive use of their prerogative to decide what they consider workable and insist on calling necessary" (1969, p. 68). Devereaux (1978) writes: "The sociology of knowledge predicates that each ethnic group and each historical period has its preferred thought models and therefore patterns most or all of its theories upon these models" (1978, p. 266). LeVine (1973) points out that it is incongruent with reality to find pathology in persons who are living socially adaptive and productive lives simply because their ways of thinking and behaving deviate from the norms of established theories.

Psychoanalysis is not unique insofar as its phenomenological analysis amalgamates novel exploration with re-presentation of history and culture-bound beliefs. While the cultural embeddedness of psychoanalysis presents a perplexing epistemological problem for those of us who would like it to be the foundation for a broad conception of personality, it is not a flaw particular to the psychoanalytic system. All intellectual systems, no matter how objective and value-neutral they may seem, and indeed our personalities themselves, are inextricably bound up with the particular social-cultural-historical matrix in which they originate. If there is a flaw, it is the monistic tendency of the user of the system to deny the contextual embeddedness of psychoanalysis and to believe that it is a totalistic or universalistic way of conceiving of personality. But this, too, is not unique to psychoanalysts.

Implications of the indigenous or culture-bound quality of psychoanaly-tic theory are explored in subsequent chapters. Correcting the problem in-volves more than recognizing the monistic fallacy, heeding the cautionary notes of people like Horney, Erikson, Devereaux, and LeVine, and adopting a more modest attitude about the boundaries of psychoanalysis, as well as more respect for culture-related differences in personality. Is the theory hopelessly indigenous? Is it possible to separate universal from particularistic elements? Are there fundamental principles of the theory that can be elaborated to create a new theory that is more applicable to persons from all cultures?

CHAPTER 8

Indigenous Psychologies of the East and West: Psychoanalysis and Buddhism

Twentieth-century Western culture, with disciplines such as psychology and psychoanalysis, is far from unique in attempting systematic conceptions of personality. Philosophy, theology, myth, and folklore have all served this function in other cultures and historical epochs. I have chosen to contrast psychoanalysis, a youthful centenarian, with Buddhism, an indigenous psychology of Eastern culture which has survived two and a half millennia, and whose purpose, like that of psychoanalysis, is to enable people to remediate needless emotional suffering.

There appear to be some striking resemblances between Buddhism and psychoanalysis. Each is based on a specific and disciplined form of personal reflection or introspection (meditation and free association, respectively). Each is based on a modal personality construct modeled, at least in large part, after the self-understanding gained by its founder. Each system postulates that self-deception is an inevitable aspect of the human condition and that, as a consequence, the core or essence of mind which one must reach in order to be liberated from needless suffering is inaccessible to ordinary conscious awareness. The theory and method of reflection developed by each discipline attempts to free the subject from these unconscious mental constraints. The

Tibetan word for Buddhist literally means "insider," one who seeks the truth in the nature of mind. Other areas of agreement include the fact that both Buddhism and psychoanalysis accept the inevitability of emotionally disturbing events in human life, and both conceive of suffering as the product of disharmony or division within the mind.

Despite these surface similarities, psychoanalytic and Buddhistic views of the person and of suffering are very different. In some instances they are seemingly opposite, with regard to what is considered normal and abnormal. As a result, the naive application of one system to members of the other may have results far different from what the teacher or analyst might expect, given the ordinary meaning of the system in his culture of origin. In other words, both systems are limited in scope by virtue of being indigenous psychologies, however interesting, perhaps even therapeutic, may be the consequences of their use with persons of other cultures.

In chapter 7 I described how psychoanalysis, as an indigenous psychology, is constructed around a modal self-centric personality. Classical psychoanalysis views the self or mind, derived from a genetic heritage of desire and aggressiveness and from early experiences with others both caring and uncaring, as the mediating instrument between the biological aspect of the person and the external world. It is a psychology of dualism: subject in apposition or opposition to object; mind versus body; conscious versus unconscious aspects of self; wishful self versus realistic self. The self of the classical theory, as we have seen, is a tripartite construction of dynamic conflicting forces: an unconscious part, initially comprising our biological heritage of instinctual uncivilized wishes, and subsequently including elements repressed during the course of development; a rational, reality-perceiving self, and the accretion of paternal authority, which is a source of civilizing guilt feelings. The self strives not only to survive but seeks gratification and aggrandizement of ambitions in work and in love. Conflict in the mind is held to be an inevitable consequence of the incompatibility of biological or instinctual human nature—its vital, passionate, desirous, destructive, nonrational elements—and the law of the father, which constitutes civilization and culture and enables us to survive in a world with others as biologically bent on gratification and destruction as ourselves. The self is internally alienated from some of its parts and externally alienated from other persons. Although psychoanalysis describes the relation of the self to others, it is in fact an explication of the individual mind; other persons are conceived of, in partial or objectifying terms (psychoanalysis aptly refers to them as objects), as embodiments or symbols of desire or representatives of patriarchal authority. Conscious awareness of the various elements comprising the self, in their conflictual and synergistic combinations, is a sign of maturity.

While some of the newer theories differ in particulars from the classical model, they retain the modal perspective of psychoanalysis. Kohut's (1971) teleological system of motivation centers around a quest for personal coherence or cohesion, which initially requires the assistance of others he called selfobjects. Kohut's theory of development traces the emergence, from the empathic attunement of parent with infant, of a complex cohesive sense of self in the form of ambitions and ideals. Different as Kohut's theory seems, like its predecessors it is based on a conception of personality as self-preoccupied, self-aggrandizing, or narcissistic, and of a world in which other persons exist only as one-dimensional objects who are or are not sufficiently empathically attuned to the needs of the emerging self. Although Mahler used observation of mother-infant behavior as data rather than subjective reports from adult analysands, she too was unable to free herself from the solipsistic perspective of individualism. She referred to the infant's initial conception of itself as intimately bound up with an undifferentiated mothering figure as a delusion. She perceived the task and the outcome of normal development to be separation and the attainment of personal autonomy and self-sufficiency and considered continuing states of dependency to be pathological.

Buddhism is also based on a modal personality construct, albeit a very different one. It teaches a kind of disciplined selflessness related to the sociocentric personality that is modal for Eastern culture. Buddhist meditation requires a disinterested form of attentiveness to the very process of experiencing, which Suzuki characterized as "the point of absolute subjectivity" (1960, p. 25). The Buddha taught that the conscious preoccupation with things, including a self reified as a concrete entity, and the active organization of life around the satisfactions of individual personhood are illusions (*sem*) to be dissolved in the quest for *annatta*, the negation of a self-attitude.

Psychoanalysts, including Freud, have often claimed that the Buddhist quest for no-self is regressive and involves a pathological state of fusion and loss of boundaries between self and world. However, beginning with Suzuki

(1960) and Fromm (1960), numerous psychologically sophisticated students of Buddhism have pointed out that meditation is far from being a regressive state of loss of self. It requires much cognitive-affective sophistication as well as purposefulness and self-control. It must be learned from a teacher through an arduous process of mental maturation. It is a particular kind of reflection involving attention both to process and to content, albeit in a special way free from the dualistic self-object way of perceiving that characterizes Western thought. In fact, the meditative state involves psychic work and training, and the process and the result are quite consistent with the maintenance of a firm sense of identity, however impossible this may be to translate into Western concepts of self or no-self. "Selflessness is not a case of something that existed in the past becoming non-existent; rather, this sort of 'self' is something that never did exist. What is needed is to identify as non-existent something that always was non-existent" (Gyatso, 1984, p. 40).

Psychoanalytic dismissal of the Buddhistic meditative state as regressive is an example of monistic thinking as well as the failure of the psychoanalytic model to conceive of certain particular complex mental processes. Similarly, the path of self-development normally taken by Westerners cannot be conceived of in Eastern models like Buddhism. As a result, complex and adaptive (at least in Western culture) self-state achievements that have taken years of effort and maturation may be naively dismissed by Buddhists as illusions or causes of suffering, markers of insufficient attunement to, harmony with, or respect for the natural world, family, and tradition, and preoccupation with self-aggrandizement, objectification, and reason. In other words, these differences between psychoanalysis and Buddhism in conceiving of self and being cannot be reconciled by the linear expedient of asserting that one is abnormal and the other is not. On the one hand, the self of Buddhism is neither self nor selfless in the psychoanalytic sense. On the other hand, the self-centeredness that Buddhism calls the "alienated way of perception," illusion, or *sem*, is normal and adaptive in Western society. The very concepts of self and mind have different meanings in Buddhism and psychoanalysis.

What I am suggesting is that some of the differences in orientation between psychoanalysis and Buddhism may be understood as consequences of the very different cultural contexts in which they are embedded and the ways in which each describes its members, which cannot be transferred or translated into the culture of the other. Western self-centric personality involves an objectified concept of self as a reified entity. In contrast, the identity-organizing system in Eastern culture—which is not, by the way, conceptualized in Buddhism—is a holistic gestalt comprising interpersonal and social relationships as well as the relationship between the person and his or her environment.

How, then, can we compare the two systems' ways of understanding personal suffering? To begin with, the distinctions between what is normal and what is not are more complex in Buddhism than in psychoanalysis. Buddhism addresses itself to *samsura*, the suffering everyone experiences consequent to a self-attitude—the personalization of ordinary expectable human events, such as loss of persons or possessions, illness, aging, and death. Buddhism teaches that the attitude of self-investment, which alienates the person from the world, leads to unnecessary suffering by weighting events with significance. Such suffering is remediable by dissolution of the self-attitude and attainment of an attitude of *annatta*. As Watts (1975) expressed it, the idea of self is a conceptual cancer. While at first glance it might seem that the person who suffers is looked upon in Buddhism as deviant, a study of the Buddhist stages of enlightenment suggests instead that what is involved is a complex idea of personal development or maturation. At the same time, Buddhism recognizes a category of psychopathological suffering, which appears to be outside the scope of its model. Buddhist teachers, at least in Western culture, generally make a point of screening and identifying disturbed persons when they seek Buddhist guidance, and referring them to other sources. Psychoanalysis, in contrast, clearly distinguishes between human suffering that is expectable and inevitable, and pathological or neurotic suffering that is remediable. Most people do not have the choice of whether or not to suffer, but, given the possibility of psychoanalytic treatment, they can choose between pathological forms and attitudes of suffering that are destructive to the self, and more normal ones that are not. Pathological suffering may be remediated by therapy designed to enhance or strengthen elements of self by expanding conscious awareness of the conflictual elements of the mind, involving the self and the real world.

From their very different perspectives on the qualitative organization of personality, Buddhism and psychoanalysis necessarily respond in different, almost diametrically opposed ways to suffering persons, regardless of their culture of origin and typology of personality. To the Buddhist, personal characteristics that make an individual stand out from others and be a "self" which possesses a separate intrinsic reality, including desire, aggressiveness, competitiveness, acquisitiveness, and orientation toward power and domination, are products of illusion and causes of suffering. The dualistic distinction between self and object, the preoccupation with an external reality, and even the objectifying modes of thinking upon which psychoanalytic thinking is based are aspects of the illusion. Suzuki says, "Our consciousness is nothing but an insignificant floating piece of island in the Oceanus encircling the earth" (1960, p. 14). He adds, "the scientific direction of study is to be reversed and the Self is to be taken hold of from within and not from the outside" (p. 25). Erich Fromm says that the Buddhist aim "becomes that of overcoming alienation, and of the subject-object split in perceiving the world . . . arriving at . . . the state of the immediate grasp of reality . . . without interference by intellectual reflection" (1960, pp. 135–136). He adds, "The method of Zen is, one might say, that of a frontal attack on the alienated way of perception."

Psychoanalysis, in contrast, views certain forms of suffering as a normal and inevitable consequence of being a mature person in a world that is inevitably less than completely gratifying and that makes certain civilizing demands on its members. The classical model focuses attention on the ordinary suffering consequent to expectable internal conflict or alienation among wishes, reality, and conscience. Such suffering usually takes the form of feelings of anxiety and guilt. Klein's theory emphasizes feelings of envy, guilt, and depression and related efforts to make amends as the person struggles to sustain loving relationships with others and to control the rage and related tendencies to perceptual distortion that threaten to disrupt his or her efforts. In contrast to the classical model of suffering, which Kohut called "guilty man," self psychology focuses on another kind of suffering that all of us are familiar with: the sense that no one understands us, which he called "tragic man." Such pain may be the inevitable consequence of failure of empathic attunement by even the most devoted caregivers, and the intensive and often painful internal stimulation a person must cope with as he or she matures and becomes more inwardly motivated and goal-directed. Finally, Mahler focuses on mastery of painful reactions to physical and emotional separation from others, especially feelings of anxiety and depression, in the expectable course of internalizing the mental processes and functions we all require to be separate and self-sustaining.

As for the pathological forms of suffering which psychoanalysis views as remediable by maturation of the self, the classical theory describes neurotic suffering, which is the outcome of serious unresolved unconscious conflicts between parts of the self. It includes disabling inhibitions of personality, intense anxiety, symptomatic distress (obsessive-compulsive and phobic), and repetition of unsatisfying behavior patterns. Classical psychoanalytic thinkers beginning with Jones (1923), Ferenczi (1913), and Freud himself (1930) have speculated about psychotic suffering related to regressive loss of self-boundaries, but this has not been a central or particularly important element of the theory. Klein's theory describes suffering related to the persistence of or regression to infantile forms of thinking characterized by a split or fragmented self that is poorly differentiated from others. It takes the form of paranoid or persecutory anxiety, that is, frightening misperceptions of the world based on projection of unconscious hostile aspects of oneself; excessive rage and envy as well as pathological guilt, and an internally shifting sense of self associated with an equally inconstant sense of others. Kohut defines pathological suffering as the result of a person's inability to integrate and cohere a sense of self from its normal infantile parts because of fundamental failures of empathic attunement on the part of others, past and present. The individual is incapable of sustaining a rudimentary good feeling about himself, and so functions in an aimless, contradictory, disoriented, and chaotic fashion sometimes referred to as psychic disintegration or fragmentation, unable to be goal-directed and constructive in life. He experiences overstimulation because he cannot channel his energies constructively, and he suffers from the manifestations of archaic precursors of self-esteem, including states of grandiosity and paranoia. Because he has no one to hold him and to assist him psychologically, he turns for compensation instead to autoerotic and perverse forms of gratification for compensation, and these may create secondary forms of suffering. Mahler writes about the suffering of the person who is insufficiently autonomous, separated, and individuated from others, who forms obligatory dependent relationships, and who experiences anxiety and depression, an inconstant sense of others, and perhaps psychotic symptoms, rather than feelings of inner well-being and trust.

What happens when psychoanalytic therapy is applied to an Eastern, sociocentric personality, whose identity is centered in the family, the society, and the ancestor world rather than in his corporeal self? His sense of identity is based not on intrapsychic integration (stable character traits and values) but on an interrelated complex of context-dependent familial and social role configurations. The requirements of one of these configurations may be externally inconsistent with those of another, which leaves little room for "individual" variability or social mobility. Such persons do not tend to manifest self-centered behavior, emotional volatility, aggressiveness, or competitiveness and may demonstrate passive acquiescence, lack of ambition, selflessness, and a willingness to accept mistreatment. To the Western observer they may seem like selfless and psychically fragmented cogs in larger social wheels, "part-objects" who accept social inequality without question. Their thinking may reflect a contextual or situational subjectivity and personalization that lends itself more to religious than to scientific forms of thinking, and that, from a Western vantage point, appear internally inconsistent, concrete, nonrational, and lacking in objectivity, a sense of personal boundaries, and self-other differentiation. All of these modal sociocentric personality traits may be viewed as pathological causes of suffering by the psychoanalytically oriented practitioner.

As Shakespeare writes in *Hamlet*: "There are more things in heaven and earth, Horatio, than are dreamt of in your philosophy." Because current psychoanalytic models of self-centric personality, derived from Western culture, are inadequate to conceptualize Eastern personality and identity, including the intricacies of Buddhism, and Buddhist models of sociocentric personality are reciprocally inadequate to conceptualize the sophistication of the Western self, it makes sense to beware of simplistic, therapeutically misguided efforts to apply doctrine derived from one to the evaluation, analysis, or remediation of members of another. The result of "educating" or "treating" persons of one culture with models from another, particularly when the effort is accompanied by the belief that what is being taught is somehow superior, more mature, or healthier than that which they know, probably depends on the age of the student and on whether the teacher is a part of the culture whose way he is teaching, or whether he, too, has learned it later in life. Because of critical periods in neuropsychological maturation and developmental stage specificity, lessons about basic personality organization given by a teacher to an adult will necessarily be assimilated very differently than lessons given by parents, as an encompassing way of being, to a child, beginning in infancy. Will the adult learn to be pathological and maladaptive with regard to the culture of which he is a member? Will he learn a technique while not disturbing his fundamental personality organization? Perhaps a Western scientific theoretical framework, useful as it might be, is no more valid than a model generated from another culture, which to Western eye may appear more like religion or philosophy.

Gender, Personality, and Culture

Although all cultures have specific, differentiating, gender-related conceptions of personality, it is only in the later years of the twentieth century that a serious effort has commenced, ideologically in the women's movement, and then in the human sciences, including psychoanalysis, to ascertain whether these are products of acculturation or whether female personality is innately or constitutionally different from male, or both, and to formulate the differences in a way that is not nullifying or devaluing to one sex or the other. In this chapter I review some of the psychological, psychoanalytic, and anthropological findings and theories about gender and gender-related differences in personality in light of my previous discussion about its constitutional substrate. I hypothesize that differential core gender identity, which contributes to qualitative differences in personality organization, is related primarily to differences in the brains of males and females. Finally, I note the striking parallel between gendered differences in personality, and the broad dichotomy between sociocentric and self-centric culture-related personality typologies noted in chapters 6 and 8, and I speculate that the relationship between gender and culture is more complex and reciprocal than has hitherto been suspected.

All cultures elaborate personality differences between males and females, and they codify behaviors and assign social roles accordingly. Division of labor according to gender is one such difference. It has been speculated that differences in strength and divisions of child-care responsibility play a part in such assignments (Anderson, 1966). Power and authority, social group definition, and control over resources are usually structured around males. What do these differences signify?

The great debate between conventional psychoanalytic constitutionalists, who have concretely interpreted external genital differences as evidence for a classical theory that considers females to be inferior, and revisionist feminist culturalists, some of whose theories are thinly disguised judgments on the male-dominated society they hold accountable, probably has as much to do with the longstanding dominance-submission struggle between the sexes as it does with scientific issues. With the benefit of hindsight we now know that Freud (1925, 1931) confused gender with one of its attributes, male sexuality. He substituted fantasy for reasoned inquiry when he went directly from gross anatomical observation to the conviction, embodied in his now infamous assertion that anatomy is destiny, that females are genitally defective males. He believed that gendered aspects of personality emerge from a common (primordially male) matrix. From this fantasy it was but a few short steps to the conclusion that females are incapable of experiencing and resolving a normal Oedipus complex, and are therefore defective with regard to ego (sublimations) and superego (moral or ethical) development (Freud, 1925, 1931). Freud felt that, because of their presumably untamed sexuality and emotionality, women are especial enemies of culture and civilization (Freud, 1930). At a more subtle level, Freud's theory of sexuality or libido, including pleasurable tension discharge and a phallic developmental stage, appears to be a projection or abstraction of male phallic physiology. He articulated a modal development endpoint for both sexes consisting of separation, objectification, conflict, and the quest for intimate knowledge of and control or domination over the animate and inanimate worlds based on idealization of then-predominant male traits.

Female analysts, initially and notably Karen Horney (1933, 1939) and Clara Thompson (1943, 1950), took up the gauntlet they felt that Freud had flung down. They argued, quite plausibly in terms of what is commonly accepted today, that Freud's ideas about women were products of his cultural bias. They offered a proposal that continues to bear fruit, that there is a primary female gendering which is entirely separate from that of males. The ensuing feminist outcry of protest has matched Freud's ideas in extremism. Some (for example, Miller, 1976) have attempted to rewrite psychoanalytic theory and demonstrate that females are superior and males are deficient. Others have adopted a radical culturalist position. They assert that gender differences either are products of cultural mandate or are themselves culturally fostered illusions and that actual (constitutional) gender differences are minimal (Maccoby and Jacklin, 1974). In the throes of reaction against naive biological reductionism the tendency has been to overlook entirely the differentiating effects of constitution (chapter 5; Blier, 1991). In this seething ideological and counterideological cauldron it is difficult to distinguish sound ideas from polemicism and to begin to specify and objectify the data that might support or refute them.

The influence of culture on the gendered aspects of personality is indisputable. It is so great that seemingly contradictory gender attributes and behaviors are encountered in personalities typical of different cultures. LeVine (1973, 1981, 1990) notes the existence of cultures where females occupy what are stereotypically thought to be male roles, and Benderley (1987) cites the existence of cultures such as the Mbuti, who are characterized by mutuality and cooperativeness and whose creation myth involves a primal womb. In any given culture there is more communality than difference with regard both to innate potential and typical outcome of male and female personality. And it is true that, regardless of gender, all humans develop capabilities for autonomy and separateness as well as relatedness or connectedness. These are by no means statistically reliable differentiating features of gender in individual instances (Berlin and Johnson, 1989).

Turning first to psychology, most studies are limited by the fact that the subjects are from Western cultures. Among neonates the female sensory apparatus seems more sensitive—for example, to sounds and to touch (Garai and Scheinfeld, 1968; Korner, 1974; Maccoby and Jacklin, 1974). Psychophysiological studies of dichotic listening patterns, which would seem to approach measures of pure brain functioning, show consistent differences between males and females (Gorski, 1991). Female infants seem more interpersonally responsive. They smile more and are less irritable and easier to calm. They vocalize earlier and more frequently than their male counterparts.

Males manifest more total body activity. Around one year of age infants tend to look and vocalize more toward the same-sex parent (Lewis and Weinraub, 1974; Spelke, Zelazo, Kagan, and Kotelchuck, 1973). Maccoby and Jacklin (1974, 1980) and Parke and Slaby (1983) claim that gender differences in aggressiveness and assertiveness are observable from very early in life in almost all cultures. Among adults, males have been observed to require more interpersonal space and females to manifest more nurturant behavior. Females tend to be more empathically attuned to personal and interpersonal nuances and to be more dependent on their social and interpersonal environment (Tyler, 1956; Witryol and Kaess, 1957).

Gilligan (1982) investigated Freud's belief that females are morally inferior because of superego weakness consequent to failure to negotiate and resolve an Oedipus complex. It is her observation that female morality is simply different from that of the typical male—not so impersonal and abstract, but structured in a more personalized and contextual way around specific caring human relationships.

As I have noted earlier, Witkin and his associates (1962) have proposed a systems differentiation theory that has been demonstrated to be capable of distinguishing among members of cultures of varying degrees of complexity (hunter-gatherer through urban industrial) on the basis of perceptual and spatial tests of field-dependence. These tests have been given to males and females in a variety of social-cultural groups including New Guinea Telefomin, Native American Cree and Athapaskan, Nigerian and Nsenga Africans, Fiji Islanders, Japanese, Indians, and Mexicans, and in every instance females have been found to be more field-dependent (less differentiated) than males (Witkin and Berry, 1975; Maccoby and Jacklin, 1974). The overall difference between the genders is small in comparison to the range of variation within each gender, however, and there is much overlap. The difference appears to be greater in more stratified societies, where females tend to assume more dependent roles, than in less stratified societies, where they are more independent (Berry, 1966, 1971; MacArthur, 1967). Although these tests seem to differentiate styles of relating, some have speculated that the measures chosen for field-dependence, which involve perceptual-spatial abilities, may simply reflect innate male superiority in that cognitive dimension. Moreover, the very terms chosen to describe the variable that is being discriminated (dependence and independence) have unfortunate value connotations and do not embrace the possibility that what is being measured is a different kind of sensitivity in females.*

In an effort to separate the constitutional contribution to gender difference from cultural influences, anthropologists have studied primate societies. The gendered differences in behavior reported in such studies appear to support the hypothesis that there are significant structural and functional differences between the male and female primate brains. Among chimpanzees, males from infancy through adulthood tend to be more aggressive than females. For example, Hamburg and van Lawick-Goodall (1974) and Bygott (1974) report that females rarely attack one another, and they tend to be more passive and submissive toward males, except in situations where their young appear to be threatened. In the presence of hostile conflict among other chimps, mother chimps will collect their infants and move away. When their infants exhibit rageful and destructive tantrums, mother chimps rarely retaliate but instead tend to initiate comforting and remediating activity. Hrdy (1981), in contrast, observes that aggressive competition among females for resources is one of the most striking and consistent findings in primate cultures.

It is difficult to know how to interpret these studies of humans and primates. Behavioral commonalities do not necessarily imply similar underlying psychological and neurobiological processes. Moreover, data that elucidate the relation of gender and personality are most difficult to distinguish from re-presentations of bias. The culture, gender, and personality of the observer-theoretician determine the nature of his or her hypotheses about gender differences, the design of studies, and the interpretation of data, in ways at once powerful and obscure. As the title of her book (*The Woman That Never Was*) suggests, Hrdy (1981) believes that some of the currently popular feminist conceptions of women as more caring, affiliated, interrelated, nurturing, and less aggressive and seeking of power and control may be mythical (p. 190). She speculates interfemale aggression may have escaped observer attention because its manifestations may be less blatantly obvious than inter-male aggression. It is possible that female aggression, rather than being quantitatively less than male, may be contextually confined to important relation-

---

* Readers who wish to pursue this subject further are referred to literature reviews—for example, Ember, 1981; Notman and Nadelson, 1991.

ships, which are often private, whereas male aggression, being more indiscriminate and public, may be more readily apparent to the casual observer. The assumption that primate differences are entirely constitutional is also debatable; who is to say that chimps do not create cultures of their own? Turning to the human studies, most have been conducted by Western males on other members of Western culture (Divale, 1976). Critics have suggested that "findings" of gender difference are simply reifications of existing bias (Restak, 1979: Blier, 1991; Notman and Nadelson, 1991). Studies that purport to verify stereotypic gender differences often select paradigmatic experimental situations in which males tend to be more practiced and involved rather than settings more typically involving females (such as family situations). Were males and females compared in situations in which females are more experienced, the direction of the observed gender differences might well be reversed. Moreover, the significance of any personality differences between males and females remains unclear, for many studies have now documented the differential treatment afforded to male and female infants by their caregivers starting at birth. For example, male infants in Western culture typically receive more attention and vigorous stimulation than females (Korner, 1974; Maccoby and Jacklin, 1974; Moss, 1974).

Keller (1985) has gone so far as to suggest that science itself, the traditional bastion of masculinity from which not only psychoanalysis but other disciplines that study gender originate, may be a reflection of the male mental apparatus. With it, "man" attempts to distance himself from the natural world, to objectify it, to struggle to conquer it, to make it reveal its inner secrets, and, ultimately, to possess and control it. Keller's ideas raise the most profound questions about the validity of scientific methodology, observations, and conclusions.

Let us turn from behavioral and observational data and inferences of psychology and anthropology to psychoanalytic theory, which considers meaning as well as behavior and affords the most comprehensive synthesis of information about gender difference currently available. Overall, there has been a gradual evolution from Freud's male model of gender, based on an economic theory of psychosexual maturation and on the epistemology of genital awareness and its dynamic (conflictual) and structural (superego) consequences, toward dichotomous conceptions of identity and relationships, involving autonomy, separateness, impersonality and abstract objectivity, conflict, power, and control, on the one hand; and emotional interrelatedness, subjectivity, and contextuality, on the other. These contemporary concerns are remarkably similar to Fairbairn's position a half-century ago. He not only discarded the concepts of separate drives and psychosexual stages but also proposed (1952) a theory of dyadic relationship commencing with a primary undifferentiated dependency on mother, initially experienced as a part-object (the breast). Fairbairn maintained that our primary psychological identity is female, a belief at odds with Freud but consistent with more recent biological findings. "It is more than doubtful, however, whether the child at first appreciates the genital difference between the two parents. It would appear rather that the difference which he does appreciate is that his father has no breasts" (1952, pp. 122–123, first published 1944). He believed that the Oedipal conflict is not so much a determinant of personality structure (the superego) as it is a derivative of the endopsychic configuration resulting from the infant's dyadic experience with its mother.

Before describing some of the newer psychoanalytic models, it is worth noting some of the problems encountered in psychoanalytic efforts to revise accounts of gender. As Benjamin (1988) has pointed out, some of the most vociferous proponents of equity in gender theory have actually advocated models that stereotypically devalue one gender at the expense of the other. For example, Clower (1981) labels as "female" such characteristics as subjectivity, interdependency, and loose boundaries, but subtly devalues them in contrast to "male" characteristics by likening the female mind to a primitive, borderline-like organization. Similar bias with a reverse twist is found in the writings of Chodorow (1978), Miller (1976), and some of her colleagues at the Stone Center. Miller idealizes the very "female" traits Clower seems to devalue subtly by constructing a countermodel of female maturity relative to male personality, which is conceived of as the product of deficiency and defense (see also Benjamin, 1988; Hrdy, 1981). The movement to model the emancipated woman around the same "masculine" characteristics that women have found objectionable and thought themselves victimized by is another example. Most of these re-presentations probably fit the criterion of sociopolitical ideologies formulated by a revolutionary minority group more than that of theories with scientific merit.

One of the newer concepts in the psychoanalysis of gender is core gender identity. This refers to a differentiating bedrock of identity that is postulated to exist from the earliest stage of life, before the developments of gender role identity and sexual orientation. Karen Horney (1933, 1939) was one of the first to advance the concept of primary femininity based on genital sensations. This core of gendered differences in personality is generally believed to develop within the first two years of life (Amsterdam, 1972; Lewis and Brooks-Gunn, 1979; and Emde, 1983), probably antecedent to or independent of the differentiating influences of culture. It cannot be accounted for by a primordial male model and secondary responses in infants of both sexes to an awareness that one of them is missing something. Female core gender identity is generally thought to commence with the earliest sensory-perceptive-entero-ceptive-cognitive-affective awareness of her body, mirrored in primary relationship with the mother (Erikson, 1968; Kestenberg, 1968; Mahler et al. 1975; Stoller, 1976; Roiphe and Galenson, 1981; Mayer, 1985; Person and Ovesey, 1983). It is generally understood to be the product of emerging body awareness, gender-differentiating early object relations, normal developmental conflicts, and selective identifications (Grossman, 1994; Tyson, 1994).

Although derived from different schools of psychoanalytic thought and history, most of the newer theories of female personality share a model of female identity as interpersonal or socially collective, in contrast to male identity, which is perceived as individualistic, autonomous, or self-centered.

Over four decades investigators from three areas separately developed an interpersonal or intersubjective model. The first is the interpersonal school of psychiatry, founded by Sullivan (1953) and currently represented by Hoffman (1983, 1987, 1991) as social constructivism. Edgar Levenson (1985, 1991) writes: "The interpersonal matrix is a self-perpetuating and self-equilibrating system that depends not on the fuel of fantasy for its viability, but on repetitive interactions" (1991, p. 219). The psychic realities of the participants in a relationship continually shape what the interpersonalists call the interactional field, which more traditional analytic constructivists would describe as the intrapsychic worlds of the participants.

Quite independent of one another, two other groups of theorists committed to a relationship model of personality constructed hypotheses around the central organizing concept of "intersubjectivity." One group (Stolorow, Atwood, and Ross, 1978; Atwood and Stolorow, 1984; Stolorow and Atwood, 1992), come to the concept through Kohut's self psychology and have not applied it to gender. The other group, beginning with the work of Dinnerstein

(1976) and Miller (1976), was influenced by the theory of Margaret Mahler and drew also upon the work of Stoller (1964, 1968), Greenson (1968), and Lynn (1969). Others who have contributed to this model include Gilligan (1982), Lykes (1985), Sampson (1988), Keller (1985), Benjamin (1988), and Flax (1990).

One of the foremost proponents of this interpersonal or collective identity model is Nancy Chodorow (1978, 1989), who employs Mahler's theory and proposes that mature women, more often than mature men, may achieve an advanced state of separation-individuation. This state requires a higher level of differentiation and integration and includes a more mature form of dependency that she calls intersubjectivity, defined as the recognition of another subject, similar to the self. She suggests that such modal female personality traits as affiliation, empathy, nurturance, and contextual morality, hitherto derogated in Western male-dominated society, may actually indicate a higher level of female maturity. This has led to speculation that it is the male and not the female whose development may in some respects be defensively crippled. Characteristics that society has traditionally valued as more mature—separateness, autonomy, objectivity, impersonal and logical thinking, and firmness of boundaries—are socially valued because they are prototypically masculine, but if viewed from a different perspective, as fear of intimacy, rigid boundaries, objectification, alienation, and domination, they may not be so mature after all. These ideas are suggestive of Fairbairn's (1952) schema of a normal developmental line for dependency, from less to more mature forms.

Expanding on Greenson's (1968) work, Chodorow (1978, 1980) postulates a primal conflict in male gender identity development between primary identity and relatedness with mother and more mature identity as a male. The male is hypothesized to repudiate relatedness to mother in order to shift identification from mother to father. She believes such conflict is exacerbated because mothers tend to treat their sons as different from themselves, thus promoting a sense of alienation (1980). In females, by contrast, development of core gender identity is hypothesized to be enhanced by mirroring relatedness to another female. It does not require repudiation of relatedness with mother (Chodorow, 1978, 1980; Keller, 1985; Flax, 1990).

The use of Mahler's theory as a framework for intersubjectivity models is problematic, however. It is based on a modal personality, regardless of gender, characterized by such traits as separation, autonomy, and objectivity. It reifies the very Western male bias that intersubjectivity theorists deplore.

In addition to being gender-differentiating, Chodorow's model is gender-prejudicial in that the female is considered to be a more mature species. The model is based on the belief that relationships between females, including mother and daughter, are qualitatively different from those between males, less aggressive and conflictual and more related and intersubjective. On the basis of her extensive studies of primate societies, Hrdy (1981) believes that such ideas are fantasy. Studies of same-sex relationships have tended to focus on more traditionally masculine-competitive realms, outside the family. But it is commonplace to observe aggression and conflict, overt or covert, in inter-generational relationships among females (mother-in-law–daughter-in-law or mother-daughter). While male *gender* identity formation may require some degree of aggressive repudiation of relatedness to mother, female *personal* (as contrasted with gender) identity and boundary formation, out of a primary identification matrix, may also require a degree of interpersonal aggression. In my own clinical experience, predominantly with a more disturbed group of patients whose primitive thinking and early experiences are highlighted, I have found that while female patients may be more adaptable than males, they have roughly comparable problems around dependency, conflicts with mother, identity, capacity for intimacy, and recognition of otherness.

Benjamin (1988) and Keller (1985) propose similar schemata for gender-related development which are less gender-prejudicial than Chodorow's model. Along with Winnicott (1971), Stern (1985), Ogden (1989), and Blatt and Blass (1990), they view separateness and intersubjective connectedness as poles of a dialectic process. Benjamin suggests the need for simultaneous complementary but qualitatively different one-person and two-person psychologies or psychoanalytic models in order to comprehend each of these poles or dimensions. Whereas the more primitive intrapsychic states of domination and submission can be conceptualized adequately with an intrapsychic model, she believes that a two-person psychology is necessary to conceptualize the mature intersubjective state. Recognition of the other and the wish to be in harmonious relationship with her are gradual processes requiring maintenance of a state of intersubjective tension and mutuality. This is in dynamic conflict or tension with a more fundamental motivation toward either a state of identification with the powerfully perceived nurturing person, which may take the form either of sadistic obliteration of the otherness of the object, or masochistic submissiveness to that person and consequent self-obliteration. Benjamin's two-person model stresses the importance of a circular, self-reinforcing process in which these societal perceptions of mothers (and all females) are both a reflection of primitive or infantile forms of thinking and a force perpetuating them.

Gendering of the male mind emphasizes difference, autonomy and separateness, and cognitive skills of abstraction and objectification. It involves development of polarized concepts of self/object, masculine/feminine, separation/connection, autonomy/intimacy, and power, domination, and control/submissiveness. In order to establish an appropriate gender identity, males must emphasize their differences and their separateness from others. As a consequence men tend to treat women as objects of use and domination rather than as people (Chodorow, 1978, Flax, 1990). Females, in contrast, are able to be closer to and more subjectively involved with others, as this reinforces rather than threatens their identity-based sense of gender. For this reason Benjamin believes that the alternative of submission is more typical of females, and that of dominance is more typical of males.

Possibly Benjamin has confused the important distinction between the state of psychological identity-fusion or undifferentiation, whether selfless (submission) or otherless (domination), and the state of differentiation that allows for awareness of the other and intersubjectivity, with the equally important distinction between the power and scope of intrapsychic and interpersonal models of personality. An intrapsychic model ought to be capable of representing both states, differentiation and undifferentiation. What it *cannot* do is to serve as an adequate model of an identity sense that is interpersonal and collective.

Keller's (1985) ideas are similar to Benjamin's. She contrasts dynamic and static aspects of autonomy associated with intersubjectivity and objectivity, respectively. Static autonomy involves sharp boundaries between self and other. When the subject is dominant, he stands in opposition to an object, that is, another who is not perceived as being alive. When the subject is submissive she relinquishes her aliveness. In both of these static states aggression, conflict, and dominance-submission characterize relationships. In contrast, dynamic autonomy involves flexible boundaries between self and other; a Winnicottian subjective-empathetic transitional area. Keller believes that far from being flawed by subjectivity, such typically female thinking may actually enable a more authentic form of knowledge.

The models of Benjamin and Keller, less gender-prejudicial or devaluing than Chodorow's, emphasize the contrast between solipsistic, boundary-less relations and ones characterized by flexible, mutually interpenetrating boundaries. They appear to be very similar to Klein's solipsistic paranoid-schizoid (splitting) position and her more mature depressive position, respectively. Klein, however, included an important dimension of emotional development and regulation which these later theories do not, involving integration of drive derivatives, achievement of the capacity for intrapsychic conflict, and toleration of ambivalent feelings about others. Klein was also an epistemologist. She was less concerned with the firmness or flexibility dimension of boundaries than with their developmental transformation from a solipsistic state of self-splitting that creates, through projective identification, the phantasy of relatedness in a kind of power struggle, to a more mature cognitive-affective differentiation of self and other enabling true mutuality.

Perhaps the new feminist theories tend toward concreteness insofar as they confuse the capacity to establish differentiated boundaries between conceptions of self and other with walls or barriers to relatedness. When they refer to the rigid boundaries that seem more characteristic of males, perhaps they are referring to barriers against relating with appropriate empathy and affect, and not to the capacity to perceive self and other with relative accuracy and express and modulate affects accordingly. Whereas Keller utilizes Winnicott's transitional object concept (1971) as a new model for mature intersubjective relations and perhaps for science itself, Winnicott himself was conceptualizing an area of private or shared illusion, not of reality.

Fast (1984) proposed the outlines of an overarching, non-gender-discriminatory model for early development, also utilizing Mahler's theory as a reference point. She emphasized the role of cognitive processes, specifically differentiation, as an organizing developmental concept and pointed out that, whatever their earlier constitutional predispositions and interpersonal/cultural experiences may have been, infants do not begin to make gender differentiations until the time they make basic identity differentiations, during the second year of life. She believes that gender differentiation may or may not become confused with separation-individuation concerns, and the two issues may become conflictual for females as well as males. Similar ideas have been proposed by Witkin and his associates (1962) in the form of a psychological differentiation model of culture and personality, described earlier.

For the most part, these accounts of gender tend to paint personality in broad brushstrokes. With some notable exceptions, such as Gilligan's work, they do not appear to be anchored in specific clinical data but seem to have originated from scholarly anecdotal group discussions among women. What constitutes data, and how are we to differentiate data from ideologies in revolution? What emerges most clearly from these studies is not so much a new theory of personality and gender as a general agreement, even among persons with different ideological biases and scientific and theoretical orientations, that there are important and probably qualitative differences between modal male and female minds and personalities. Sampson (1988) refers to the unique aspect of female personality as "ensembled individualism." Following the conceptual schema I developed in earlier chapters I prefer to designate these typical gendered differences in personality, arising under average expectable circumstances, sociocentric (female) and self-centric (male). These are overlapping, not clearly dichotomous typologies, because all human beings are much more similar than different. Moreover, all of us grow up in proximity to both kinds of thinking, self-centric and sociocentric, and tend to be dually gendered from birth.

To synthesize the hypothesis of qualitative differences between modal male and female personalities and the data on gendered differences in the brain dating from neonatal life, I propose that we re-define the concept of core gender identity. The commonly accepted definition does not take into account constitutional differences in the brain but starts with differentiating organizations of the sensory-perceptual-affective experience of the body, beginning in the neonatal period in the context of the primary relationship. It is held to be a process completed in infancy and very early childhood involving the creation of self-object-affect representations. Tyson, for example, writes, "with an awareness of the sense of self and sense of bodily zones, a basic sense of belonging to one sex and not the other, and having certain characteristics of that sex accrues" (1994, pp. 451–452). While the sensory-perceptual significance of the sexually distinctive body configurations is an important dimension of core identity, it is constitutional differences in the brain and the endocrine system in relation to differently designed and functioning bodies, in the context of culturally average or expectable early interpersonal interactions with caregivers, that lead to a gender-differentiating organization and functioning of mind.

In order to illustrate my contention that sociocultural attitudes and beliefs have led us to more or less disregard the gender-differentiating significance of differences in the brain, I should like to contrast the current sociocultural attitude about the etiology of schizophrenia (that it is an organic illness) with the popular bias about the origin of gender differences (that they are largely sociocultural artifacts). In so doing, I do not mean to imply that gendering is a disease. Genetic factors appear to account for slightly more than one-third of the variance in schizophrenia (Robbins, 1993a). But despite the absence of more definitive evidence, it is now generally accepted that schizophrenia is an organic disease of the brain and the effects of the cultural and interpersonal environment on development of the illness are negligible. In contrast, constitution accounts for much of the variance in sex, and there is much more definitive evidence for brain differences between males and females than between schizophrenics and nonschizophrenics. Although it is not possible to make definitive morphological distinctions between individual male and female brains, or schizophrenic and "normal" brains, and differences are encountered only when one statistically averages large groups, there is much more substantial agreement about the nature of gender differences. And there is a much higher probability that one can successfully ascertain, using neurochemical tests, whether a given individual is male or female than whether he or she is schizophrenic or normal.

My point is that powerful social attitudes and values are at play in determining what we view as data and how we construe it. In the instance of schizophrenia the predominant sociocultural belief that it is an organic illness leads people to discount the absence of definitive organic findings. In the instance of gender, reaction against the cultural bias that led people to misconstruction of organic (anatomical) differences in support of a theory devaluing of females tempts us to ignore differentiating neurobiological findings.

I think little doubt exists that there is a constitutional predisposition to be typically gendered, and that the concept of core gender identity should be redefined to take this into account. Under ordinary circumstances of parenting, constitutional elements lead to the emergence of those aspects of personality we characterize as gender-related. Under unusual circumstances of parenting these developments may be thwarted or altered. The interaction of neurobiological and social-interpersonal experiential forces that constitutes gendered development is not a static process, but one that evolves over the life span of the individual. Organic gender-specific changes in the brain and mind characterize puberty, mature adult procreativity, aging, and senescence, every bit as much as the more readily apparent somatic changes do. We may conclude that core gender identity comprises constitutional gender-related differences that have qualitative consequences for how personality is constituted and evolve throughout the life cycle as part of a reciprocal interactive process with the environment.

Core gender identity formation is but one element of the evolution of gendered aspects of personality. Others include developmental interactions with parents and with one's culture as mediated through caregivers and social institutions. These may elaborate, alter, or abort the usual and typical gender development sequences. Culture not only influences structural development, it also ascribes meaning, hence some of the confusion between "real" differences and culturally created beliefs or illusions. Part of the complexity stems from the fact that the constitutional-organic factors and interpersonal-cultural factors, far from being static forces, are each evolving at the same time they are interactive. Cultural, social, and interpersonal experience modify the brain (neural plasticity), and the brain, probably the temporal-limbic system whose role is perpetuation of learned patterns, both evolves and shapes the cultural and interpersonal worlds.

In her best-selling book on male-female communication (You Just Don't Understand), Tannen (1990) used the analogy of different cultures to describe differences between men and women. However, her definition of culture is an abstract one—shared differences in style and meaning—and she does not consider actual cultures and the differences among them. There are remarkable parallels between the gender-related dichotomy of personality (self-centric and sociocentric) and the dichotomy between modal personality in Western and Eastern cultures noted in chapters 6 and 8. Using systems theory and the nonlinear dynamics of transformational systems, I hypothesize in chapter 14 that constitution, personality, and culture comprise recursive systems, and that there is a constitutional substrate of gender differences, and a gendering both of personality and of culture.

CHAPTER 10

Psychoanalytic Monism and Intracultural Diversity

Every culture establishes its own standards of normal or modal and deviant personality typologies. The local systems or indigenous psychologies that each culture constructs to conceive of personality, such as psychoanalysis and Buddhism, use these standards as references. The modal personality organization tends to be the centerpiece of a linear scale, and what is unusual tends to be viewed as abnormal or deviant from it. In earlier chapters I demonstrated how the scope of psychoanalysis has been limited by its monistic model with regard to conceiving of personality differences among cultures (intercultural) and between the genders. In this chapter I turn to the psychoanalysis of intracultural diversity of personality, which is similarly limited by monistic thinking. I argue that the concern of many analysts (for example, Wallerstein, 1988) that contemporary psychoanalysis has become a theoretical babel of tongues and needs to be more unified masks the fact that all these apparently different theories actually share, more or less, a common set of underlying principles of mental functioning. As a result, existing psychoanalytic models cannot encompass intracultural personality diversity. They do not suffice to comprehend persons who are more deeply disturbed (primitive personalities including borderline, narcissistic, paranoid, and schizoid), individuals with clear constitutional differences (for example, schizophrenics), other statistically uncommon personality types such as homosexuals, or even some unusual personalities who never come to psychoanalytic attention. I have deliberately avoided use of the term *psychopathology* to designate this group, because in this context it is a null reference concept with regard to normalcy which commits us to the very linear monistic mode of thinking that I believe is the source of the problem. As I proposed self-centric and sociocentric variations of personality related to the genders and to the major culture variants, so I now propose that there are qualitative differences in personality organization within Western culture itself (and no doubt within any culture) that also require qualitatively distinctive models for adequate exposition.

Unfortunately, discussions of the adequacy of psychoanalysis' existing model structure tend to be suffused with a polemical quality, emanating from two groups whose superficial polarization masks an underlying commonality of belief: the flexible evolutionists and the revolutionaries or revisionists. The flexible evolutionists take issue with the claim that psychoanalysis is a single-model theory, pointing to such developments as ego psychology in support of their contention that the theory is sufficiently elastic to meet clinical needs and to evolve in whatever direction is necessary. They fear that those who use the single-model argument are constructing a straw man in order to discard what has been tried and tested for something radical and unproven. When faced with questions about the scope of psychoanalysis—that is, its applicability to more seriously disturbed persons, statistically unusual subpopulations, or persons from different ethnic and cultural groups—this faction divides into two subgroups.

The first subgroup of flexible evolutionists defines psychoanalytic theory and its patient population in such a way that the question of whether the theory is monistically limited never arises. They regard these other populations as outside the scope of psychoanalysis and they do not wish to make immodest claims for the field. In the instance of more disturbed persons, the unique elements of their personality are not looked upon as having intrinsic psychological meaning. They are a null category, reflecting a defect or deficiency, perhaps reductionistically dismissed as organic. With the rationale that it is not the theory that is lacking but the patient, such persons are classified as psychoanalytically "untreatable," even though they may be statistically numerous and, in the case of mental illness, may comprise the bulk of the population.

Flexible evolutionists in the second subcategory are convinced that the existing model is sufficiently plastic to treat all types of patients, regardless of diagnosis, although, in practice, few members of this group actually attempt to do so. With regard to more seriously disturbed persons, the Kris Study Group in New York is perhaps the principal representative of this belief, reflected in the work of Arlow and Brenner (1964, 1969) on schizophrenia, and in Abend, Porder, and Willick's (1983) book on borderline personality. However, the case examples they use to support their argument are persons who seem hardly ill enough to satisfy accepted diagnostic criteria of schizophrenia and borderline personality.

The revisionist or revolutionary element, in contrast, believes that psychoanalysis is constrained by a "classical" theory that may need to be replaced with an alternative model, such as Kleinian theory, Kohutian self psychology, or one of the hermeneutic theories (interpersonal, intersubjective, or social constructivist). However, on close inspection the new theories turn out to share many of the limitations of the old theory and are not as fundamentally different as adherents and critics alike seem to believe (Robbins, 1980, 1993a, 1993b).

I should like to outline what I believe are some of the basic postulates of psychoanalytic theory that are responsible for its monistic limitations with regard to the intracultural diversity of personality. I shall not reiterate those monistic aspects of the theory that are particularly relevant to culture (self-centric) or those related to gender (phallocentric), which are discussed in chapters 7 and 9, respectively.

Despite Freud's often-cited statement (1915) that constitution and early experience form a complemental series, a position which allows for a variety of beginnings and developmental pathways, the model postulates that all persons—at least all who fall within the scope of a psychoanalytic model of personality—are endowed with a more or less similarly organized constitutionally determined psychic "apparatus." Personality epigenetically unfolds according to a single, constitutionally determined blueprint. Psychoanalysis postulates paradigmatic, qualitatively similar familial and sociocultural configurations and experiences for all individuals, at least for all individuals defined as falling within its scope. These include a nuclear family, more or less good-enough mothering, certain kinds of training and expectations, among which are exposure to a primal scene and to paternal authority. Such a paradigm may even be an expression of human phylogenetic inheritance. The basic model postulates that the person develops from common constitutional and environmental beginnings via a single developmental pathway toward an ideal end point of modal personality comprising stable, self-contained individuality and the capacity to function autonomously, separate from other "objects." In the classical neurosis model the modal personality achieves psychosexual maturity and genital primacy, more or less, as well as a tripartite mental structure. In Kohut's model it achieves self-cohesion around the poles of ambitions and ideals.

The basic model consists of the modal personality and a null category; that is, there is no such thing as equally weighted but qualitatively different personalities. With reference to the modal personality there is a linear scale of quantitative deviation. Both immaturity and the varieties of psychopathology are mapped as points and related patterns of arrest, fixation, regression, and symptom formation. The actual or potential patient in the analyst's consulting room is either presumed (at times erroneously, judging from some outcomes of treatment) to have the qualitative modal personality organization I shall describe, or is consigned to a null category, in part or entirely beyond the scope of the theory and technique. Because the null category is believed to comprise conditions of immaturity or deficiency, these do not need to be conceptualized as differences in their own right. In his valedictory statement about what constitutes psychoanalysis, Theodore Shapiro, former editor of the *Journal of the American Psychoanalytic Association* and a notably broad-minded representative of contemporary psychoanalysis, states succinctly both the qualitative organization of the basic model and the null hypothesis: "Psychoanalysis warrants the appellation science as well as being a profession that is sincerely devoted to furthering the understanding of human mental processes in conflict and deficiency" (1993, pp. 924–925).

All psychoanalytic theories share certain core assumptions about the modal personality. He or she has achieved a significant degree of psychic integration and differentiation. He or she is presumed to have achieved, more or less, a state of functional self-containment and self-sufficiency, self-caring, and self-esteem. Dependent and symbiotic structures have been resolved in the course of development as the individual has internalized the identity-sustaining functions formerly served by others, and they have become intrapsychic structures. Interpersonal group and social formations are considered secondary achievements rather than cornerstones of a collective identity. The personality structure includes:

1. Representation of cognitive-affective experience regarding self and other that is reasonably constant or sustained;
2. A mind that is more reflective or representational than enactive;
3. Differentiation of representations of self from representations of other;
4. A secondary or dynamic unconscious system wherein representations of conflicted past experience with related drive and affective components live on to influence contemporary life;
5. An integration of the various elements of the mental world, conscious and unconscious, into an organization based on intrapsychic conflict, defense, and ambivalence; and
6. Appropriate and adaptive self-regulatory and self-control functions with regard to sensation, perception, and related action.

Freud did make a place in his theory for different theoretical levels or systems: his much-maligned metapsychology. Originally he included economic, topographic, and dynamic points of view. Rappaport (1960) believed that a gestalt or systems viewpoint is implicit in psychoanalytic metapsychology. Noy (1977) and Ellman and Moskowitz (1980) believe that inherent in the various metapsychological viewpoints is a multiplicity of levels for comprehending data and tools for manipulating it. Nonetheless, most of the numerous efforts to revise, expand, and replace the basic monistic model have turned out, instead, to reiterate many of its basic elements in new guises. Many of these efforts involving theories of Klein, Fairbairn, and perhaps Kohut, as well, are subsumed within the concept of object relations theory, a loose umbrella for theories that attribute motivation and organization to human relatedness rather than to innate biological elements.

Melanie Klein (1935, 1940, 1946) is generally considered the first of the object relations theorists, probably because of her homuncular conception of instinctually driven infantile phantasy. From Freud's (1920, 1937) death-instinct hypothesis she elaborated a theory of inherent infantile rage and its normal and pathological developmental consequences. She recognized the importance of the mother-child relationship, and her theory paved the way for other dyadic theories and for more recent efforts to conceptualize interpersonal relationships. But her conception of instinct is like Freud's. The infant in her theory is almost entirely self-engrossed, so that its sense of the other person is little more than a figment of its hostile imagining. She implicitly recognized the fundamental importance of integration and differentiation in psychic development, for she traced the evolution of the paranoid-schizoid position, characterized by splitting (weak integration) and projective identification (partial undifferentiation), to the depressive position characterized by whole object relations (differentiation) and depressive ambivalence (integration). However, she couched her observations in the basic model framework of intrapsychic conflict and defense (splitting and projective identification). Her theory has been subjected to much criticism based on doubts that such mental states as conflict and defense, which seem to require significant maturation in the form of integration and differentiation, exist from the very start of life. She never faced this seeming contradiction and it did not occur to her that she might have stumbled upon primitive global mental states that require a different model of personality, based on immaturity of integration and differentiation. As a consequence, while the conceptual language Klein chose is sufficiently different from Freud's as to lend her theory an air of novelty, her theory, in its fundamentals, retains a more basic conceptual identity with the core of psychoanalytic theory than her proponents or detractors commonly acknowledge. Klein's theory postulates the presence of a psychic organization more cognitively sophisticated in terms of integration and differentiation than seriously disturbed individuals seem to be capable of. Such an organization presumably enables the neonate and the seriously disturbed patient to mentally represent affect-laden ideas and to maintain sufficient integrative linkage between disparate ideas to be able to represent primal conflict, utilize intrapsychic defense mechanisms (splitting and projective identification) and maintain cathectic connection with the object while differentiating the self from the projectively identified other. Waelder was aware of the basic similarity between the theories of Freud and Klein in 1936, when he wrote of Klein's contribution: "the theories in question abandon none of the views with which we have long been familiar but merely add to them" (p. 124).

The psychoanalytically conceivable person in the theories of Fairbairn (1952) and Kohut (1971, 1977) is also organized along the lines of the basic model I have described. Fairbairn, whose work emerged from a dialogue with Klein, postulates that we are all schizoid (more or less). His schizoid personalities are said to be capable, from earliest infancy, of such neurotic level mental attitudes as defensive splitting of the undifferentiated amalgam of self and ego, object and drive, related to early unsatisfactory object experience, into ideal and "bad" parts, repression of the "bad" part, and further splitting of it into exciting and rejecting parts.

Kohut's psychology of the self, like Fairbairn's object relations theory, rejects the classical notion that innate human motivation is biological, consisting of lust and destruction, and that a mental apparatus evolves from biologically based conflict. He offers, instead, a teleological motivation system based on self-cohesion around the narcissistic poles of ambition and ideals, and an appreciation of the maturational or pathogenic role of the empathic or frustrating parent in this process. Beginning in the middle of the second year of life the infant is deemed capable of archaic self-cohesion, realistically differentiated selfobject transferences and representation of affect. He can also experience intrapsychic conflict, though it does not have an important place in Kohut's model. Psychopathology is described as fragmentation of the self and is believed to be the result of major failures of empathic selfobject attunement. Kohut's view that infants in the first year and a half and seriously disturbed patients (including borderline personalities and schizophrenics) lack these integrating and differentiating capacities—and hence are a null category, psychologically meaningless, and beyond the scope of psychoanalytic theory—highlights the monistic character of his theory. Kohut's monism is also expressed in the belief in the possibility of empathy between analyst and all patients with actual or potentially cohesive selves, a possibility that requires one to postulate a qualitative similarity of minds.

John Gedo and a theoretically related group variously known as interpersonalists, intersubjectivists, and social constructivists have made the only genuine efforts to move away from monistic models of personality. Gedo alone (1979, 1984, 1986), and with Goldberg (1973), has considered the possibility of qualitatively different mental organizations that cannot be accounted for by the basic assumptions of psychoanalysis. He has constructed an epigenetic transformational hierarchy comprising five models of psychic function, each organized around a major task or achievement that heralds the new concepts and principles of organization that will characterize the next "higher" model. From the most primitive level these tasks are as follows: state regulation or homeostasis, a variable which was identified through infant observation and is based on the reflex-arc model; integration (or cohesion of the self), which might have come from Kleinian theory or from self psychology; self-esteem regulation, including acceptance of reality and relinquishment of illusion and grandiosity, which comes from self psychology; resolution of intrapsychic conflict, from the structural theory of the classical model; and self-actualization beyond conflict, a notion derived from Maslow and Erikson. The supraordinate variable around which Gedo's hierarchy of models is organized is not the drive-based psychosexual maturation of the classical model, but the teleological Kohutian conception of cohesion of the self around aims and goals.

A miscellaneous group of theorists who share a sense of the importance of interpersonal relations and hermeneutics, comprising interpersonalists (Sullivan, 1953; Levenson, 1985, 1991); intersubjectivist descendants of Kohut (Atwood and Stolorow, 1984; Stolorow and Atwood, 1992), intersubjectivists in the feminist movement descended from Mahler (Chodorow, 1978), and social constructivists (Hoffman 1983, 1987, 1991), have also attempted to move beyond some of the assumptions of the core model. The major contemporary exponent of the interpersonal school, Edgar Levenson (1985, 1991), writes that "The interpersonal matrix is a self-perpetuating and self-equilibrating system that depends not on the fuel of fantasy for its viability, but on repetitive interactions" (1991, p. 219). The psychic realities of the participants in a relationship continually shape each other; the result is what is known as the interactional field. Interpersonal theory is more interested in this evanescent field than in a relatively fixed (structured) intrapsychic template. Independently, from the field of feminist studies, Chodorow introduced the same term *intersubjectivity* in her efforts to define the relational field she believes characterizes modal female personality. Other contributors to this new paradigm include so-called hermeneuticists from philosophy, particularly Habermas (1971), Ricoeur (1970, 1981), and Spence (1982), and from psychoanalysis, including George Klein (1976), Gill (1976), and Schafer (1976). For the most part, however, these ideas have not been articulated into true psychoanalytic theories of personality but have been utilized more as nontraditional perspectives on or orientations toward the clinical treatment situation. Moreover, they are also monistic models, albeit of a different kind than the core theory.

Some personality typologies within the culture just do not seem to fit the basic model and appear to differ in complex ways from the modal personality on which it is based. It may be nullifying of their diversity to characterize these persons as pre-genital, ego-defective, non-cathecting, immature, and the like. In chapters 4 and 7 I reviewed how the concept of modal personality, which is central to psychoanalytic theory, was derived from a relatively limited and skewed sample of patients, preponderantly the "worried well," who are able to conduct reasonably constructive lives and make office visits. Although the Rat Man and the Wolf Man were seriously disturbed (Tausk, 1919; Binswanger, 1956; Reichard, 1956), Freud's experience with such patients, and particularly with schizophrenics, was limited. Yet his statements about schizophrenia, which are few and modest, are responsible for the widespread psychoanalytic conception of it as a null category, a deficit or defect syndrome that cannot be treated psychoanalytically. Those most influential in psychoanalytic theory have tended to work with typical analytic populations, heavily weighted with mental health personnel and even other analysts in training. Some have attempted to generalize their findings, as Freud did—for example, Arlow and Brenner (1964, 1969) and Abend, Porder, and Willick (1983), from the Kris Study Group in New York. When I had occasion to review the psychoanalytic literature on schizophrenia for my 1993 book, for example, and to talk with some of those considered experts in the field, I was amazed to learn how few of them had ever worked personally and intensively with schizophrenics. In fact, relatively few psychoanalysts have worked intensively with unusual populations of any kind.

There have been some studies by psychoanalysts of another atypical or exceptional group, comprising persons who might well be labeled pathological if encountered in a clinical setting but who do not seek treatment and therefore do not ordinarily come to the attention of psychoanalysts. Artson (1978) and Vaillant (1977, 1993) studied members of this group, persons with unusual albeit constructive adaptations to life's exigencies; they separately conclude that the range of so-called normal adjustment is not fully represented within the modal end points of ordinary psychoanalytic developmental theory.

In 1981 I suggested that the idea of achievement of autonomy is an illusion or myth and that obligatory symbiotic dependences normally persist throughout life. Although I do not disavow this idea, I now believe that it did not go far enough. I have since suggested (Robbins, 1983, 1988, 1989, 1993b) that many of the more seriously disturbed personalities in the borderline, narcissistic, paranoid, and schizoid spectrum, as well as schizophrenics, are organized in qualitatively different ways that cannot be conceived of by the core model or by quantitative deviations from it. The pathology of these primitive personalities originates not from defenses, compromises, and constrictions that are products of a dynamic unconscious and intrapsychic conflict, but from an agenda expressed at the somatic, behavioral, and interpersonal levels, which appears to have evolved as a rudimentary survival adaptation within their families of origin. This adaptation has never gained symbolic representation in the mind and proves, in the ordinary adult world, to be fundamentally maladaptive, even to the point of jeopardizing the very maintenance of life. What follows is a summary of conclusions I reached in earlier publications about some of the major elements that differentiate these primitive personalities from the core theoretical configuration.

The borderline, narcissistic, paranoid, and schizoid personalities to whom I refer are seriously maladapted, inept in at least some of the basics of self-care, and self-destructive in their personal lives. However, their serious self-destructiveness is often concealed by a shared network of non-acknowledgment, and many of these persons are capable of considerable work and social accomplishments that lead others also to overlook their problems. This probably contributes to the common belief (to which I do not subscribe) that their personalities are mixes of more mature and more primitive levels of functioning, rather than being basically and qualitatively different. The work of Fraiberg (1969), Piaget (Flavell, 1963; Gruber and Voneche 1977), Fairbairn (1940), and Winnicott (1960) may help us to understand this phenomenon better. Fraiberg utilized the work of Piaget to distinguish between the capacities for human object constancy (which primitive personalities have not attained) and inanimate "thing" constancy (which they do have). In other words, they can keep in mind a conception of themselves and others as things, denoted by name and formal qualities, even when lack of personal integration and differentiation renders them incapable of synthesizing and sustaining constancy in human terms, that is, ones involving subtle attributes of feeling and character. Fairbairn wrote of the schizoid personalities' skill in role-playing, to which Winnicott gave the felicitous name "false self." These individuals have a special facility for observing and complying with formal social rules, using the capacity for "thing" constancy, probably developed as an offshoot of the extraordinary adaptive skills they required in early infancy. So long as they are able to maintain a certain distance from intimate affect- and need-arousing relationships, they are adept in masking their problems. In the area of personal intimacy, however, they more clearly manifest the features I am about to describe: (1) a relative absence of psychic integration and differentiation, (2) a rudimentary capacity to represent and regulate affect, (3) a reliance on sensorimotor-affective thinking and pathological symbiotic relationships in lieu of internalized mental capabilities, and (4) resultant profound disturbances in their self-esteem and object relations.

An absence of integration. Affect-laden ideas which relate to a single ideational system—that is, which are about the same person or thing—but are affectively different and even contradictory are experienced in isolation from one another, and affects are not appropriately linked to ideas. The person is likely to mistake his mental state at any given moment for the totality of his belief rather as a part (*pars pro toto* thinking). He presents a shifting, fragmentary, contradictory self, or, more accurately, selves. Klein (1946) was the first to call attention to this phenomenon, but, along with most who have followed, she believed this was a primary defense against otherwise overwhelming rage. In contrast, as I shall elaborate below, I believe that the primitive mind lacks the capacity to experience intrapsychic conflict, conscious or unconscious, or mature ambivalence.

An absence of differentiation. Characteristics of self and object are confused in ways we are accustomed to think of in terms of defenses, projective and introjective. As with lack of integration, Klein was probably the first to observe the projective aspect of misidentifying aspects of the self in the other (1946). The introjective process—that is, the self's acceptance or incorporation of attributions or projections of disavowed undesirable characteristics from the other, which serves as a perverse and self-destructive form of self-organization—has received less attention. It is phenomenologically similar to what Fairbairn described as the splitting and repression of the "bad" part of a frustrating object relationship, which then becomes part of the self-structure.

Absence of affect representation, related affect control, and other affect disturbances. Primitive personalities manifest a range of somatic symptoms and a predominance of global dysphoric affect, which they do not conceive of as an internal predisposition, autonomous from current experience, and are unable to name and to regulate. Their unawareness of the nature of feeling states was initially described in two papers by Marty, de M'Uzan and associates (both 1963), and was named alexithymia by Sifneos (1967). I have also written about it (Robbins, 1993b). Because of their sense of innocence about their hostility these persons present themselves as victims of mistreatment by others. Because of their lack of psychic integration, affect may not be appropriate to mental content. It may be missing where expectable. For example, affects appropriate to important childhood memories tend to be enacted in current relationships rather than experienced in their appropriate context.

Sensorimotor-affective thinking, most commonly in the form of repetitive enactment of affective disturbance, in lieu of internalized thought (Piaget [see Flavell, 1963]; Robbins, 1981). Primitive personalities are like infants, whose minds and thoughts are undifferentiated from sensory-perceptual-motoric action on the environment. They cannot distinguish between thoughts and acts, and their actions speak louder than their words. Action, including somatic channels of expression and involving perception, motoric expression, somatic sensation, and language that is used concretely to manipulate the environment rather than symbolically to express and communicate, serves in lieu of representing, reflecting, and remembering. Unlike ordinary infants, they repeatedly enact scenarios that come not from contemporary efforts to adapt to the environment and to meet needs, but from infantile affective-somatic-motoric patterns encoded at the neurobiological level but never mentally represented. The presence of these affects may not be noted at all by the patient, or may be noted but misinterpreted as an unremarkable response to a current situation. Action, in the sense I use the term here, is not confined to the gross destructive sexual and aggressive behavior patterns commonly labeled "acting out," but also includes the interpersonal dramatization of all sorts of mental patterns which in a more mature person would be experienced as thoughts, feelings, and memories—what McDougall (1985) felicitously referred to as theaters of the mind.

Pathological symbiotic relationships serve in lieu of non-internalized mind because essential aspects of mind are not represented, differentiated from action patterns and from the object world, integrated as thought-patterns, or maturely regulated. Seduced by concern for the sufferings of individuals with primitive personalities, others, including therapists, often take on the impossible task of ameliorating and equilibrating their behavioral and emotional states and providing them with essentials of care. In the process the caregivers become projection screens upon which the primitive personality can recognize non-internalized dysphoric aspects of identity, and participants in a drama in which he seeks to coerce compensation for them. Because of their personal deficiencies, these individuals attract not only well-meaning caretakers such I have just described, who struggle to absorb, process, and compensate for their noxious attributions and for their obvious self-care deficits, but also another class of persons who manipulate them. The users exploit the primitive person's undifferentiated tendency to introject and make him a repository for the user's undesirable qualities. Of course, as none of us are all good or all bad, these using and compensating activities may in some instances be embodied in the same person. In this manner other persons furnish ongoing introjective aliment for an auto-destructive sense of self or identity (a core sense of badness associated with attacks on elements of self) and enact compensatory struggles against the primitive personality's destructive tendencies. This accounts for primitive personalities' common attraction to and overvaluation of persons who are objectively not good for them. At the same time they require and seduce, but also attack, reject, and devalue, persons who attend to and care about them, often including their therapists. Previously (especially 1983) I have referred to these reciprocal symbiotic patterns as possession configurations.

Problems with self-esteem and object relations. The problems these persons experience in their object relations are apparent from the preceding descriptions. Although Kohut modified his position in 1984, his early work has fostered a belief that self-esteem problems and archaic narcissistic configurations are unique to so-called narcissistic personalities, and it may be less apparent that, in lieu of mature self-esteem, tendencies to be arrogant and devalue others coexist unintegrated with inappropriate idealizations of others and related forms of self-hatred and self-devaluation.

Much of the issue of whether primitive personality is qualitatively different centers around whether we understand the absence of psychic integration as a defense against intrapsychic conflict or as an adaptive development. I have deliberately written *absence* of integration rather than disintegration or fragmentation, for those terms presuppose a defensive regression from a prior state of integration. The phenomenon of non-integration was first noted and called schizoid by Klein (1935, 1946) and Fairbairn (1940, 1944), and subsequently remarked on by many others including Kernberg and Kohut. Klein considered it to be defensive against primal rage, whereas Fairbairn viewed it as defensive with regard to a frustrating primary object relationship. With the exception of Kohut, who viewed non-integration as a normal, nondefensive, primal state of mind and its persistence as the product of a developmental failure, it has been interpreted generally as a neurotic phenomenon of defense against conflict, biological in the case of Klein, environmental in the case of Fairbairn. Despite her theory of primal paranoid-schizoid conflict, Klein's belief that the capacity for ambivalence is a depressive position development suggests she also believed that integration of the mind is a gradual process. Sandler and A. Freud (1983) also seem to believe that the capacity for intrapsychic conflict and defense develops gradually, for they write that projection and introjection have respective primary process precursors, displacement, and condensation. While reflexive avoidance or defensive *behavior* is a characteristic of all living organisms, it is not a uniquely human aspect of mind and might better be conceptualized as a primary adaptation than as an intrapsychic process. Stern seems to concur, asserting that earliest developments occur in the realm of affect, cognition, and adaptation and only later in the realm of conflict and defense. There is "a non-psychodynamic beginning of life in the sense that the infant's experience is not the product of reality altering conflict resolution. . . . Deficit is the wrong concept, however, for these reality-based events. . . . It is the actual shape of interpersonal reality . . . that helps determine the developmental course. Coping operations occur as reality-based adaptations. Defensive operations of the type that distort reality occur only after symbolic thinking is available" (1985, p. 255).

Schizophrenia is another condition of personality that seems qualitatively incomprehensible by the core psychoanalytic model. The ensuing comments are a brief abstraction of issues I have explored elsewhere (Robbins, 1992a, 1993a). It is likely that a particular genetically determined organization of the central nervous system activates development of a characterological vulnerability phenotype unless parenting is exceptional and compensatory. Studies of organic findings as well as lengthy and intensive therapeutic work with schizophrenic patients have led me to hypothesize two areas of constitutional vulnerability. The first is a general hypersensitivity to stimulation, both external (sensation and perception) and internal (drive and affect), and a particular difficulty processing it, which leads to mental and interpersonal avoidance patterns. The second area of vulnerability I call affinity-organization. This includes difficulty with psychic integration and differentiation, lack of mental cohesion and personal ownership of mental content, as well as the characteristic passivity and alienation or failure of attachment to other persons, all of which Bleuer originally described in 1911. I consider the failures of attachment to others and differentiation to be related, insofar as mental organization develops in the context of attentive, holding human relationships. These two core vulnerabilities, in organization and affinity and intensity and processing of stimulation, combine to produce a third: nihilism. This is a deep aversion to the basic mental work involved in thinking, feeling, and being responsible for the content of one's mind. The resulting protosymbiotic state of the schizophrenic mind and parasitic form of relatedness to others are characterized by passivity, avoidance of others, and absence of adaptive mental organization. It is easy to doubt the concept of mental nihilism in the face of the pseudological organization of schizophrenic thinking—for example, the pseudo-logic of a delusional system. But such activity depends on intelligence, the innate capacity of mind, whereas mature mentation requires, in addition to innate capacity, the mental work involved in ownership or responsibility for one's thought, feelings, and actions, and maintenance of accurate perceptions of reality. Because these persons cannot actively employ sensorimotor-affective thinking and symbiotic relating to organize their minds and establish a sense of identity, as do the primitive personalities I described above, they are extraordinarily vulnerable to and dependent on the structure and meaning imposed by the family system and by societal institutions and attitudes.

To return to some of the limitations of the basic theory, not all humans start out with a qualitatively similar central nervous system organization. There is considerable evidence for significant variability in the neonatal brain. Furthermore, clinical experience teaches that the interpersonal and social environments of infancy and childhood vary enormously, and that the idea of universal paradigmatic environmental provision is not only a heuristic over-simplification, but a monistic way of thinking that blinds us to the multi-dimensioned aspect of experience and development. There are idiosyncratic pathogenic environmental configurations, some related to external configurations of family, others to the very qualitative variability of parental personality to which I am alluding. Singly or in combination, these may initiate alternative developmental pathways leading to different organizations of adult personality. Analysts who work with more disturbed patients are often caught in a contradiction between theory and practice. In their clinical dealings they are usually respectful of the profound and idiosyncratic psychological effects of the parenting a patient has received and of his familial-cultural background, and the equally profound influences of the patient's unique psyche on other persons in his life, including his children. With regard to schizophrenia it is even widely held that the patient, through his "illness," may wreak emotional havoc on his parents and be responsible for familial pathology; at the same time, the possibility that parental pathology might have played a significant role in the development of the patient's illness is denied. Dissenting voices have been raised, ranging from Fromm-Reichman's unfortunate concept of the schizophrenogenic mother (1948) to the current revival of Freud's original seduction hypothesis in the form of readiness to perceive patients as victims of child abuse and incest, but these popular movements have never been securely incorporated within the corpus of psychoanalytic theory. Fairbairn and Kohut are notable exceptions, but each has a unidimensional conception of pathogenic parenting as frustration, and a single model of personality outcome.

It follows that the concept of a universal linear path of development toward a modal personality end point, with quantitative deviations and a null reference, is also a fallacy. The fallacy of isomorphism among normal and pathological development and the tendency to combine normal maturation and psychopathological development in a single model (that is, to equate childlike with pathological) seems egregious in Kleinian theory (Peterfreund, 1978). But such a reasoning process is characteristic of most theories, including innovative ones such as Gedo's hierarchical epigenetic theory.

Half a century ago (1939–1955) the anthropologist A. Hallowell raised objection to such an equation of immaturity and primitiveness. While some of the mental and behavioral peculiarities that characterize patients with more serious forms of pathology such as absence of affect representations and sensorimotor-affective (enactive) thinking appear to have normal infantile counterparts, other elements may not. Pathological symbiotic relationships that compensate for developmental failures at pre-neurotic levels of function, for example, are not simply perseverations of developmentally normal symbiosis, but are unique configurations (Robbins, 1981a and 1989). Like Fairbairn (1952) and Kernberg (1975), I doubt that self-esteem vacillations from grandiosity to extreme and destructive shame and devaluation are normal in infancy. And, contrary to Kohut and Gedo, I believe that lack of self-cohesion or disintegration of aims and goals is not a normal part of childhood. Although psychological differentiation and integration may be rudimentary in early childhood (note that I do not refer to capacities inherent in the neonatal brain, which Stern [1985] has demonstrated, but to the conscious and symbolic mind, which arises only through socialization), such a state does not necessarily imply an antecedent state of disintegration or fragmentation. Young children do not demonstrate the singularity of goal directedness and purpose which may characterize some mature adults, but can we truly say they are psychologically unintegrated and disorganized? It seems more useful to apply Werner's (1940) orthogenetic principle that symbolic psychological development normally proceeds from globality through less mature forms of integration and differentiation to more mature ones. The normal infantile mind is neither differentiated nor integrated (see also Fairbairn's [1952] concept of self), though it possesses innate capacities to make distinctions. Only as differentiation occurs can organization and integration follow; in the global state disintegration is a meaningless concept. Perhaps the phenomenon of unintegration is encountered only in pathological situations.

Qualitatively distinctive models may also be necessary to conceive of developmental transformations in normal personality development, as Gedo and Goldberg (1973) have indicated. I find it heuristically useful to postulate a model of primitive mentation in normal development whose beginnings consist of a highly competent perceptual-cognitive apparatus that is nonetheless neither differentiated nor integrated in the biologically representational and structural sense and is characterized by an enactive, sensorimotor-affective form of mentation such as Piaget described. Development, with the assistance of a caring and mirroring symbiotic object, involves progressive psychic integration and differentiation, which leads in turn to qualitative reorganizations of mind, which in turn require different concepts and rules to comprehend. Piaget was the first to consider development in terms of such a transformational systemic hierarchy (Tanner and Inhelder, 1956). This process involves increasing representation of and control over the affects, ideas, and conscious states that are first perceived and enacted within the symbiotic orbit, but that come to characterize the gradually discovered self. It includes development of the capacity for accurate differentiation between self and object and the acquisition of an integrated capacity to experience both intrapsychic conflict and ambivalence. The developmental process eventuates, through qualitative transformations, in a mental apparatus that is relatively self-contained, integrated, and internally regulated and functions by a different set of principles, for example, involving intrapsychic conflict and defense, in a world of differentiated others. I return to this subject in chapter 14.

By now an apparent similarity in personality organization among the sociocentric personalities of Eastern culture, females, and the primitive personalities described in this chapter will be evident. In each instance, identity maintenance is conceptualized within an interpersonal or social network. However, there are significant differences. The primitive personality in Western culture has achieved but a rudimentary state of integration and differentiation, and one that requires not only the participation but also the compensatory assistance of others. The sociocentric personality characteristic of Eastern cultures and the mature female personality, in contrast, use the ancestral, natural, and social environments as part of a sophisticated, exquisitely developed and refined, identity-maintaining system of integration and differentiation.

As I have noted, neither the sociocentric personality of Eastern cultures nor the intracultural diversity of personality can be encompassed by the basic psychoanalytic model. Indeed, the notion that such diversity can be conceived of as a linear variable on a single distribution curve on which deviations can be specified in quantitative or positional terms like deficit, deficiency, arrest, fixation, and weakness, seems barely credible. It is more likely that we must learn to conceptualize or signify qualitative differences in personality by employing different systems with different principles of organization, which evolve from a diversity of constitutional and environmental (interpersonal) configurations and traverse different developmental pathways toward a variety of outcomes.

CHAPTER 11

How Models Become Movements: The Ideological Dimension

In previous chapters I explored the human tendency to fabricate monistic models of the phenomenological world and the resulting reductionistic impoverishment of our ability to appreciate diversity and complexity. This tendency is exacerbated by the ideological fervor that tends to possess model-makers. Ideologies are founded on the conviction that a particular system of thought is not simply a model of the world, but a way of life. They tend to rigidify models and guard them against change, and to generate action in the form of proselytizing and propagating them as faith. Ideological "isms" are encountered in the political sphere (imperialism, colonialism, totalitarianism), in matters of ethnicity (racism), and in religions, where the elements of biblical encoding and rituals of worship are concrete and blatant. But ideologies assume new and insidious guises in each historical epoch, so that the panaceas and nostrums of one era are ridiculed as the fads and quackery of the next.

As I noted in chapters 3 and 4, science has acquired an ideological aspect. In this chapter I examine the psychoanalytic movement, the sociopolitical structure with ideological overtones that Freud constructed to advance his ideas. Ironically in light of the fact that a major function of ideology is preservation and propagation, it is the ideological expression of psycho-analysis that has tended to sequester it from forces of change that might enable it to evolve and adapt, and that today is threatening it with obsolescence.

In an early paper (1914a) Freud characterized the organizational aspect of psychoanalysis as a movement, to distinguish it both from his theory of development and psychopathology and from the therapeutic profession and clinical practice derived from it. Freud worked diligently to develop the movement, because he saw it as necessary to preserve the identity of his fledgling field and help it to grow. As noted in chapter 2, patriarchal, even authoritarian tendencies played a role in Freud's own personality, and they re-emerged as central concepts in his theory. The same personality characteristics that led to his particular point of view about personality also led him to develop psycho-analysis as a movement.

Unfortunately for psychoanalysis as a theory of personality, the boundaries between it as a theory, a clinical practice, and an ideology or movement have never been clear. Evolution of the basic model of personality has been impeded by the patriarchal authority that transmits the right to call oneself an analyst from one generation to the next and grants stature within the movement. Orthodoxy is maintained through a power structure responsible both for training procedures and for validation of ideas. This power resides in the license to train and certify psychoanalysts, originally granted by Freud himself and passed down by more or less authoritative decree first to his small group of disciples, whom he betrothed with rings, and subsequently to the larger International Psychoanalytical Association (IPA). In the United States the American Psychoanalytic Association was until the 1980s the literal and exclusive embodiment of psychoanalysis, by virtue of a unique agreement with the IPA. The position of training analyst has always been the most powerful in the movement. It is one that is acquired at least as much through conformity to authoritarian requirements as through creative contributions. The method of training disciples with a combination of education and individual analysis yields a hybrid product of personal and professional maturity alongside passive conformity. This viewpoint is seldom voiced in psychoanalytic discussions, but there are some exceptions, for example, Kohut's (1979) remarkable confession that his personal training experience was in large measure a kind of brainwashing.

The movement has also managed to retain the power to validate psychoanalytic ideas. There has never been a way to differentiate the objective validity of a new idea from the relationship of its author to Freud or his successors in power. Acceptable ideas were naively referred to as "Freudian" until the personalization became embarrassingly unacceptable to an aspiring science. In contrast, unacceptable ideas have tended to be labeled with the name of their author or termed "not psychoanalytic." Such personalization sometimes takes the form of authoritative "interpretation" of the dissident as immature or pathological, and dissenters have been shunned and even excommunicated as heretics.

My language may seem extreme to some, but it has been chosen deliberately. Robert Michels, one of a handful of reputable analysts who have succeeded in expressing criticism with regard to the shape and effect of the movement, says of psychoanalysis: "Arguments from authority are more common than arguments from data. As a result Psychoanalysis is organized more like a religious movement than a science" (1990, p. 6). This organizational structure resulted from Freud's isolation from the University of Vienna and its medical school, which one might argue resulted both from external reactions against his novel ideas and personal religion, and from elements of his own personality. Whatever its origins, the structure concentrated power and authority in the hands of individuals who were hardly unbiased. The dogmatic element of psychoanalytic organization is strikingly at odds with the noncensorious, truth-seeking character of psychoanalytic theory and therapy, much of which seeks to liberate the individual mind to make choices free of both biological and cultural-authoritarian imperatives. This incompatibility between elements of the theory and practices of the movement constitutes a basic flaw of psychoanalysis.

Like other ideological or authoritarian social structures, psychoanalysis has tended to oscillate between rigidity and stagnation, on the one hand, and revolution, on the other. Melanie Klein's successful effort to have her theory accepted within the legitimate corpus of the psychoanalytic movement is perhaps the major revolutionary achievement. Through the crucible of the "controversial discussions" in Britain during World War II and the subsequent controversies between psychoanalysis in the United States and in other countries, she proved that there is room within the movement for more than one theory.

Shortly after the death of Freud, the emigré analysts Anna Freud, representing direct patrilineal and ideational descent from her founding father, and Melanie Klein joined the British Psychoanalytic Society. Debate soon polarized around their theoretical systems and centered around differences in conceptual language. From the perspective of half a century of hindsight, as I noted in chapters 7 and 10, we can say that Klein was actually trying to expand Freud's theory, and the similarities far outweigh the differences. Nonetheless, for reasons that probably had as much to do with the patrilineal power structure of the psychoanalytic movement as they did with the ideas in question, controversy erupted over whether Klein's contribution could be construed as psychoanalytic. The dispute commenced, not surprisingly, with power issues regarding the governance of the society, the freedom of expression of ideas, and the training of candidates. Many of the participants in both camps were emigré Jewish analysts escaping Nazi totalitarianism. As the debates became acrimonious, the Freud camp, representing patriarchal repressive elements in the society, labeled as dictatorial those who strived for more freedom of expression and respect for their ideas. In a memo published by King and Steiner in their excellent review of these controversial discussions (1991, pp. 632–633), Anna Freud actually asserted that the efforts of Klein and other dissident analysts to advance their ideas were akin to Nazism. By managing to remain within the psychoanalytic movement in the United Kingdom despite this persecution, Klein struck a major blow against the ideological element of psychoanalysis that may ultimately prove more important than her specific theoretical contributions for the survival of psychoanalysis and for its scientific aspirations.

Meanwhile, similar controversies between "Freudian" analysis and various dissident analysts, including Horney and Alexander, were occurring in the United States. The evolution of the psychoanalytic movement in America has in some respects been unique. Prior to World War II it became intertwined with the development of medicine, under whose umbrella it took refuge during the battle against therapeutic quackery which culminated in the Flexner Report (Wallerstein, 1994). As World War II approached and emigrés swelled the ranks of analysts in the United States, the newly formed American Psychoanalytic Association was able to negotiate a unique agreement with the International Psychoanalytical Association consisting of an exclusive mandate to educate and certify analysts in America. The authoritarian and ideological opposition to the free exchange of ideas that has always characterized the psychoanalytic movement thus became linked to the marriage of the American Psychoanalytic Association and the medical establishment.

The effects of granting autocratic powers over psychoanalysis and psychoanalysts in a democratic society to a single organization are not difficult to see. The influence of the American alliance of psychoanalysis with medicine is in some ways more insidious, for medicine and the medical establishment have also attained something of an iconic or ideological quality, as the medical establishment is generally held to be synonymous with the unquestioned best in the care of human ills. Nonetheless, medicine and psychoanalysis are strange and probably incompatible bedfellows. The bedside manner of the late-lamented and much-fabled general practitioner notwithstanding, medicine is synonymous with scientific materialism and with organic reductionism. It has no primary conceptual or practical place for the mind, conceived of in terms of the meanings, values, and feelings, conscious and unconscious, to which each of us, psychoanalyst and neuroscientific reductionist alike, ascribes our actions and attributes our uniqueness. The alliance with medicine has conferred a transient power and status on medical analysts, as the big bad wolf in the fable accorded to Red Riding Hood, ill concealing his devaluation of her behind his guise as grandma. But medicine and neuroscience, like the fabulous wolf, are eager, when the opportunity presents, to proclaim that mind is epiphenomenal and to consume psychoanalysis in an embrace that obliterates its uniqueness and reduces meaning to molecules.

Discontent with the personally and intellectually stultifying aspects of the psychoanalytic movement on the part of younger analysts has become progressively more vocal in recent years. The gradual attrition of the second and third generation of analysts, those who personally knew or were analyzed by Freud himself or his direct descendants, has weakened the power of authoritarian transmission and also shifted financial (organizational dues-paying) control to a new generation. The manifestations within psychoanalysis of the minority rights movements that have swept postwar America—in particular the demands of two vital and creative groups, women and psychologists— have been a force for change, as well. These pressures, culminating in a major lawsuit, have resulted in some liberalization within the American Psychoanalytic Association, along with loss of its near-exclusive power to control psychoanalysis in the United States.

Nonetheless, control of education still resides in more conservative and less creative elements of the analytic societal structure, primarily in the American Psychoanalytic Association and the training analysts who receive their imprimatur through it. Not even a training analysis and graduation from an institute accredited or accepted by the American Psychoanalytic Association are sufficient to guarantee a young analyst full parity within that major guardian of the movement, and acknowledged contributions to the scientific aspects of the field do not officially count for advancement. Those who design and enforce the certification requirements and who devote their careers primarily to indoctrinating the young still have the highest status the movement can confer. These persons tend to practice in their private offices on a clientele of relatively healthy individuals, a high percentage of whom comprise psychoanalytic candidates and other mental health professionals. Most of them are not psychoanalytic innovators, nor are they likely to encourage others to be.

An unacknowledged omission in the clinical theory of psychoanalytic termination tends to perpetuate this authoritarian structure and inhibit professional and personal maturation. Termination work does not include and facilitate the establishment of subsequent mature relations between the analyst and his or her erstwhile analysand. The implication that newly graduated analysts ought to be peers with their training analyst and their generational cohort is not accompanied by any formal procedure to bring this about. In fact, as the recent social furor about analyst-patient sexual relationships has highlighted, there is no sanction within psychoanalysis much less the broader society for peer intimacy between an analyst and his or her graduated and presumably mature analysand. One way or another, the senior generation and its ideas always retain authoritarian status and the younger generation cannot achieve parity.

In these respects psychoanalysis is quite different from other human sciences. Its model structure, the society / institute, is a complex entity that fuses the training, personality alteration, and certification of the trainee with evaluation of the value of psychoanalytic ideas and contributions. Other human sciences do not undertake the right to alter the personalities of those who enter them to begin with, and they have generally achieved a structural separation between educating and certifying parts, professional movement parts, and scientific contribution and application parts. In other human sciences, training and certification power resides within the university, whereas the application and adjudication of ideas, including publication and meetings, resides substantially outside the university. On graduation there are career paths at least as powerful and prestigious as becoming a teacher. As the saying that there are "those who teach and those who do" suggests, in academia, in contrast to the situation within psychoanalysis, teaching is a labor of love more than one of power, control, and status.

So, while the ideological aspect of psychoanalysis appears to be eroding, the theoretical model of personality that it has managed to preserve relatively intact seems less socially relevant than it once did. Whether ideological liberalism will evolve in time to rescue psychoanalysis from obsolescence remains to be seen.

CHAPTER 12

Summary of the Monism-Pluralism Debate

As a prelude to my synthetic endeavor in the concluding chapters, I should like to summarize salient aspects of our efforts to conceive of personality thus far.

There appears to be a qualitative diversity of personality organization—among different cultures, within each culture, and across gender lines at any particular time in history. Each of these changes over historical time, as well. This diversity is not encompassed in existing monistic models such as psychoanalysis as it is currently constituted, and, indeed, it appears to be beyond the conceptual power of such models.

Broad classes of constitutional difference in the central nervous system, of which sex differences are the most obvious example, seem to have a deterministic impact on personality organization. Qualitative differences in brain organization seem related, in complex reciprocally interactive ways, to qualitative differences in personality organization. Psychoanalytic theory was originally articulated by Freud in terms of concepts and relationships appropriate to nineteenth-century biological science, long since outdated. Analysts remain divided about whether a model based on a biological drive theory should be retained, whether a new model related to current findings and theories in neurobiology is needed, or whether psychoanalysis as an hermeneutic discipline needs to divorce itself from neuroscience entirely. Respected analysts including Fairbairn (1952), George Klein (1976), Gill (1976), and Kohut (1971) have rejected biological motivational concepts. At the same time, psychoanalysis is under attack from neuroscientific reductionists. If there are broad classes of constitutional differences in brain organization related to qualitative differences in personality, as the findings presented in chapter 5 suggest, it is difficult to see how psychoanalysis can avoid relating its models to these findings in some way, or what is to be gained by ignoring them.

There is some evidence to support the existence of transformational systemic hierarchies of personality organization, particularly in human development or maturation, in the relation among constitution, gender, and culture, and in the broader constitution-personality relationship as well.

Models of personality based on modal constructs in relation to a null category are necessarily limited in their scope to a particular qualitative organization, for example, male, Western, or "neurotic."

Two broad classes of personality organization found in reference to cultural variation and to gender differences have been identified: self-centric and sociocentric. While the sociocentric type superficially resembles the primitive personality organization of Western culture, closer scrutiny of the complexity and maturity of each typology indicates clear qualitative differences. Since dichotomizing is a feature of the rational dualistic thinking characteristic of the self-centric mind, and perhaps of all minds, can it be a feature of the natural world as well? Is the hypothesis of sociocentric/self-centric gender and cultural personality typologies simply a mental artifact? Evidence for a neurobiological substrate of gender differences in personality suggests that, in this case, dichotomizing is a natural phenomenon and not simply an artifact of mind. Neurobiology may set in motion the kind of recursive, transformational dynamic I have outlined, leading first to the major gender dichotomy in personality and then to broad differences in personality characteristic of the major cultures. The idea of discrete personality types, of course, is valid only in large group comparisons and not in individual instances. And within each culture there exist clearcut gender-related differences in personality. Most cultures, Eastern or Western, tend to be patriarchal, with males exercising power and domination. Female personality is typically more separated and individuated in Western culture than in Eastern. Western females tend not only to be more autonomous or independent than their Eastern counterparts, but perhaps more individually assertive than even male members of Eastern cultures.

However open, flexible, and creative the mind of a person who undertakes to conceive of personality may be, his creation is inevitably embedded in the particulars of his individual constitution and personality, including gender, and circumstances of culture and the historical period in which he is living. This opens, to the conceiver, particular avenues of perception and thought while it shuts off both access to a diversity of data about personality and the capacity to conceptualize diversity. These monistic inclinations are enhanced by ideological thinking, which leads the conceiver to overlook his limitations, to overgeneralize the significance of his product, and to conclude that he may have stumbled upon universal truth. It is difficult to avoid the conclusion that the results of our attempts to conceive of ourselves must be taken with the proverbial grain of salt.

Personality models at best, as in the case of Freud's generation of psychoanalytic theory, reflect a combination of universals about personality and particulars of historical perspective and culture- and gender-embeddedness. In circumstances where the creator is a relatively normal individual in relation to his particular time and culture, capable of a reasonable degree of differentiation of his personality idiosyncrasies from his or her general theoretical model, expectable mental scotomata still limit his or her capacity to appreciate minds and personalities that are qualitatively different. The same lack of perspective subtly limits the person's ability to comprehend the uniqueness of minds like his or her own. The result is best looked upon as a form of local knowledge. At worst, in the instance of Wilhelm Reich and his orgone theory, the model will express idiosyncratic elements of personality that are not even typical for its creator's time and culture, much less for humankind.

As for limitations of the data of personality available to any individual conceiver, chaos theory or dynamics of nonlinear nonequilibrating systems informs us not simply that it is difficult to identify and specify initial conditions sufficient to reach a stable, predictable outcome but also that it is theoretically impossible to do so (Mandelbrot, 1983; Barton, 1994; Prigogine and Stengers, 1984; Stewart, 1989). This means that it is theoretically impossible for the human mind ever to achieve the Archimedean leverage necessary to conceive of personality adequately.

One apparent solution may be to collect persons who represent the dimensions of diversity, that is, different cultures, genders, and intracultural personality types, and encourage them to have a dialogue. LeVine (1973) made such a suggestion, involving collaboration between a Western analyst and an Eastern cultural informant. There is no question that such team efforts, particularly among persons of different cultures, are potentially fruitful, and they are increasingly being undertaken (for example, Berry and Kim's 1993 collaboration). But if the minds and personalities of the collaborators are in fact qualitatively differently, as much of our evidence implies, how are they to communicate at more than a superficial level, and how might they avoid unwittingly sinking into a swamp of misunderstandings? The surface structures and concrete referents common to most languages readily permit the illusion if not the substance of communication. There is a small group of Western theorists who are multicultural. Some natives of Eastern sociocentric cultures (Kakar from India and Doi from Japan are two of the more prominent exemplars) migrated to the West relatively early in life and obtained analytic training. And there are others whose indigenous culture is being assimilated by the West (Native Americans, for example) and who have struggled with the experience of living in two cultures. These persons might possess a unique perspective. Bakhtin captures something of the problem when he writes, "It is only in the eyes of another culture that foreign culture reveals itself fully and profoundly, but never exhaustively, because there will be other cultures that see and understand even more" (1986, p. 7).

Yet another cautionary note is hardly necessary, but so long as we confine ourselves to ways of looking which are considered to be scientific, we may be sentencing ourselves to a prisonhouse of monism. Suzuki (1960) points out that there are other equally valid ways of looking at the person, and Wilber (1990) elaborates his belief that there are three separate, equally valid, and nonmergeable modalities: sensory-empirical (scientific), rational, and contemplative-transcendental. From a somewhat different perspective Keller (1985) suggests the possibility of an alternative or female science. Whereas the primary focus of the science of the past has been to search for order by reduction of complexity, the science of the future may need to emphasize richness, diversity, and dialogue.

It is my intention in the concluding chapters to explore further the debate between proponents of monistic or universalistic models and those who endorse pluralistic or relativistic ones, and to pursue the implications of each for conceiving of the diversity of personality. In the intellectually vexing situation I have described, it is tempting to abandon the quest for order and simplicity and to retreat to the position of enlightened subjectivity, relativity, and indeterminacy adopted by some postmodern philosophers, which appears to offer a new intellectual rigor in the form of critical deconstruction. However, such an eclectic approach may be subtly permissive of a kind of nihilism, a retreat from values and even from the mental effort of synthesis. Insofar as the postmodern "enlightenment" has the potential to be little more than a deconstructive "analysis" of all positions, it is similar to the passion of early twentieth-century science for "taking things apart," which has proven to be a more destructive activity than was anticipated. Once Humpty Dumpty is in pieces, we may have neither the knowledge nor the ability to put him back together again. The certainty associated with monistic thinking and the flexibility associated with pluralism each have their unique intellectual appeal. However, each has potential drawbacks: the rigidity and monochromatic impoverishment associated with monism and the intellectual nihilism and amoral pragmatism associated with pluralism. Is it necessary to choose between the two, or is it possible to view pluralism and monism in a nondichotomous manner, as complementary dialectical aspects of theory and ways of looking at the phenomenology of personality?

CHAPTER 13

Systems in Transformation: A Model for the Dialectic between Discovery and Creation

In this chapter I sketch the outline of a model that might subsume human phenomena, individual and collective, in a manner that incorporates the strengths of monistic and pluralistic ways of thinking and enables an epistemological dialectic between discovery and creation. The notion of an overarching theory of systems in transformation arises from a confluence of historical developments in several disciplines. One of the earliest suggestions of such an approach may be found in the nineteenth-century work of Hughlings Jackson (1931–1932), who suggested that organisms are integrated in a hierarchical series of increasingly complex neural levels, and that in the course of development the expression of lower levels is progressively inhibited by the functioning of higher ones. In the early twentieth century Adolph Meyer (1957) took the next step and introduced the concept of psychobiology to denote that human beings are meaningfully integrated at a mental level as well as a neurobiological one. He believed that phenomena characteristic of one level, such as the organic, may affect events and processes at other levels, such as the mental.

As with so many other developments in the study of mind and personality, Freud anticipated developments in systems theory. He was aware of Jackson's work, and he conceived of a transformational hierarchy of systems both neurological and psychological, with recurring analogous structures. In 1913 he wondered about the reasons for the choice of one type of neurosis rather than another and stated that the determinants of a neurosis "are in the nature of [hereditary] dispositions and are independent of experiences which operate pathogenically" (p. 317). Elsewhere (1915) he wrote: "The physiological events do not cease as soon as the psychological ones begin; on the contrary, the physiological chain continues. What happens is simply that, after a certain point in time, each (or some) of its links has a psychical phenomenon corresponding to it. Accordingly, the psychical is a process parallel to the physiological—a 'dependent concomitant'" (p. 207). He later (1916, p. 362) proposed but did not elaborate the concept of a complemental series. Toward the end of his life Freud (1940) restated this position: "We know two kinds of things about what we call our psyche (or mental life): firstly, its bodily organ and scene of action, the brain (or nervous system), and, on the other hand, our acts of consciousness, which are immediate data and cannot be further explained by any sort of description. Everything that lies between is unknown to us, and the data do not include any direct relation between these two terminal points of our knowledge. If it existed, it would at the most afford an exact localization of the processes of consciousness and would give us no help towards understanding them" (p. 144).

The first full expression of these ideas is to be found in the scientific philosophy known as general systems theory, popularly attributed to biologist-philosopher Ludwig von Bertalanffy (1952, 1967a, 1967b, 1968). Systems philosophy originated during the 1920s and 1930s as the creation of a group comprising prominent German biologists and persons from disciplines as disparate as fiction writing (Arthur Koestler [Koestler and Smythies, 1969]), psychology (Heinz Werner, 1926); the Gestalt school (Perls, Hefferline, and Goodman, 1985); and physics (Heisenberg, 1958). The biologist Paul Weiss, whose earliest writing on the subject, a paper first published in 1925 and republished in English in 1959, slightly antedates the work of von Bertalanffy, is in my estimation the most articulate spokesperson of this group and possibly the originator of these ideas.

Systems theory begins with recognition of the insufficiency of monistic thinking and the related idea that the phenomenological world is naturally organized in systemic groupings. Von Bertalanffy (1969) asserted that, "compared to the analytical procedure of classical science, with 'linear' causality connecting two variables as basic category, the investigation of organized wholes of many variables requires new categories of interaction. . . . This leads to a 'perspective philosophy.' . . . Reality is a hierarchy of organized wholes" (p. 14). Weiss (1969) says that "all living phenomena consists of group behavior" (p. 8). He adds, "the ordered state (organization) of a living entity can, therefore, not be conceived of as the blind outcome of microprecisely defined serial cause-effect chain reactions, as in an assembly plant" (1977, p. 29). The physicist Niels Bohr (1937) introduced what he called the principle of complementarity in an attempt to apply Heisenberg's uncertainty principle to the human sciences and argued for the separate study of the human as a system. Von Bertalanffy (1968) maintained that living systems "maintain themselves in a state of high order and improbability, or may even evolve toward increasing differentiation and organization as is the case in organismic development and evolution" (pp. 143–144). He proposed the concept of *anamorphosis* to describe the progressive differentiation and reorganization of biological systems at hierarchically higher levels into wholes that cannot be accounted for by summing their parts. He emphasized that such terms as *higher* and *lower*, used to characterize levels, simply denote differences in perspective, not in importance or validity. Weiss wrote that nature is ordered as a hierarchical continuum in which more complex, larger units are supraordinate to less complex, smaller ones. He used the terms *larger* and *smaller* in the same way von Bertalanffy used *higher* and *lower*. He commented that "it is one thing not to see the forest for the trees, but then to go on to deny the reality of the forest is a more serious matter, for it is not just a case of myopia, but one of self-inflicted blindness" (1969, p. 11). This observation, that disciplines devoted to different systems levels of a phenomenon may study it simultaneously, exhaustively, and profitably, is most germane to the current reductionist dispute in which neuroscientists attempt theoretically to consume psychology and psychoanalysis. We might say that each tree, with its microstructures, the individual forest with its component trees, and the larger ecosystem of forests comprise separate levels of systems discourse.

In other words, we may view personality and the human sciences which study it as a multidimensional hierarchy of systems, ranging from the "lowest" molecular biological system through the individual psychological system to various sociocentric systems, culminating with culture itself. The physicist Werner Heisenberg (1958) writes:

The degree of complication in biology is so discouraging that one can at present not imagine any set of concepts in which the connections could be so sharply defined that a mathematical presentation could become possible. If we go beyond biology and include psychology in the discussion, then there can scarcely be any doubt but that the concepts of physics, chemistry, and evolution together will not be sufficient to describe the facts. On this point the existence of quantum theory has changed our attitude from what was believed in the nineteenth century. . . . We would, in spite of the fact that the physical events in the brain belong to the psychic phenomena, not expect that these could be sufficient to explain them. We would never doubt that the brain acts as a physical-chemical mechanism if treated as such; but for an understanding of psychic phenomena we would start from the fact that the human mind enters as object and subject into the scientific process of psychology. (1958, pp. 105–106)

Hence, personality may be viewed as the organization of human phenomena at each of a multiplicity of different systems levels.

As Weiss (1969) described it, "hierarchical concepts of organization . . . imply some sort of discontinuity encountered as one crosses interfaces between lower and higher orders of magnitude" (p. 8). Each level of organization, from the microscopic to the macroscopic, depends on its predecessor but is theoretically autonomous and freestanding, based on new principles of structure, function, and meaning that can be neither predicted from that predecessor nor entirely reduced to it. Systems may be arranged in hierarchies according to successive transformations or reorganizations along the continua or dimensions of time (growth, development, evolution), size or magnification (microscopic to macroscopic), and complexity (level of concreteness-abstraction).

During the mid-1980s the concept of systems as dynamically related groupings in transformation was reincarnated in the form of what is most commonly (and somewhat misleadingly) known as chaos theory (Gleick, 1987; Hayles, 1990), and perhaps more aptly described as complexity theory (Spruiell, 1993), universality theory (Feigenbaum, 1980), or nonlinear dynamics of nonequilibrating systems. In the following discussion it is important to keep in mind the distinction between the realm or system of mathematics and physics, within which the new theoretical system was developed, and the verbal metaphors used to describe it. Barton notes, "Terms that refer to specific and limited ideas in mathematics and physics should not be confused with the broader characteristics of self-organizing psychological systems. Using these terms as metaphors may be acceptable as a heuristic device, but the two are not the same. Although useful at times, all metaphors eventually break down and lose their validity when more and more exacting parallels are drawn between them and reality" (1994, p. 12).

What has been misleadingly described in the new theory as chaos is not really disorganization, but a particular kind of organization which is believed to be inherent in the world we live in. Contrary to the belief of the eighteenth-century philosopher Laplace and the assertions of the logical positivists and the scientists of linear dynamics, we cannot derive or predict the future from present conditions. This is not because of our ignorance, or the limitations of our techniques of measurement, but because of what is termed sensitive dependence on initial conditions, and the theoretical impossibility of precisely measuring these conditions, which requires infinite precision (Barton, 1994; Prigogine and Stengers, 1984; Stewart, 1989; Mandelbrot, 1983). Mandelbrot demonstrated in his classic 1967 paper, *How Long Is the Coast of Britain?* that the answer is system- or scale-dependent and, hence, that the length of the coast-line is infinite. The larger implication is that initial conditions cannot be determined precisely.

Scientists of all persuasions, including classical logical positivists, are well aware, when they conduct causal experiments, of the relation between sensitive measurement of initial conditions and the accuracy of the outcome. Complexity theory has added a crucial element: it is that the initial conditions on which the qualitative organization of systems and their iterations are sensitively dependent are ones of infinite and hence unmeasurable complexity and variability. They can at best be approximated, but never exhaustively determined. The clear implication is that no single model of systemic organization can suffice to account for the qualitative variability and complexity of outcome.

This observation has profound ramifications for monistic theories in general, and for the adequacy of psychoanalysis as a single-model theory in particular. No single or universal model can begin to do justice to the variability of initial conditions or the qualitative diversity of systemic iterations. By yet another route we reach the inescapable conclusion that monistic models of systemic phenomena like personality are inadequate. However, there may remain a place for a monistic model which helps us to understand the general origin, evolution, and transformation of all systems.

Chaos theory articulates that systems are related to one another according to a causal pattern of nonlinear dynamic transformation that differs from the linear causality of logical positivism. They follow a predictable course involving iterations of symmetry groups (Mandelbrot, 1983) or recursive structures: to chaos, and then, entropy-rich and far from conditions of equilibrium, to order or self-organization, and back again. This course involves folds in their iterative paths (Feigenbaum, 1980; Lorenz, 1963) or coupling-points between micro- and macro-levels involving what are known as "strange attractors" (Shaw, 1981). There are recursive invariant symmetries or constants between scale levels, recognizable by analogy in their morphology, but novel and unpredictable in their specific manifestations. Information is not constant; it is created and it disappears. Crutchfield, Farmer, Packard, and Shaw (1986) refer to this as patterned unpredictability in phase-space.

Vital or biological systems appear to follow this course. During their life span they appear to maintain themselves in a state of equilibrium or homeostasis or cohesion, solving routine problems, self-monitoring and self-adjusting in the process. Moreover, they tend to evolve or transform themselves creatively toward greater complexity or specialization, into systems of higher order. In other words, a motivational or energic factor is characteristic of systems. Some of the mathematics of these transformations has been worked out by Mandelbrot (fractal geometry) and by Wilson (1983; renormalization groups).

There is a remarkable complementarity between chaos theory and general systems theory, the former spelling out the dynamic mechanism of transformations among the hierarchical systems defined by the latter. There is also a remarkable similarity between elements of chaos theory and postmodern philosophy (Derrida, 1967). A major difference, however, is that postmodernists tend to consider chaos as an elemental bedrock of disorder, whereas scientists believe it reflects a new conception of orderliness (Hayles, 1990). The complementarity between chaos theory and systems theory suggests that they may be aspects of a more encompassing theory. As there is as yet no consensus about the name for what is variously known as chaos theory, complexity theory, or nonlinear dynamics. I should like to offer a name—

systems-in-transformation theory—that embraces both the significance of systems, in all their diversity, and the principles governing their iteration, or transformation.

Some of these developments have begun to penetrate psychiatry, in its interface with general medicine, and psychoanalysis. Probably the most important of these applications are Gedo and Goldberg's (1973) hierarchy of mind-models related to human development and psychopathology, which I noted in chapter 10, and Engel's (1977, 1980) biopsychosocial model. Engel focused on the relationships among the human sciences of personality in his role as a medical-psychiatric liaison physician and proposed a hierarchical schema known as the biopsychosocial model. However, Engel was primarily interested in teaching the relevance of psychoanalytic ideas to physicians working with organically ill patients. Although his biopsychosocial model possesses some of the formal characteristics of a theory of systems in transformation, for the most part it has been used simply to affirm the importance of a psychological level of understanding in persons with a coexisting but distinctive organic illness. Instead of considering the phenomenon under study, the illness, as a part of the personality, and conceptualizing the whole personality at various hierarchical levels, personality and illness have been treated as separate entities, the latter monistically, as organic, and the former pluralistically, at various psychological and social levels. The result is very different if one begins with the monistic premise that the condition to which the biopsychosocial model is applied is entirely organic and that psychological, interpersonal, and social manifestations are restricted to coping mechanisms, than it is if one begins with the pluralistic premise that the condition itself may be viewed as a hierarchy of recursive systems or structures that are related by analogy, each of which is valid and meaningful.

The advance afforded by systems-in-transformation theory is to alert us that phenomena do not "exist" monistically at any single level of organization and, therefore, that no single or monistic conceptual system provides a comprehensive account of them. Conceiving of a specific individual personality, from the vantage point of multisystemic complexity, implies that it is organized simultaneously on various levels: organic, individual psychological, interpersonal, familial, societal, and cultural. These systems are related not by linear causality but by the nonlinear transformational dynamics of recursive systems, similar by analogy but different in terms of an unpredictable creative emergence. Elements of a lower-level system are necessary to the emergence and continuity of a higher-level system but are not sufficient to account for it; nor can the elements of the higher-level system be reduced to those of the lower. In general, new and unique principles of structure, organization, meaning, and function characterize each level of a system hierarchy.

Differentiation and integration are core processes in the transformations and re-assemblages that comprise the evolution of systems toward greater complexity and specialization. The fundamental significance of differentiation and integration in the organization and functioning of vital systems and their evolution from a global state was first noted by Werner in 1926. He proposed what is known as the orthogenetic principle: "Wherever development occurs, it proceeds from a state of relative globality and lack of differentiation to a state of increasing differentiation, articulation, and hierarchic integration" (1947, p. 126). In other words, personality organization may be elucidated by a kind of calculus model. Witkin, Dyk, Faterson, Goodenough, and Karp explored some of the implications with regard to personality in their 1962 monograph.

A systems-in-transformation model encompasses the conceptual systems that are applicable to any given entity or whole and studies the structure and function of each system or level, the principles and processes of transformation and reorganization at successive levels, and the nature of the interdependency of one level with another. Weiss (1969) said, "what the 'level' we are speaking of signifies, is really the level of attention of an observer whose interest has been attracted by certain regularities of pattern prevailing at that level, as he scans across the range of orders of magnitude . . . as he would turn a microscope from lower to higher" (p. 16). Systems may be studied in evolution, over the course of time, or at a particular moment. Examples of systems in evolution might include a neurobiologist observing the function of an organ system, a psychologist observing human development, a therapist observing the course of family life, a biologist observing evolution, or a cultural anthropologist observing social change. The study of systems at a static moment in time, in terms of their recursive hierarchical layering, involves successively using the different lenses peculiar to different sciences such as molecular biology, neurobiology, neurochemistry, psychoanalysis (intrapsychic psychology), interpersonal psychology, family systems, sociology, and cultural anthropology. Although the perspectives of every systems level are necessary if we are to begin to account for the complexity of personality, no single systemic explanation is sufficient. Because the relationship among systems is not linear but transformational and recursive, involving different dimensions and concepts, systems cannot subsume other systems, nor can one system be used to predict, construct, or reconstruct another.

At this point the reader may object that I have succumbed to the very pitfall of monistic thinking I have taken such pains to debunk; that is, the fallacy of overgeneralization, the notion that a single model might be sufficient to account for everything. It is true that systems theory and chaos theory are monistic or universal model structures. But they differ from the universalizing or globalizing trend of logical positivist science insofar as they generalize in a different way, by emphasizing recursive or correlative movements from one system level to another. In a sense, they combine or synthesize monism and pluralism. It is no longer necessary to confine ourselves, when conceiving of personality, to the unsatisfactory choice between the Scylla of monothetic rigidity and egocentrism and the Charybdis of pluralistic anarchy and nihilism. The pluralistic model allows us to exercise all the flexibility we are capable of, at the same time that we retain a belief in universal principles: lawful if unpredictable transformations among systems. By analogic reasoning we may apply insights gained from one systemic perspective to hypothesis-making and observation at another.

CHAPTER 14

Modeling the Dialectic between Discovery and Creation

The model I proposed in chapter 13 based on the orthogenetic principle, a kind of calculus of mental development (differentiation and integration) and on the theory of systems in transformation, enables us to conceive of personality, whether at the particular individual level or at the level of generalization and typology, in a flexible, dialectic manner. With it we need not choose between the monistic rigidity of logical positivism and universalism and the pluralistic nihilism of extreme postmodernism. It enables us to search for essence and lawfulness, for universal structure, in each qualitatively unique personality system without having to generalize our conclusions to all systems, and it helps us to understand context dependency or instability of personality systems and hence their evanescence.

I shall try to schematize some of the multidimensional complexity involved in conceiving of personality. To begin with, it is important to recognize that personality is a pluralistic concept. That is, not only does one individual personality differ from another, but there are broad classes, typologies, or systems of personality organization that are qualitatively different from one another. Some of these differences or variants are intercultural (self-centric and sociocentric). Others are intracultural, including self-centric and sociocentric typologies related to gender, and psychopathological variants (neurosis, primitive personality, schizophrenia), and yet other statistically unusual personality typologies that it might not be appropriate to label as pathological at all.

The model of systems in transformation can be applied to any personality typology or to the understanding of any single individual, and it can be applied in two broadly distinctive ways that relate to the variables of systemic magnification and of time. In the first instance time is fixed, like taking a snapshot, and the perspective of multiple systems or levels is achieved by varying the magnification with which the system is viewed. This is what Mandelbrot described in his 1967 treatise on the impossibility of measuring the coast of Britain—or, more precisely, on the existence of multiple equally valid, scale-dependent systems for measuring it. Personality may be viewed with regard to systemic iteration or transformation through the lenses of neurobiology, individual psychology, interpersonal relations, family relations, and social and cultural structure.

The second way the model can be applied is to study transformations of a single system, whether individual or typological, over time. This requires holding the magnification or perspective constant and tracing systemic iteration as time elapses: for example, studying how modal personality evolves over historical time (chapter 3), or studying the development or maturation of an individual personality or of a particular typology—normal (self-centric or sociocentric) or pathological (neurosis, primitive personality, schizophrenia). This is the province of a psychoanalytic theory that is pluralistic and dialectic.

I shall begin by using the model of systems in transformation, based on the orthogenetic calculus of integration and differentiation, to study the systemic-hierarchical relationship among the organic, intrapsychic, interpersonal, familial, social, and cultural spheres of personality, and among the various human sciences, each with its unique conceptual lens, that study them. In chapters 5, 6, and 9 I gave an example consisting of the relationship between constitution, gender, and culture, consisting of the reiteration of self-centric and sociocentric systems. I noted the remarkable similarity between descriptions of male and Western personality, on the one hand, and of female and Eastern personality, on the other, as well as their dependence on constitutional elements, and I speculated about the nature of the transformational schema that might help to account for this. Now I shall return to schizophrenia, a complex systems hierarchy that was discussed in chapter 10.

If we think by analogy as we observe each successive level of the systemic iteration—interpersonal, familial, social, and cultural—it is possible to observe recursive transformations or repeating configurations of basic schizophrenic characteristics. In fact, much of what is commonly thought of as treatment of schizophrenia, if viewed from the perspective of a recursive systems hierarchy, might more accurately be considered enactment of the schizophrenic process itself.

In chapter 10 I hypothesized two phenotypical characterological vulnerabilities to schizophrenia: weakness of affinity-organization (mental cohesion in the form of integration and differentiation, and bonding to others) and hypersensitivity, as well as regulatory difficulties with regard to processing external and internal stimulation. Some of the psychological characteristics of the individual schizophrenic personality system, including lack of mental cohesion, ownership of a realistic sense of self and mental content, and passive withdrawal and alienation from others, can be accounted for, at least in part, by these vulnerabilities.

Turning from the psychological system to the family system, families tend to infantilize the schizophrenic member and invalidate his perceptions of the family and of himself. They attribute agency and responsibility not to the disturbed member or to other members of the family but to external forces. They supply meanings for his actions, usually grandiose and special as well as hostile and devaluing. In this way they alienate themselves from the disturbed member, reinforce his weak affinity for them, and encourage his tendency not to organize and integrate his mental contents. This combination of reinforcement of and compensation for the elements of schizophrenia ensures continuing dependency of the ill person on the family.

At the social system level the label *schizophrenia* signifies that the person's thoughts are deemed meaningless and incomprehensible, "crazy" products of organic forces outside his mind, which neither he nor his family are responsible for—not an integral part of his personality. He is considered disabled, incapable of handling stresses and responsibilities of ordinary living. He is looked upon as alien or less than human, fundamentally and irremediably different from others and special, either in the sense of sensitive, creative, and even supernatural, or in the sense of being pitiable and defective. Treatment may involve administration of what were formerly and aptly called "tranquilizing" medications to remove the unwanted thoughts, along with removal of the patient from "normal" people and the mainstream of life. Once again the basic elements of schizophrenia appear to be recombined at a "higher" systems level.

Turning from examples of the application of systems-in-transformation theory to the static analysis of personality typologies, to psychoanalysis, I shall suggest some ways in which it might incorporate the principles of systems organization and systems transformation in order to make it more useful, both universally and specifically, as a theory of development and organization of diverse personality typologies. Beginning with some general principles or postulates, a kind of metapsychology, if you will, I shall turn to a different way of looking at the late twentieth-century controversy between proponents of intrapsychic and interpersonal theories, and then to a discussion of two perspectives on psychoanalysis: the first as a general or universal theory of systems structures and their transformation, and the second as a multiplicity of local, indigenous content-rich theories. As a general theory of systems and their transformations, psychoanalysis can be a theory of systemic structure and process: personality evolution in complexity and specialization, equilibration, and entropy.

As the first postulate, Werner's (1926, 1940) orthogenetic principle of psychological integration and differentiation out of an initial global unity is critically important to understanding both the structure and transformation of systems, as well as their diversity.

As resistance to entropy, maintenance of homeostasis, and transformation to different levels of complexity are characteristic of all vital systems, the theory also requires dynamic concepts of energy or motivation. The very theory of systems informs us that these dynamisms can be conceptualized simultaneously and equally vividly at multiple levels: biological, psychological (appetites, affects), interpersonal, and social-cultural. It is probably tautological or teleological (in relation to structure) to conceptualize them in terms of self-cohesion.

Next, the theory must be highly sensitive to initial conditions, as variability in the smallest of these will result in iterative trajectories and resultant organizations of personality that are qualitatively different from one another.

Finally, the overarching or universal theory I am proposing accounts for transformation among personality systems according to the principles of non-linear dynamics of nonequilibrating systems and recursive iterations of structure. These transformations may take place along the dimension of time or development-maturation, or the dimension of magnification, that is, the lens power of the various sciences that attempt to comprehend personality.

The result is a theoretical structure as free as possible of specific content, which is left for articulation and representation in various local or indigenous theories related to particulars of gender, culture, or intracultural typology. Werner (1962) summarizes these principles as follows:

Firstly, the concept of differentiation refers to formal rather than to material properties of organization; it thus makes it possible to interrelate the various functional areas and their unfolding in an individual in terms of formal as against content characteristics. Secondly, it is a concept dynamic rather than static in its essence; it thus makes possible the study of ways of experiencing and behavioral patterning in terms of processes rather than achievement. Thirdly, it implies a temporal element; it ties together present behavioral and experiential characteristics—of individuals or groups—with those of the past; in other words, it binds the state of being to that of becoming. Fourthly, it is a concept capable of defining ways of behavior in terms of their universality and generality as well as in terms of their specificity and individuality; that is, it makes it possible to characterize behavior by a developmental principle which, defined as a basic law, refers to the uniform nature of genetic change—but at the same time, allows for multiformity of experience and articulation. (p. vi)

The model I am outlining affords us a different way of viewing the late twentieth-century controversy between proponents of intrapsychic and interpersonal models. This controversy may actually be an artifact of the Western individualistic-dualistic bias that equates personality with the particular corporeal person and otherness with the animate and inanimate environment. Instead, I propose that we adopt a broader concept of identity which may be defined with equal validity in individual or collective terms using the integration-differentiation calculus. It may no longer be necessary to choose among theories of the individual psyche, of the symbiotic or selfobject relationship, or of the interpersonal relationship. The concepts of integration and differentiation, applied broadly to the understanding of identity, enable us to adopt an intrapsychic (self-centric) or interpersonal (sociocentric) viewpoint as the moment requires. Although such a unified structural metatheory may ulti-

mately prove to be as bound to specifics of history and culture as its predecessors, it can serve as the framework for a plethora of content-rich indigenous
psychologies.

In other words, the most obvious local concept that has mistakenly been
generalized as universal in psychoanalytic theory is that of self, which is
indigenous to self-centric cultures. Its meanings in Eastern and Western cultures are actually very different. A concept like identity, which may be applied
to self-centric and sociocentric personalities alike, might be preferable (Erikson, 1950, 1959). From a self-centric standpoint identity connotes an internal
experience; from a sociocentric standpoint it describes an interconnectedness
to the social-cultural and natural worlds. Because identity has a structural
(what persists over time) as well as a dynamic connotation, it represents
constancy of personality. Erikson states that "The term identity . . . connotes
both a persistent sameness within oneself . . . and a persistent sharing of some
kind of essential character with others" (1956, p. 57). The identity concept is
compatible with models of development and of deviance. Identity is not only
subjective (one's personal awareness) but objective (the social and cultural
referents by which one is identified). Depending on the social-cultural milieu
in which the person develops, the sense of identity may evolve to be primarily
self-contained in a world of differentiated others, intrapsychically integrated
and regulated, including the capacity to experience intrapsychic conflict and
ambivalence and initiate related adaptations and defenses. Or it might evolve
to become part of an exquisitely differentiated and integrated social-cultural
system. In other words, Erikson's suggestion that identity resides "within
oneself" may not apply to sociocentric as much as to self-centric personality.

The sense of identity of sociocentric personalities is structured in terms of
complex patterns or networks of interrelatedness or interdependency within
entities larger than the individual person. These entities may be familial,
interpersonal, social, cultural, or ancestral. There may not be a structural
distinction between elements from the animate and the inanimate or natural
worlds. Sociocentric persons are not self-preoccupied, aggressively self-inter-
ested, or competitively self-aggrandizing, and to the extent they are personally
emotive it is not in the service of individual self-interest but as part of a
collective cause. They could be described, from a typically devaluing self-
centric point of view, as worker bees or ants who perform specialized functions in larger social hives or colonies, "part-objects" who tend to accept social

inequality as a fact of life. Their personalities may appear inconsistent over the range of these social roles, even unintegrated by self-centric standards, but this appears to be because these elaborately structured interpersonal and social networks play the functional and subjective stabilizing role that a more exclusively internal organization comprising various intrapsychic structures plays in constitution of the self-centric personality. The complexity of these identity-sustaining networks that extend beyond the individual parallels the individual intrapsychic complexity of mind that characterizes the self-centric personality organization. It is not a rudimentary or primitive organization, and in that sense it is very different from immature or pathological forms of personality organization encountered within Western culture and the self-centric dimension.

The identity of self-centric personalities is primarily structured intrapsychically, around the sense of a separate and autonomous self. Self-centric identity is based on stable cognitive and affective configurations which we refer to variously as character traits and as values, and which are constant across social role boundaries. Self-centric relationships, with the exception of the most intimate, are subject to mobility and change; except under conditions of immaturity or in pathological formations, their stability is not so essential to the person's sense of identity. Expressions of feeling by self-centric persons make them stand out from the group. Characteristic self-preoccupation and quest for self-enhancement may lead these personalities into conflict with established social-cultural groupings and lend a self-centeredness to their thinking and qualities of rebelliousness, competitiveness, and strivings for social mobility to their social dealings. They may try to control or manipulate the external world as though it were intended for their own use.

Each personality typology represents psychological complexity of a different kind; each has a developmental sequence of its own, from primitive to mature forms. Some of the most important maturational lines and achievements of sociocentric personality, which involve subtle and refined identity-sustaining participation in holistic or interdependent networks of thinking, feeling, and relating to others, are simply not conceived of in existing Western psychoanalytic models. Reciprocally, traditional Eastern modes of thought such as Buddhism insufficiently comprehend and articulate the richness and complexity of self-centric autonomous self-development and function. Theories based on integration-differentiation from an initial global state enable us to bridge these differences and to contrast mature personalities typical of different cultures, as well as immaturity and exceptional maturity within a particular culture, without concretizing and nullifying any one as a "hole" or deficit condition. They permit distinctions between pathological primitivism of personality, on the one hand, and immaturity, on the other, and between a variety of mature or modal typologies. They make possible the nonjudgmental contrast of personalities in different cultures, including the identity outcomes characteristic of sociocentricity and self-centricity, however difficult if not impossible it may be to find an observer and a viewing position with which to perceive both simultaneously.

Why is it that a majority of the world's cultures appear to be sociocentric (female) rather than self-centric (male)? Axiomatic in chaos theory is the proposition that it is impossible to specify all the initial conditions in any system. As a result, while the general recurrence of structural patterns can be predicted, the particulars cannot be. If we presume that cultures have arisen from multiple loci of human interaction throughout the world, initial conditions (in this case a core gender dichotomy) may seem to have been identical, but obviously were not in the details of personality and circumstance. So it should not be surprising that broad culture groupings have emerged in part along gendered lines, but that the specifics of cultures are quite heterogeneous.

Personalities in different cultures, of different gender, and with varying degrees of intracultural normality-psychopathology will differ in the ratio and manner in which structures and functions are personally or autonomously regulated and are interpersonally, interactively, or socially regulated. Another way to articulate this idea is that there is an interdependence or interplay between social and interpersonal representational and regulatory systems, on the one hand, and intrapsychic ones, on the other, so that for each culture there is a unique ratio or balance between the two. As I mentioned in earlier discussions about culture and gender, Witkin and associates (Witkin, Dyk, Faterson, Goodenough, and Karp, 1962; Witkin and Berry, 1975; Witkin and Goodenough, 1976; Berry, 1992) have applied an integration-differentiation model to the study of the relationship between individual psychology and society-culture. Using their rating of individuals in various cultures on a visual-spatial variable called field-dependence, they concluded that there is an inverse relationship between individual and social complexity. Persons from more complex cultures tend to be less psychologically differentiated and more field-dependent than those from less complex ones. According to their studies, field-independent people tend to be more separate, autonomous, and capable of abstract thinking than field-dependent persons. It apparently did not occur to them to study qualitative systemic differences in culture and personality and to apply their integration-differentiation model to more complex kinds of diversity. LeVine employs similar thinking but contemplates some of the qualitative questions when he asks, "Is there a complementarity of structure between the psychic order of the individual and the social order of the community such that certain necessary functions can be fulfilled through mental or social organization? Do some societies rely more heavily on customary, institutionalized social organization and others on internalized mental organization (personality structure) for fulfillment of functions that are necessary for human adaptation?" (1990, p. 468). He adds, "The expectation that a particular ego function will become self-regulated, that is, organized as intrapsychic rather than interpersonal structure, varies from one society to another in accordance with the cultural models of a people and their priorities for the development of competence in their children" (p. 469).

A psychoanalytic systems model based on integration and differentiation might begin by postulating a highly competent perceptual-cognitive apparatus in the sense that numerous observer-experimenters of infants have noted in recent decades. However innately competent this apparatus, it is nonetheless neither differentiated from immediate sensory-perceptual experience and related motor patterns nor integrated in the fashion of mature mentation, but is characterized by an enactive, sensorimotor-affective form of mentation such as Piaget (Wolff, 1966; Flavell, 1963) described. Might there be a basic array of expectable cognitive-affective capacities universal to most human beings regardless or independent of cultural context? I suggest four such capacities: focus, attention, or concentration; discrimination; affinity or organization; and tolerance for mental (probably affective) intensity.

Such a list could be expanded and elaborated by observers of infants in conjunction with neuroscientists, to include constitutional variations on these basic capacities comprising gender and personality phenotypes at the normal end and predispositions or vulnerabilities to various forms of psychopathology—for example, schizophrenia—at the abnormal end. From the basic capacities it can be hypothesized that development occurs with the symbiotic assistance of others who are at once personalities in their own right and members of a particular culture. This developmental process ordinarily involves intrapsychic and interpersonal integration and differentiation, including increasing representation of and control over affects and related thoughts, as well as over actions. The many paths development may take depend on the constitutional givens of the infant, including gender and special vulnerabilities, the cultural milieu, and particular personality configurations of caretaking figures, ranging from the relatively normal variants to the diverse pathological ones. The qualitative permutations and combinations of infant constitution, culture, and parental personality within a culture are potentially numerous.

Psychoanalysis needs to increase the sensitivity of its developmental theory to initial conditions. Although Freud was not totally consistent in his belief, he postulated a qualitative constitutional mental endowment more or less common to all humankind, as I suggested in chapters 7 and 10. So far as environmental provision was concerned, he postulated either paradigmatic experiences common to all humans, or a kind of phylogenetic inheritance that rendered vicissitudes of environment relatively inconsequential. Personality typologies that could not adequately be described by a model with these uniform and general initial conditions, such as female psychology and schizophrenia, were thought of as null categories of defect or deficiency, rather than equally valid, if qualitatively different forms of personality. The theory has never been re-worked to account for the kinds of constitutional variability I discuss in chapter 5. As for the variability of early environmental provision or nurture that is now being popularized in trauma theories, its importance is recognized at a commonsense level by most analysts in their clinical work, but its possible implications for differences in qualitative organization of adult personality remain more or less unexplored.

I have noted in chapter 10 that Gedo (1979, 1984, 1986; Gedo and Goldberg, 1973) has explored the potential of hierarchical systems concepts, a succession of mind models in which earlier and more primitive organizations appear to be transformed into progressively more complex or higher-level ones, to account simultaneously for the mental diversity encountered in normal maturation and in the normal and pathological variants of personality. As Gedo's success in basing the levels of his epigenetic hierarchy on existing psychoanalytic conceptualizations (for example, reflex arc, self-cohesion, intrapsychic conflict) implies, it is not necessary to reformulate psychoanalysis radically or to look beyond the hypotheses we utilize in our daily work to find the suggestion of qualitative systemic reorganizations, transformations from one mind model, and emergence of another that depends on the developmental achievements of its predecessor as a foundation, functions analogously, but is constructed of new concepts and relationships that cannot be predicted from them. In classical theory, for instance, the most obvious transformation, which we may comprehend by analogy, is from the neonatal psychosomatic condition of limited control; to a system of external dyadic or symbiotic regulation and control of the person, with a related emerging identity sense; to a relative emphasis on internalized control and identity formation through the agency of superego, via resolution of the Oedipus complex. In Klein's theory, a process of integration and differentiation serves to transform an inherently split (schizoid) and undifferentiated (projectively identifying) personality, fueled by rage and envy, and functioning as part of a dyad, into a more integrated and autonomous one. This more mature self is depressive, having achieved coherence, differentiation from others, and more self-regulatory capacity by a process of internal self-attack and self-repair involving a combination of love and guilt. Mahler's theory similarly marks a fundamental and qualitative transformation from a symbiotic mode of thinking and relating involving cognitive and functional dependency to a more autonomous, integrated, self-regulating one. Finally, in Kohut's theory a model of unintegrated functioning involving grandiose, mirror-seeking, and idealizing configurations in undifferentiated relationship with selfobjects is transformed through a process of transmuting internalization, impelled by phase-appropriate disillusionment, into a model of self-cohesion and self-regulation around more integrated ambitions and ideals.

Implicit in each of these theories is a developmental progression involving psychic integration and differentiation with internalization of structure and control, including a shift at some point from obligatory self-completing and self-sustaining dyadic dependencies to analogous self-sustaining internal processes requiring new concepts and modes of organization, which enable the person to have more freestanding autonomous relations with others. Of course, all these are indigenous aspects of Western self-centric development.

Turning from the general or universal in a theory of personality to what is local or particular, the kind of unified theory of personality I propose serves as a superstructure for various parochial, content-rich theories that are bounded by the particulars of historical time, culture, gender, and intracultural typology. Employing concepts related to integration and differentiation each of these local or indigenous psychologies might outline identity-structuring appropriate to a unique set of circumstances which makes a particular organization of personality qualitatively different from others.

An examination of the existing psychoanalytic theory suggests that some of its concepts and constructs are more applicable to the overarching universal theory I am proposing, whereas others belong in individual, content-rich indigenous psychologies. Examples of the more universally applicable structural and regulatory concepts include unconscious mental functioning and transference. Unconscious process and content in the individual psyche results from interaction (secondary unconscious) or the lack of interaction (primary unconscious) between child and caregivers. The primary unconscious comprises repeated behavioral and affective patterns that have never gained mental representation through social learning, and the secondary unconscious consists of thoughts and feelings which have been repressed as part of the child's adaptation to the particular exigencies of his family and culture. Therefore, unconscious process and content are probably universal attributes of mental life. Levels of consciousness and identity regulation may be represented in a model of progressive complexity and directionality of differentiation and integration. Does the structuring of the unconscious and its functional manifestations differ in self-centric and sociocentric personalities? The unconscious mental functioning of self-centric individuals takes the form of individual dreams, parapraxes, and symptoms. In sociocentric cultures similar functions may be served by what Jung (1964) referred to as the collective unconscious, that is, shared mythology, archetypes, imagery, and even group hallucinatory phenomena. These elements may be expressed less in individual symptoms and behavior and more in larger social enactments or dramatizations. Mythology, after all, does not exist apart from the people who recount it and are governed by it. The relationship between mythology and the people who create and use it may be more or less differentiated; in sociocentric cultures it is less so. The Japanese psychoanalyst Kitayama introduced a recent lecture on the mythology of his people (1994) by remarking, in what he considered to be a personal anecdote or an interesting aside to his major exposition, that the Japanese, particularly the generation born before World War II, do not differentiate their mythology from what is accepted as sociocultural reality, as Westerners do. They feel themselves to be a part of their mythology. For example, the emperor is believed to be a living descendent of the gods, and the Japanese islands are believed to be the result of the primal procreation of the gods. Kitayama goes on to elaborate recurrent mythological themes that appear to him to reflect dynamic unconscious issues which Japanese share. In such a system idiosyncratic aspects of a person's unconscious might be represented by his or her selective attachments to aspects of the culture's mythology. Similar phenomena are also characteristic of native American cultures.

The concept of transference probably represents another universal phenomenon, which may also be conceptualized in content-free energic and integration-differentiation terms. Like the unconscious, however, the transference field may encompass broader elements in sociocentric than in selfcentric personalities, including various social groupings and aspects of the natural world.

Numerous psychoanalytic concepts probably need to be particularized with regard to their local contexts and specific applicability, for example, as part of indigenous Western psychology, or as part of a modal personality organization within Western culture which does not necessarily represent the entire range of personalities within that culture. Such concepts include narcissism, symbiosis, separation-individuation, autonomy, and the Oedipus complex. In sociocentric cultures, what psychoanalysis refers to as separation and autonomy is considered abnormal, and what psychoanalysis refers to as narcissism and symbiosis and looks upon as immature states to be relinquished in favor of complex internalizations, are looked upon as normal conditions to be developed and refined by elaborate external structural and regulatory linkages. As for the Oedipus complex, it may be an indigenous Western identity-crystallizing and impulse-regulatory configuration—an aspect of maturation of a separated, individuated, autonomous self. It is made possible by successful completion of earlier stages of psychic integration, including acquisition of the capacity to experience intrapsychic conflict and to tolerate ambivalence. It also involves differentiation from the parental regulatory figure by means of identification, or integration of new intrapsychic capabilities (both ego and superego). Sociocentric personalities may acquire analogous mental content and capabilities through elaboration of social linkages. Such an idea was proposed by Japanese analysts such as Doi (1973), who introduced the concept of amae, and Okonogi (1979), who writes about the Ajase complex (see chapter 6). Cohler (1993) also writes about the cultural relativity of ways of integrating sexual taboos and intrafamilial impulse control into one's identity.

However tantalizing the theoretical prospect I have presented may seem, a fundamental question remains unanswered. It is not sufficient to try to envision a unified metapsychology that subsumes a multiplicity of more content-specific subtheories without considering who is capable of the special perspective and mental flexibility necessary to construct such a schema. After all, every observer-theoretician, no matter how sensitized to the issues discussed here and how much exposed to cultural and personality diversity, is inextricably embedded in a limited way of thinking about personality. The cognitive blindness into which each of us as observer-theoreticians is inevitably locked by virtue of our own gender, culture, and personality typology within the culture renders us simultaneously ideologically overcommitted to certain elements related to our own personalities and incapable of perceiving and therefore potentially signifying forms, structures, and functions of personality which are foreign to us and represent a trajectory in which our mental capabilities have not developed. Another way to look at the problem is that we must supplement common notions of intelligence—based on our understanding of interaction of biologically innate capabilities with enriching or retarding elements of the interpersonal world—with the idea that there are specialized forms of intelligence or dimensions of mind that are mandated and facilitated by each culture. Sociocentric and self-centric modes of development each specialize in unique and sophisticated pathways of integration and differentiation. LeVine (1973) has suggested that, in order to effect a comprehensive analysis of personality in a particular (non-Western) culture, a collaboration may be necessary between a Western analyst-theorist and an indigenous observer. At the point when he wrote this he did not question the ultimate verity of the Western point of view, nor did he address how communication and collaboration between two qualitatively differently organized personalities could occur. With the benefit of LeVine's groundwork, Shweder is better able to elaborate some of the complexity of the problem: "'Thinking through others' in the first sense is to recognize the other as a specialist or expert on some aspect of human experience, whose reflective consciousness and system of representations and discourse can be used to reveal hidden dimensions of ourselves. . . . In its second sense [it] is a process of representing (and defending) the other's evaluations of and involvements with the world. . . . Then there is . . . the sense favored by . . . postmodern deconstructionists . . . passing through the other . . . revealing what the life and intentional world of the other has dogmatically hidden away, namely its own incompleteness" (1991, pp. 108–109). He adds that in the alternative, postpositivist philosophy, subjectivity and objectivity are inextricably linked, and that "The objective world is incapable of being represented completely if represented from any one point of view, and incapable of being represented intelligibly if represented from all points of view at once" (p. 66).

I have made the case that conceiving of personality is best looked upon as a dialectical process. While there is no single essence of personality to be discovered, there may be invariant principles that enable us to conceive of personality in all its qualitative variability, multisystemic complexity, and transformational iteration, whether individual, or typologically related to historical epoch, culture, gender, or intracultural variability. I have articulated such principles in the form of a model of systems in transformation, based on the calculus of integration and differentiation, and tried to demonstrate its potential to liberate us from the dilemma of having to choose between two equally impoverishing conceptual positions: monistic rigidity and pluralistic nihilism. I have made some suggestions for an expansion of psychoanalytic theory based on this model which would enable it to distinguish more accurately between the universals of personality and those elements that are particular or indigenous. The model I envision can also serve as umbrella for a plethora of indigenous psychologies that are neither unwittingly overgeneralized nor so relative to particulars of time and place as to be hardly more useful than folklore. Unfortunately, the dialectical model I propose is only as useful as the persons who employ it, and we must recognize that, as conceivers of personality, each of us is forever imprisoned in unique particulars of time, culture, gender, and intracultural experience.

CHAPTER 15

Conceiving of Personality: The Warp and the Woof

The recent flood of relativist, perspectivist, subjectivist, postmodernist rhetoric has highlighted the naivete of the positivist conception of a world of absolute substantial reality and truth, external and internal, there to be discovered. The notion of a world out there awaiting capture, naming, comprehension, and control by an elite cadre of trained objective (scientific) male observers, and a world within, similarly awaiting empathic comprehension and ultimate objectification by therapists more invested in relating clinically to others than in conducting experimental research, is an illusion. Monism, the mode of thinking predicated on such a belief, is rigid, reductionistic, and mentally and spiritually impoverishing. The conceptual entity we call personality is contextually created and qualitatively diverse, relative to a multiplicity of contexts, ever-changing, evanescent. As yet the models of personality on which we depend remain constrained by the old ways of thinking. For the most part they are unselfconsciously indigenous or ethnocentric, imbued with egocentrism and promulgated as ideology.

The phenomenon I am describing is certainly not limited to the world of ideas, of theorizing about personality, but may readily be appreciated in the realm of enactment (for example, religious crusades, nationalism, imperialism, colonialism and slavery, racism and genocide). Each of these movements is driven by a conception of "the" personality type, a normative center from which a spectrum of abnormality or deviation—which must be controlled, reformed, or eliminated—radiates. Each tends at best to ignore and devalue difference and diversity and, at worst, to use totalitarian dogma as justification to annihilate them. Any substance to the claims of fundamental and universal truth made by the adherents of such thought- and action-systems is so embedded in the particularistic content of their belief system and the ideological stridency of their presentation as not to be readily visible.

When we turn from appearances, what we think of as being out there, to epistemology, how we know about it, it is even more unsettling to realize that particular personalities (ourselves), idiosyncratically embedded in the very qualitatively particularistic circumstances of history, constitution (including gender), culture, and intracultural typology, create the theories or conceptions of personality to which we accord the status of truth. Our theories are contextually relativistic not simply because that reflects a fact about the personalities we are conceiving, but also because of the idiosyncratic vantage points and limited data bases of ourselves as conceivers. If we accept that notions of universality and verity represent at best unattainable theoretical fictions like the concept of infinity, and at worst, when they become ideologies, movements, or "isms", misleading and distorting ways of thinking; and that meaning and knowledge appear to be contextually limited to time, place and person, as well as shifting and inconstant, then the task of conceiving of personality is truly and literally a mind-boggling one. It requires that we question how generally applicable are the core assumptions, the very roots and foundations on which each of our identities as well as our sense of what comprises personality are based, without the solace afforded by the belief that we may find an alternative form of certainty with which to replace them.

Nonetheless, monistic thinking—the search for universals, for comprehensive models and overarching principles—is based on the mind's constructive quest for order and organization and should not be abandoned lightly. To reject the general for the particular, and to look upon the choice between one model and another as purely pragmatic, is just as reductionistic, value-repudiating, and intellectually impoverishing as the kind of thinking it proposes to supplant. Such an approach leads inexorably to a nihilistic cul-de-sac. Moreover, since personality is bounded and limited by constitutional factors, it seems unlikely that it can be adequately comprehended in terms that are exclusively relativistic.

The universal value of the insights into personality which psychoanalysis has provided is difficult to distinguish from its bias as a monothetic theory—an indigenous psychology of the modal self-centric Western male psyche, colored by the personal idiosyncrasies of its creators, and propagated by a "movement" in quasi-ideological form. But most of these limitations, particularly an embeddedness in self-centric modes of thought, are shared by the other human sciences and by science in general. It may be an impossible task to frame a comprehensive theory of personality with any Western science. Perhaps such a theoretical framework has no more inherent validity than a model generated from another culture. This awareness is probably one factor responsible for the heightened contemporary popularity of Eastern religions. The fact that Eastern belief systems do not enjoy even greater popularity says much about how much more readily apparent the folkloric or religious essence of an indigenous psychology may be to the beholder located in another cultural context.

The universal we search for is not a substantive truth or fact, nor a particular model or system of personality, but an overarching model or unifying perspective, which, in itself, is content-free, that might help us to understand personality system transformations or iterations. Such a model or schema would allow for the dialectic between discovered truth or essence and relativistic creation or evanescence. Confusing as it may seem to those of us accustomed to the commonsense reasoning that monistic and pluralistic approaches are mutually exclusive, and that one is bad and the other good, I conclude that these are necessary dialectical orienting poles, "strange attractors," if you will, of a unitary reasoning process, and that true creativity involves sustaining an ongoing tension between the quest to discover, the process of experimenting with tools to do so, and the flexibility to create, analogically, while accepting the qualitative unpredictability of the result. Monistic and pluralistic viewpoints each take on added richness as part of such a dialogue. I have drawn upon two related theories—systems theory and chaos or complexity theory—in order to elaborate a model for conceiving of personality that combines the orthogenetic principle or calculus of integration and differentiation with the theory of systems in transformation. The orthogenetic calculus enables us to comprehend the basic organization of qualitatively different personality systems without sacrificing our appreciation for their idiosyncratic richness of content and organization. The theory of systems in transformation, both in magnification and over elapsed time, enables us to understand the iteration of qualitatively different personality organizations; how they change and become different in unpredictable ways, yet how in the process of change they remain the same. Nested within the parameters of this model, like the Russian Matrioschka dolls, are pluralist hierarchies of personality models related to the diverse circumstances and contents of personality: historical and maturational time, and level or perspective of observation (individual, constitutional, interpersonal, social, intracultural, and intercultural).

In taking into account personality diversity related to cultural differences, to gender, and to other factors of constitution, I proposed a dualistic typology of personality, self-centric and sociocentric, that is susceptible of finer gendered distinctions or subgroupings. I hypothesize that these may reflect a hierarchical sequence of systemic transformations beginning with what is now known as core gender identity, which, in turn, is based on the constitutional neurobiological substrate of personality, and undergoing progressive systemic transformations through the interpersonal and psychological levels to the level of culture itself. In other words, broad differences among cultures may at root stem from biological gender differences, although it is also true that culture is ultimately an autonomous and self-sustaining system at a different level of organization, and also has reciprocal influences on individual personality expressions of gender difference. I have outlined the organization of systems underlying some of the qualitative differences in personality within Western culture, particularly ones related to modal personality, to gender, to primitive personality, and to schizophrenia. And I have suggested some of the conceptual and organizational revision that might be required in order to integrate the contributions of the orthogenetic calculus and the systems-in-transformation model into psychoanalysis as a theory of normal development and psychopathology, in the hope of making it a more powerful tool for engaging in the dialectic of personality.

It is evident that no single person or representative of a single cultural or ideological group is capable of creating a comprehensive picture of personality. And yet the potential of collaborative or conjoint operations by mutually respectful theorists and data-gatherers who represent the spectrum of personality diversity must be tempered by awareness of the pitfalls and limitations related to the very qualitative differences in the personalities of the collabora-tors. The possibility of sharing surface structures and meanings of language encourages well-intentioned efforts to communicate, but the profound differ-ences in mind which exist, for instance, among sociocentric and self-centric personalities, may readily and unwittingly result in mistaking the illusion of communication for the substance, and in confusion rather than clarification and insight.

The theoretical implications of the conception of personality I have pro-posed are perhaps more apparent than the clinical-therapeutic ones. As clini-cians we cannot afford to be nihilistic, but we had better be modest and avoid the hubris that inevitably attends each new epistemological fad and fashion that serves to reassure us that we truly know what is going on, whether it be the model of the objective, truth-detecting analyst; that of the wonderfully empathic analyst, or that of the humble, non-authoritarian analyst who simply assists his patients to construct a story that seems satisfying. We must beware our natural tendency to overinvest in our models and to overgeneralize them, and the modal value-laden assumptions on which they are based. It is easier to realize that we may not be able to help everyone than it is to accept that we may not even be able to understand the other person much less comprehend the meanings and ramifications of changes in his life for which we may serve as the vehicle. It is paradoxical that, if we can accept these things, the therapeutic scope of a field such as psychoanalysis might actually be broadened so that it could become truly useful to a wider spectrum of patients.

Conceiving of personality—our own and those of our fellow humans—is a dialectical process more than a goal. The challenge appears Herculean, the results at best approximate or indeterminate, analogical every bit as essential, and more evanescent than enduring. The dialectic occurs within a matrix of tension between finding or discovering—a quest for certainty in the form of truth, reality and substance involving an attitude of faith in the tools or processes we use in the quest—and a more uncertain, subjectivistic, interac-tive or creative appreciation of the relativistic uniqueness of what we perceive. The two modes of conceiving of personality diversity elaborated and explored throughout this book—a unifying deterministic monism, the search-and-discover mode on which traditional science has been based—and an indeter-ministic pluralism, an artistic or creative mode—appear to be complementary aspects of a dynamic epistemological framework. One aspect gains meaning with reference to the other. These complementary attitudes are the very warp and woof of our method of conceiving of personality. Within this matrix, hedged about with the dangers of rigid ideological thinking on the one hand and nihilistic anarchy on the other, we aspire to a creative synthesis.

The process of creation and the effort at comprehension are synonymous with life itself. Attainment of a state of certainty may be beyond reasonable expectation. Perhaps this book is as much about a questing attitude of thought as it is a concrete content or product. I look to future efforts to conceive of personality in the hope that defining the necessity and purpose of a skeptical but optimistic attitude, and offering a frame of reference based on energy, process and structure, within which other more content-specific systemic frames or theories may be created, will inform and sharpen our thought processes at the same time that it renews our enthusiasm for the task.

References

Abend, S., Porder, M., and Willick, M. (1983). *Borderline Patients: Psychoanalytic Perspectives.* New York: International Universities Press.

Adler, L., Pachtman, E., Franks, R., Pacevich, M., Waldo, M., and Freedman, R. (1982). Neurophysiological evidence for a defect in neuronal mechanisms involved in sensory gating in schizophrenia. *Biol. Psychiat.,* 17:639–654.

Alejandro-Wright, M. (1985). The child's conception of racial classification: A socio-cognitive developmental model. In: M. Spencer, G. Brookins, and W. Allen (eds.), *The Social and Affective Development of Black Children.* Hillside, N.J.: Erlbaum, pp. 185–200.

Alexander, F. (1931). Buddhistic training as an artificial catatonia. *Psychoanalytic Review,* 18:129–145.

Allen, L., and Gorski, R. (1992). Sexual orientation and the size of the anterior commissure in the human brain. *Proc. Natl. Acad. Sci. U.S.A.,* 89:199–202.

Amsterdam, B. (1972). Mirror self-image reactions before age two. *Developmental Psychology,* 5:297–305.

Anderson, K. (1966). Work capacity of selected populations. In: P. Baker and J. Weiner (eds.), *The Biology of Human Adaptability.* Oxford: Clarendon, pp. 67–90.

Andreasen, N. (1988). Brain imaging: Applications in psychiatry. *Science,* 239:1381–1388.

Arlow, J., and Brenner, C. (1964). *Psychoanalytic Concepts and the Structural Theory.* New York: International Universities Press.

———. (1969). The psychotherapy of the psychoses: a proposed revision. *Internat. J. Psycho-Anal.,* 50:5–14.

Artson, B. (1978). *Mid-Life Women: Homemakers, Volunteers, Professionals.* Ph.D. diss., California School of Professional Psychology.

Atwood, G., and Stolorow, R. (1984). *Structures of Subjectivity: Explorations in Psychoanalytic Phenomenology.* Hillsdale, N.J.: Analytic Press.

Augustine. (397). *Confessions.* R. Pine-Coffin (trans.). New York: Dorset Press (1986).

Bailey, J., and Pillard, R. (1991). A genetic study of male sexual orientation. *Arch. Gen. Psychiatry,* 48:1089–1096.

Bailey, J., Pillard, R., Neale, M., and Agyei, Y. (1993). Heritable factors influence sexual orientation in women. *Arch. Gen. Psychiatry,* 50:217–223.

Bakhtin, M. (1986). *Speech Genres and Other Late Essays.* Austin: University of Texas Press.

Barfield, A. (1976). Biological influences on sex differences in behavior. In: M. Teitelbaum (ed.), *Sex Differences: Social and Biological Perspectives.* Garden City, N.Y.: Anchor.

Barton, S. (1994). Chaos, self-organization, and psychology. *American Psychologist,* 49:5–14.

Bass, A. (1994). For academic psychiatry the future looks dim. *Boston Globe,* March 28.

Baumeister, R. (1986). *Identity: Cultural Change and the Struggle for Self.* New York: Oxford University Press.

———. (1987). How the self became a problem. *J. Personality Social Psychol.,* 52:163–176.

Beatty, W. (1979). Gonadal hormones and sex differences in nonreproductive behaviors in rodents: organizational and activational influences. *Hormones Behav.,* 12:112–163.

Benderly, B. (1987). *The Myth of Two Minds: What Gender Means and Doesn't Mean.* New York: Doubleday.

Benedict, R. (1934). *Patterns of Culture.* Boston: Houghton Mifflin.

———. (1946). *The Chrysanthemum and the Sword: Patterns of Japanese Culture.* Boston: Houghton Mifflin.

Benjamin, J. (1988). *The Bonds of Love.* New York: Pantheon Books.

Berlin, I. (1976). *Vico and Herder: Two Studies in the History of Ideas.* New York: Viking.

Berlin, S., and Johnson, C. (1989). Women and autonomy: Using structural analysis of social behavior to find autonomy within connections. *Psychiatry,* 52:79–95.

Berry, J. (1966). Temne and Eskimo perceptual skills. *Internat. J. Psychol.,* 1:207–229.

———. (1971). Ecological and cultural factors in spatial perceptual development. *Canadian Journal of Behavioral Science,* 3:324–336.

———. (1992). Developmental issues in the comparative study of psychological differentiation. In: R. L. Munroe, R. H. Munroe, and B. Whiting (eds.), *Handbook of Cross-cultural Human Development.* New York: Garland, pp. 63–72.

Bertalanffy, L. von. (1952). *Problems of Life.* New York: John Wiley and Sons.

———. (1967a). *Robots, Men and Minds.* New York: George Braziller.

———. (1967b). The role of systems theory in present day science, technology and philosophy. In: K. Schaefer, H. Hensel, and R. Brady (eds.), *Toward a Man-Centered Medical Science.* Mt. Kisco, N.Y.: Futura, pp. 11–15.

———. (1968). *General System Theory.* New York: George Braziller.

———. (1969). Chance or law. In: A. Koestler and J. Smythies, *Beyond Reductionism: New Perspectives in the Life Sciences.* New York: Macmillan.

Binswanger, L. (1956). Freud's psychosentherapie. *Psyche*, 10:357–366.

Blatt, S., and Blass, R. (1990). Attachment and separateness: A dialectical model of the products and processes of development throughout the life cycle. *Psychoanal. Study Child*, 45:107–127.

Blier, R. (1991). Gender ideology and the brain: Sex differences research. In: M. Notman and C. Nadelson (eds.), *Women and Men*. Washington, D.C.: American Psychiatric Press, pp. 63–73.

Bohr, N. (1937). Causality and complementarity. *Philos. of Science*, 4:289–298.

Bourne, E. (1991). Does the concept of the person vary cross-culturally? In: R. Shweder, ed., *Thinking Through Cultures*. Cambridge, Mass.: Harvard University Press, pp. 113–185.

Boyer, L. B. (1962). Remarks on the personality of the Shamans: With especial reference to the Apache of the Mescalero Indian reservation. In: W. Muensterberger and S. Axelrod (eds.), *Psychological Study Society*. New York: International Universities Press, 2:233–254.

———. (1979). *Childhood and Folklore: A Psychoanalytic Study of Apache Personality*. New York: Library of Psychological Anthropology.

Briggs, J. (1970). *Never in Anger: Portrait of an Eskimo Family*. Cambridge, Mass.: Harvard University Press.

Broff, D., and Geyer, M. (1978). Sensorimotor gating and schizophrenia: Human and animal model studies. *Arch. Gen. Psychiat.*, 47:181–188.

Bronson, E., and Desjardins, C. (1968). Aggression in adult mice: Modification by neonatal injections of gonadal hormones. *Science*, 161:705–706.

Bruner, J. (1986). *Actual Minds, Possible Worlds*. Cambridge, Mass.: Harvard University Press.

Buhrich, N., Bailey, J., and Martin, N. (1991). Sexual orientation, sexual identity, and sex-dimorphic behaviors in male twins. *Behav. Genetics*, 21:75–96.

Bygott, J. (1974). Agonistic behavior and social relationships among adult male chimpanzees. Ph.D. diss., Cambridge University.

Cahoone, L. (1988). *The Dilemma of Modernity: Philosophy, Culture and Anti-Culture*. Albany: State University of New York Press.

Campbell, D. (1974). "Downward causation" in hierarchically organized biological systems. In: F. Ayala and T. Dobshansky (eds.), *Studies in the Philosophy of Biology*. London: Macmillan, 1974, pp. 179–186.

Cannon, W. (1935). Stresses and strains of homeostasis. *Amer. J. Med. Sci.*, 189:1–14.

Carew, T., Walters, E., and Kandel, E. (1981). Associative learning in *Aplysia*: Cellular correlates supporting a conditioned fear hypothesis. *Science*, 211:501–504.

Cattell, J. (1890). Mental tests and measurements. *Mind*, 15:373–380.

Caudill, W. (1962). Anthropology and psychoanalysis: Some theoretical issues. In: T. Gladwin and W. Sturtevant (eds.), *Anthropology and Human Behavior*. Washington, D.C.: Anthropological Society of Washington, pp. 174–214.

Caudill, W., and Weinstein, H. (1969). Maternal care and infant behavior in Japan and America. *Psychiatry*, 32:12–43.

Chodorow, N. (1978). *The Reproduction of Mothering: Psychoanalysis and the Sociology of Gender*. Berkeley: University of California Press.

——. (1980). Gender, relation, and difference in psychoanalytic perspective. In: C. Zanardi (ed.), *Essential Papers on the Psychology of Women*. New York: New York University Press, 1990, pp. 420–436.

——. (1989). *Feminism and Psychoanalytic Theory*. New Haven: Yale University Press.

Choi, S.-C., Kim, U., and Choi, S.-H. (1993). Indigenous analysis of collective representations: A Korean perspective. In: J. Berry and U. Kim (eds.), *Indigenous Psychologies*. Newbury Park, Calif.: Sage, pp. 193–210.

Clower, V. (1981). The acquisition of mature femininity. In: M. Notman and C. Nadelson (eds.), *Women and Men*. Washington, D.C.: American Psychiatric Press, pp. 75–88.

Cohler, B. (1993). Intent and meaning in psychoanalysis and cultural study. In: T. Schwartz, G. White, and C. Lutz (eds.), *New Directions in Psychological Anthropology*. Cambridge: Cambridge University Press, pp. 269–293.

Crick, F. (1993). *The Astonishing Hypothesis: The Scientific Search for the Soul*. New York: Charles Scribner's Sons.

Crow, T. (1980). Molecular pathology of schizophrenia: More than one disease process? Brit. Med. J., 280:166–168.

Crutchfield, J., Farmer, J., Packard, N., and Shaw, R. (1986). Chaos. *Scientific American*, 255:46–57.

Cushman, P. (1990). Why the self is empty. *American Psychologist*, 45:599–611.

D'Andrade, R. (1966). Sex differences and cultural institutions. In: E. Maccoby (ed.), *The Development of Sex Differences*. Stanford, Calif.: Stanford University Press, pp. 174–204.

Danziger, K. (1983). Origins and basic principles of Wundt's volkerpsychologie. Brit. J. Social Psychol., 22:303–313.

Darwin, C. (1859). *The Origin of Species by Means of Natural Selection*. New York: F. Ungar.

Davis, M., and Fernald, R. (1990). Social control of neuronal soma size. J. Neurobiol., 21:1180–1188.

Delbrück, M. (1970). A physicist's renewed look at biology: Twenty years later. *Science*, 168:1312–1315.

——. (1972). Some comments on the transduction of experience by the brain: Implications for our understanding of the relationship of mind to body. *Psychosom. Med.*, 34:355–375.

De Man, P. (1982). The resistance to theory. *Yale French Studies*, 63:3–20.

Derrida, J. (1967). *Of Grammatology*. G. Spivak (trans.). Baltimore: Johns Hopkins University Press (1976).

——. (1978). *Writing and Difference*. Chicago: University of Chicago Press.

——. (1981). *Dissemination*. Chicago: University of Chicago Press.

Devereaux, G. (1950). *Psychoanalysis and Anthropology: Culture, Personality and the Unconscious*. New York: International Universities Press.

——. (1956). Normal and abnormal: The key problem of psychiatric anthropology. In: *Basic Problems in Ethnopsychiatry*. Chicago: University of Chicago Press, 1980, pp. 3–72.

————. (1978). *Ethnopsychoanalysis: Psychoanalysis and Anthropology as Complementary Frames of Reference.* Berkeley: University of California Press.

Diamond, M. C. (1988). *Enriching Heredity: The Impact of the Environment on the Anatomy of the Brain.* New York: Free Press.

Dinnerstein, D. (1976). *The Mermaid and the Minotaur.* New York: Harper & Row.

Divale, W. (1976). Female status and cultural evolution: A study in ethnographic bias. *Behavioral Science Research,* 11:169–211.

Dodds, E. R. (1964). *The Greeks and the Irrational.* Los Angeles: University of California Press.

Doi, T. (1973). *The Anatomy of Dependence.* J. Bester (trans.). Tokyo: Kodansha International Press.

Dumont, L. (1970). *Homo Hierarchicus.* Chicago: University of Chicago Press.

Eisenberg, L. (1986). Mindlessness and brainlessness in psychiatry. *Brit. J. Psych.,* 148:497–508.

Ellman, S., and Moskowitz, M. (1980). An examination of some recent criticisms of psychoanalytic "metapsychology." *Psychoanal. Quart.,* 49:631–662.

Elshtain, J. (1995). *Democracy on Trial.* New York: Basic Books.

Ember, C. (1981). A cross-cultural perspective on sex differences. In: R. L. Munroe, R. H. Munroe, and B. Whiting (eds.), *Handbook of Cross-cultural Human Development.* New York: Garland, pp. 531–580.

Emde, R. (1983). The pre-representational self and its affective core. *Psychoanal. Study Child,* 38:165–192.

Engel, G. (1977). The need for a new medical model: A challenge for biomedicine. *Science,* 165:129–136.

————. (1980). The clinical application of the biopsychosocial model. *Amer. J. Psychiat.,* 137:535–544.

Epstein, M. (1990). Beyond the oceanic feeling: Psychoanalytic study of Buddhist meditation. *Internat. Review Psychoanalysis,* 17:159–166.

Erikson, E. (1968). *Identity, Youth, and Crisis.* New York: W. W. Norton.

————. (1950). *Childhood and Society.* New York: W. W. Norton (1963).

————. (1956). The problem of ego identity. *J. Am. Psychoanal. Assn.,* 4:56–121.

————. (1959). Identity and the life cycle. *Psychol. Issues,* Mgr. 1. New York: International Universities Press.

————. (1969). *Ghandi's Truth.* New York: W. W. Norton.

Fairbairn, W. R. D. (1940). Schizoid factors in the personality. In: *Psychoanalytic Studies of the Personality.* London: Routledge and Kegan Paul, (1952), pp. 3–27.

————. (1944). Endopsychic structure considered in terms of object-relationships. In: *Psychoanalytic Studies of the Personality.* London: Routledge and Kegan Paul (1952), pp. 82–136.

————. (1952). *Psychoanalytic Studies of the Personality.* London: Tavistock.

Fast, I. (1984). *Gender Identity: A Differentiation Model.* Hillsdale, N.J.: Analytic Press.

Federn, P. (1928). Narcissism in the structure of the ego. *Internat. J. Psycho-Anal.,* 9:401–419.

Feigenbaum, M. (1980). Universal behavior in nonlinear systems. *Los Alamos Science,* 1:4–27.

Ferenczi, S. (1913). Stages in the development of the sense of reality. In: S. Ferenczi, *First Contributions to Psychoanalysis*. E. Jones (trans.). London: Hogarth, pp. 213–239.

Ferguson, M. (1981). Progress and theory change: The two analyses of Mr. Z. *Ann. Psychoanal.*, 9:133.

Feyerabend, P. (1975). *Against Method*. Atlantic Highlands, N.J.: Humanities Press.

Flavell, J. (1963). *The Developmental Psychology of Jean Piaget*. Princeton, N.J.: Van Nostrand.

Flax, J. (1990). *Thinking Fragments: Psychoanalysis, Feminism, and Postmodernism in the Contemporary West*. Berkeley: University of California Press.

Foucault, M. (1973). *The Order of Things: An Archaeology of the Human Sciences*. New York: Vintage Books.

———. (1979). *Discipline and Punish: The Birth of the Prison*. New York: Random House.

———. (1980). *The History of Sexuality*. Vol. 1. *An Introduction*. New York: Random House.

Fraiberg, S. (1969). Libidinal object constancy and mental representation. *Psychoanal. Study Child*, 24:9–47.

Freeman, D. (1993). Precocious cognitive and visual individuation in early Japanese child development. Presentation at meeting of American Psychoanalytic Association in New York City, December 18.

Freud, S. (1887–1904). *The Complete Letters of Sigmund Freud to Wilhelm Fliess*. J. Masson (ed.). Cambridge, Mass.: Harvard University Press.

———. (1895). Project for a scientific psychology. *SE*, 1:295–387.

———. (1900). The interpretation of dreams. *SE*, 4 and 5.

———. (1901). The psychopathology of everyday life. *SE*, 6.

———. (1910). Leonardo da Vinci and a memory of his childhood. *SE*, 11:59–138.

———. (1911). Psycho-analytic notes on an autobiographical account of a case of paranoia (dementia paranoides). *SE*, 12:3–88.

———. (1913). Totem and taboo. *SE*, 13:1–161.

———. (1913b). On beginning the treatment. *SE*, 12:121–144.

———. (1914) On the history of the psychoanalytic movement. *SE*, 14:3–66.

———. (1914b). On narcissism. *SE*, 14:67–102.

———. (1914c). The Moses of Michelangelo. *SE*, 13:211–240.

———. (1915). The unconscious. *SE*, 14:166–215.

———. (1916). Introductory lectures on psycho-analysis. *SE*, 16.

———. (1920). Beyond the pleasure principle. *SE*, 18:3–64.

———. (1923). The ego and the id. *SE*, 19:3–66.

———. (1925). Some psychical consequences of the anatomical distinction between the sexes. *SE*, 19:248–258.

———. (1927). The future of an illusion. *SE*, 21:77–174.

———. (1930). Civilization and its discontents. *SE*, 21:57–146.

———. (1931). Female sexuality. *SE*, 21:223–246.

———. (1933). Why war? *SE*, 22:197–218.

———. (1937). Analysis terminable and interminable. *SE*, 23:211–253.

———. (1939). Moses and monotheism. *SE*, 23:7–137.

———. (1940). An Outline of Psychoanalysis. *SE*, 23:141–207.

Friedman, R. (1994). Homosexuality. *New Eng. J. Medicine*, 331:923–930.

Friedman, R., and Downey, J. (1993). Neurobiology and sexual orientation: Current relationships. *J. Neuropsychiatry Clin. Neuroscience*, 5:131–153.

Fromm, E. (1960). Psychoanalysis and Zen Buddhism. In: E. Fromm, D. Suzuki, and R. DeMartino, *Zen Buddhism and Psychoanalysis*. New York: Harper & Row.

Fuxe, K., Agnati, L., Harfstrand, A., Lintra, A., Aronsson, M., Zoli, M., and Gustafsson, J.-A. (1988). Principles for the hormone regulation of wiring transmission and volume transmission in the central nervous system. In: D. Ganten and D. Pfaff (eds.), *Neuroendocrinology of Mood*. Berlin: Springer-Verlag.

Garai, J., and Scheinfeld, A. (1968). Sex differences in mental and behavioral traits. *Genetic Psychology Monogr.*, 77:169–299.

Gedo, J. (1979). *Beyond Interpretation: Toward a Revised Theory for Psychoanalysis*. New York: International Universities Press.

———. (1984). *Psychoanalysis and Its Discontents*. New York: Guilford.

———. (1986). *Conceptual Issues in Psychoanalysis*. Hillsdale, N.J.: Analytic Press.

Gedo, J., and Goldberg, A. (1973). *Models of the Mind*. Chicago: University of Chicago Press.

Geertz, C. (1975). On the nature of anthropological understanding. *American Scientist*, 63:47–53.

———. (1979). From the native's point of view: On the nature of anthropological understanding. In: *Local Knowledge: Further Essays in Interpretive Anthropology*. New York: Basic Books, 1983.

Gehrie, M. (1978). The psychoanalytic study of social phenomena: A review essay. *Annals of Psychoanalysis*, 6:143–164.

Gergen, K. (1985). The social constructionist movement in modern psychology. *American Psychologist*, 40:266–275.

———. (1990). Social understanding and the inscription of self. In: J. Stigler, R. Shweder, and G. Herdt (eds.), *Cultural Psychology*. Cambridge: Cambridge University Press, pp. 569–606.

———. (1991). *The Saturated Self*. New York: Basic Books.

Gergen, K., and Davis, K. (1985). *The Social Construction of the Person*. New York: Springer-Verlag.

Gill, M. (1976). Metapsychology is not psychology. In: M. Gill and P. Holzman (eds.), *Psychology Versus Metapsychology: Essays in Memory of George Klein*. Psychol. Issues, Mgr. 36. New York: International Universities Press, pp. 71–105.

———. (1982). *Analysis of Transference*. New York: International Universities Press.

———. (1994). *Psychoanalysis in Transition*. Hillsdale, N.J.: Analytic Press.

Gilligan, C. (1982). *In a Different Voice: Psychological Theory and Women's Development*. Cambridge, Mass.: Harvard University Press.

Gleick, J. (1987). *Chaos: Making a New Science*. New York: Viking.

Gödel, K. (1962). *On Formally Undecidable Propositions in "Principia Mathematica" and Related Systems*. R. Braithewaite (ed.), B. Meltzer (trans.). New York: Basic Books (original publication, 1931).

Gorer, G. (1943). Themes in Japanese culture. *Transactions of the New York Academy of Sciences*, 5:105–124.

Gorski, R. (1991). Sexual differentiation of the endocrine brain and its control. In: M. Motta (ed.), *Brain Endocrinology*, 2nd ed. New York: Raven Press, pp. 71–104.

Gottesman, I., and Shields, J. (1982). *Schizophrenia: The Epigenetic Puzzle*. London: Cambridge University Press.

Goy, R., and Goldfoot, D. (1974). Experimental and hormonal factors influencing development of sexual behavior in the male rhesus monkey. In: F. Schmitt and F. Warden (eds.), *The Neurosciences: Third Study Program*. Cambridge, Mass.: MIT Press, pp. 571–581.

Greenberg, J., and Mitchell, S. (1983). *Object Relations in Psychoanalytic Theory*. Cambridge, Mass.: Harvard University Press.

Greenson, R. (1968). Dis-identifying from the mother: Its special importance for the boy. *Internat. J. Psycho-Anal.*, 49:370–374.

Grossman, L., (reporter). (1994). Contemporary theories of female sexuality: Clinical applications. *J. Am. Psychoanal. Assn.*, 42:233–241.

Grotstein, J. (1990). The "black hole" as the basic psychotic experience: Some newer psychoanalytic and neuroscience perspectives on psychosis. *J. Am. Acad. Psychoanal.*, 18:29–46.

Gruber, H., and Voneche, J. (1977). *The Essential Piaget*. New York: Basic Books.

Gur, R. C., Mozley, L., Mozley, D., Resnick, S., Karp, J., Alavi, A., Arnold, S., and Gur, R. E. (1995). Sex differences in regional cerebral glucose metabolism during a resting state. *Science*, 267:528–531.

Gyatso, T. (1984). *Kindness, Clarity, and Insight*. Ithaca, N.Y.: Snow Lion.

Haber, S. (1981). Social factors in evaluating the effects of biological manipulations on aggressive behavior in nonhuman primates. In: D. Hamburg and M. Trudeau (eds.), *Biobehavioral Aspects of Aggression*. New York: Alan R. Liss.

Habermas, J. (1970). A theory of communicative competence. In: H. Dreitzel, ed., *Recent Sociology. No. 2*. New York: Macmillan.

———. (1971). *Knowledge and Human Interests*. J. Shapiro (trans.). Boston: Beacon Press.

Hallowell, A. (1939). The recapitulation theory and culture. In: A. Hallowell (ed.), *Culture and Experience*. Philadelphia: University of Pennsylvania Press (1955), pp. 14–31.

Hamburg, D., and van Lawick-Goodall, J. (1974). Factors facilitating development of aggressive behavior in chimpanzees and humans. In: W. Hartrup and J. deWit (eds.), *Determinants and Origins of Aggressive behavior*. The Hague: Mouton, pp. 59–85.

Harre, R. (1981). Psychological variety. In: P. Heelas and A. Lock (eds.), *Indigenous Psychologies: The Anthropology of the Self*. London: Academic Press, pp. 79–103.

———. (1984). *Personal Being*. Cambridge, Mass.: Harvard University Press.

Hartmann, H. (1950). Comments on the psychoanalytic theory of the ego. *Psychoanal. Study Child*, 5:74–96.

Hayles, N. K. (1990). *Chaos Bound: Orderly Disorder in Contemporary Literature and Science*. Ithaca, N.Y.: Cornell University Press.

Heelas, P., and Lock, A. (eds.). (1981). *Indigenous Psychologies: The Anthropology of the Self*. Lancaster, Pa.: Academic Press.

Heidegger, M. (1962). *Being and Time*. J. MacQuarrie and E. Robison (trans.). New York: Harper & Row.

Heisenberg, W. (1958). *Physics and Philosophy: The Revolution in Modern Science*. New York: Harper & Brothers.

Herdt, G. (1990). Cross-cultural issues in the development of bisexuality and homosexuality. In: M. Perry (ed.), *Handbook of Sexology*. Vol. 7. *Childhood and Adolescent Sexology*. Amsterdam: Elsevier.

Ho, D. (1993). Relational orientation in Asian social psychology. In: J. Berry and U. Kim (eds.), *Indigenous Psychologies*. Newbury Park, Calif.: Sage, pp. 240–259.

Hoffman, I. (1983). The patient as interpreter of the analyst's experience. *Contemporary Psychoanalysis*, 19:389–422.

––––––. (1987). The value of uncertainty in psychoanalytic practice. (Discussion of paper by E. Witenberg.) *Contemporary Psychoanalysis*, 23:205–215.

––––––. (1991). Discussion: Toward a social-constructivist view of the psychoanalytic situation. (Discussion of papers by I Aron, A. Modell, and J. Greenberg.) *Psychoanalytic Dialogues*, 1:74–105.

Hofstede, G. (1983). National cultures revisited. *Behavior Science Research*, 18:285–305.

Holzman, P. (1987). Recent studies of psychophysiology in schizophrenia. *Schiz. Bull.*, 13:49–75.

Horney, K. (1933). The denial of the vagina: A contribution to the problem of the genital anxieties specific to women. In: *Feminine Psychology*. New York: W. W. Norton, 1967.

––––––. (1937). *The Neurotic Personality of Our Time*. New York: Norton.

––––––. (1939). Feminine psychology. In: *New Ways in Psychoanalysis*. New York: W. W. Norton.

––––––. (1967). *Feminine Psychology*. New York: Norton.

Hrdy, S. (1981) *The Woman That Never Was*. Cambridge, Mass.: Harvard University Press.

Hsieh, A., and Spence, J. (1981). Suicide and the family in pre-modern Chinese society. In: A. Kleinman and T. Lin (eds.), *Normal and Abnormal Behavior in Chinese Culture*. Dordrecht: D. Reidel.

Husserl, G. (1970). *The Crisis of European Sciences and Transcendental Phenomenology*. Evanston, Ill.: Northwestern University Press.

Hutt, C. (1972). Neuroendocrinological, behavioural, and intellectual aspects of sexual differentiation in human development. In: C. Ounsted and D. Taylor (eds.), *Gender Differences: Their Ontogeny and Significance*. Edinburgh: Churchill Livingstone, pp. 73–121.

Huxley, T. (1898). *Method and Results: Collected Essays*, vol. I. London: Macmillan.

Jacklin, C., Maccoby, E., and Doering, C. (1983). Neonatal sex steroid hormones and timidity in 6–18-month-old boys. *Dev. Psychobiol.*, 16:163–168.

Jackson, J. H. (1931–1932). *Selected Writings of John Hughlings Jackson*. J. Taylor, G. Holmes, and F. Walshe, eds. New York: Basic Books, 1958.

Jacobson, E. (1964). *The Self and the Object World*: New York: International Universities Press.

Johnson, A. (1992). Psychoanalysis and materialism: Do they mix? In: D. Spain (ed.), *Psychoanalytic Anthropology after Freud*. New York: Psyche, pp. 225–249.

Johnson, F. (1993). *Dependency and Japanese Socialization: Psychoanalytic and Anthropological Investigations into Amae*. New York: New York University Press.

Jones, E. (1923). Anxiety and birth. *Internat. J. Psycho-Anal.*, 4:120.

———. (1953). *The Life and Work of Sigmund Freud.* New York: Basic Books.

Joselyn, W. (1973). Androgen-induced social dominance in infant female rhesus monkeys. *J. Child Psychol. and Psychiat.*, 14:137–145.

Jung, C. (1964). *Man and His Symbols.* Garden City, N.Y.: Doubleday.

Kakar, S. (1971). The theme of authority in social relations in India. *Journal of Social Psychology*, 84:93–101.

———. (1979). *The Inner World: A Psychoanalytic Study of Childhood and Society in India.* Delhi and London: Oxford University Press.

———. (1982). Reflections on psychoanalysis, Indian culture and mysticism. *J. Indian Philosophy*, 10:269–297.

———. (1985). Psychoanalysis and non-western cultures. *Internat. Rev. Psychoanal.*, 12:441–448.

———. (1990). Stories from Indian psychoanalysis: Context and text. In: J. Stigler, R. Shweder, and G. Herdt (eds.), *Cultural Psychology: Essays on Comparative Human Development.* Cambridge: Cambridge University Press.

Kandel, E. (1978). *A Cell Biological Approach to Learning.* Baltimore: Society for Neuroscience.

———. (1979). Psychotherapy and the single synapse. *New Eng. J. Med.*, 301:1029–1037.

Kant, I. (1781). *Critique of Pure Reason.* J. Meiklejohn (trans.). London: J. M. Dent and Sons, Ltd. (1934).

Kardiner, A. (1939). *The Individual and His Society: The Psychodynamics of Primitive Social Organization.* New York: Columbia University Press.

———. (1945). *The Psychological Frontiers of Society.* New York: Columbia University Press.

Keller, E. F. (1985). *Reflections on Gender and Science.* New Haven: Yale University Press.

Kendler, K. (1992). The genetics of schizophrenia: An overview. In: S. Steinhauer, J. Gruzelier, and J. Zubin (eds.), *Neuropsychology, Psychophysiology and Information Processing. Handbook of Schizophrenia*, vol. 5. New York: Elsevier Science, pp. 437–462.

Kernberg, O. (1975). *Borderline Conditions and Pathological Narcissism.* New York: Jason Aronson.

Kestenberg, J. (1968). Outside and inside, male and female. *J. Am. Psychoanal. Assn.*, 16:457–520.

Kim, U., and Berry, J. (1993). *Indigenous Psychologies.* Newbury Park, Calif: Sage.

King, P., and Steiner, R. (1991). *The Freud-Klein Controversies:1941–1945.* London: Routledge, Chapman and Hall.

Kirschner, S. (1992). Anglo-American values in post-Freudian psychoanalysis. In: D. Spain (ed.), *Psychoanalytic Anthropology after Freud.* New York: Psyche, pp. 162–197.

Kitayama, O. (1994). Japanese tragic legends and a maternal prohibition. Paper presented to study group of the American Psychoanalytic Association, May 1994.

Klein, G. (1976). *Psychoanalytic Theory.* New York: International Universities Press.

Klein, M. (1935). A contribution to the psychogenesis of manic-depressive states. In: *Love, Guilt and Reparation and Other Works.* London: The Hogarth Press and the Institute for Psycho-analysis (1975), pp. 262–289.

————. (1940). Mourning and its relation to manic-depressive states. In: *Love, Guilt and Reparation and Other Works, 1921–1945*. London: The Hogarth Press and the Institute for Psycho-analysis (1975), pp. 344–369.

————. (1946). Notes on some schizoid mechanisms. In: *Envy and Gratitude and Other Works, 1946–1963*. London: The Hogarth Press and the Institute for Psycho-analysis (1975), pp. 1–24.

Kluckhohn, C. (1953). Universal categories of culture. In: A. Kroeber (ed.), *Anthropology Today*. Chicago: University of Chicago Press, pp. 507–524.

Knowles, D. (1962). *The Evolution of Medieval Thought*. London: Longmans, Green.

Koestler, A., and Smythies, J. (1969). *Beyond Reductionism: New Perspectives in the Life Sciences*. New York: Macmillan.

Kohlberg, L. (1969). Stage and sequence: The cognitive-developmental approach to socialization. In: D. Goslin (ed.), *Handbook of Socialization Theory and Research*. Chicago: Rand McNally, pp. 347–480.

————. (1981). *Essays on Moral Development*, Vol. 1, *The Philosophy of Moral Development: Moral Stages and the Idea of Justice*. San Francisco: Harper & Row.

Kohut, H. (1971). *The Analysis of the Self*. New York: International Universities Press.

————. (1977). *The Restoration of the Self*. New York: International Universities Press.

————. (1979). The two analyses of Mr. Z. *Internat. J. Psycho-Anal.*, 60:3–27.

Kolb, L. (1987). A neuropsychological hypothesis explaining posttraumatic stress disorders. *Am. J. Psychiat.*, 144:989–995.

Kopala, L., and Clark, C. (1990). Implications of olfactory agnosia for understanding sex differences in schizophrenia. *Schiz. Bull.*, 16:255–261.

Korner, A. (1974). Methodological considerations in studying sex differences in the behavioral functioning of newborns. In: R. Friedman, R. Richart, and R. Vande Wiele (eds.), *Sex Differences in Behavior*. New York: John Wiley and Sons, pp. 197–208.

Kraepelin, E. (1896). *Dementia Praecox and Paraphrenia*. R. M. Barclay (trans.). Edinburgh: E. and S. Livingstone. New York: R. E. Krieger, 1919.

Kringlen, E. (1987). Contributions of genetic studies on schizophrenia. In: H. Hafner, W. Gattaz, and W. Janzarik (eds.), *Search for the Causes of Schizophrenia*. Berlin: Springer-Verlag. pp, 123–142.

Kroeber, A. (1920). Totem and taboo: An ethnologic psychoanalysis. *American Anthropologist*, 22:48–55.

Kuhn, T. (1962). *The Structure of Scientific Revolutions*. Chicago: University of Chicago Press (1970).

Lannoy, R. (1971). *The Speaking Tree: A Study of Indian Culture and Society*. London: Oxford University Press.

LaPlanche, J., and Pontalis, J. (1973). *The Language of Psychoanalysis*. D. Nicholson-Smith (trans.). New York: W. W. Norton.

Lasch, C. (1979). *The Culture of Narcissism: American Life in an Age of Diminishing Expectations*. New York: W. W. Norton.

————. (1995). *The Revolt of the Elites and the Betrayal of Democracy*. New York: W. W. Norton.

Lebra, T. (1976). *Japanese Patterns of Behavior*. Honolulu: University of Hawaii Press.

Leong, F. (1986). Counselling and psychotherapy with Asian-Americans: Review of the literature. J. Counselling Psychol., 33:1996–2006.

LeVay, S. (1991). A difference in hypothalamic structure between heterosexual and homosexual men. Science, 253:1034–1037.

Levenson, E. (1985). The interpersonal (Sullivanian) model. In: A. Rothstein (ed.), Models of the Mind. New York: International Universities Press, pp. 49–67.

———. (1991). The Purloined Self: Interpersonal Perspectives in Psychoanalysis. New York: William Alanson White Institute.

Leventhal, B., and Brodie, K. (1981). The pharmacology of violence. In: R. Plutchik and H. Kellerman (eds.), Emotion: Theory, Research, and Experience. Vol. 3: Biological Foundations of Emotion. Orlando, Fla.: Academic Press, pp. 85–106.

Lévi-Strauss, C. (1949). The Elementary Structures of Kinship. J. von Sturmer (trans.). Boston: Beacon Press, 1969.

———. (1963). Structural Anthropology. New York: Basic Books.

———. (1966). The Savage Mind. Chicago: University of Chicago Press.

LeVine, R. (1973). Culture, Behavior and Personality. Chicago: Aldine.

———. (1981). Psychoanalytic theory and the comparative study of human development. In: R. L. Munroe, R. H. Munroe, and B. Whiting (eds.), Handbook of Cross-cultural Human Development. New York: Garland, pp. 63–72.

———. (1990). Infant environments in psychoanalysis: A cross-cultural view. In: J. Stigler, R. Shweder, and G. Herdt (eds.), Cultural Psychology. Cambridge: Cambridge University Press, pp. 454–474..

Levy, R. (1973). Tahitians: Mind and Experience in the Society Islands. Chicago: University of Chicago Press.

Levy-Bruhl, L. (1965). The "Soul" of the Primitive. London: George Allen and Unwin (originally published 1928).

Lewin, B. (1950). The Psychoanalysis of Elation. New York: W. W. Norton.

Lewis, M., and Brooks-Gunn, J. (1979). Social Cognition and the Acquisition of Self. New York: Plenum.

Lewis, M., and Weinraub, M. (1974). Sex of parent x sex of child: Socioemotional development. In: R. Friedman, R. Richart, and R. Vande Wiele (eds.), Sex Differences in Behavior. New York: John Wiley and Sons, pp. 165–189.

Liberman, R., Barringer, D. M., Marder, S., Dawson, M., Nuechterlein, K., and Doane, J. (1984). The nature and problem of schizophrenia. In: A. Bellack, ed., Schizophrenia: Treatment, Management, and Rehabilitation. Orlando, Fla.: Grune and Stratton, pp. 1–34.

Lichtenstein, H. (1961). Identity and sexuality. J. Am. Psychoanal. Assn., 9:179–260.

———. (1963). The dilemma of human identity. J. Am. Psychoanal. Assn., 11:173–223.

Linton, R. (1936). The Study of Man. New York: Appleton-Century-Crofts.

———. (1945). The Cultural Background of Personality. New York: Appleton-Century-Crofts.

Loevinger, J. (1976). Ego Development: Conceptions and Theories. San Francisco: Jossey-Bass.

———. (1987). Paradigms of Personality. New York: W. H. Freeman.

Lorenz, E. (1963). Deterministic nonperiodic flow. J. Atmospheric Sciences, 20:130–141.

Lowe, D. (1982). History of Bourgeois Perception. Chicago: University of Chicago Press.

Luria, A. (1976). *Cognitive Development: Its Cultural and Social Foundations.* Cambridge, Mass.: Harvard University Press.

———. (1979). *The Making of Mind.* Cambridge, Mass.: Harvard University Press.

Lykes, M. (1985). Gender and individualistic vs. collectivistic bases for notions about the self. *J. Personality,* 53:356–383.

Lynn, D. (1969). *Parental and Sex-Role Identification: A Theoretical Formulation.* Berkeley, Calif.: McCutchan.

MacArthur, R. (1967). Sex differences in field dependence for the Eskimo: Replication of Berry's finding. *International Journal of Psychology,* 2:139–140.

Maccoby, E. (1990). Gender and relationships: A developmental account. *American Psychologist,* 45:513–520.

Maccoby, E., and Jacklin, C. (1974). *The Psychology of Sex Differences.* Stanford, Calif.: Stanford University Press.

———. (1980). Sex differences in aggression: A rejoinder and reprise. *Child Dev.,* 51:964–980.

MacIntyre, A. (1984). *After Virtue.* Notre Dame, Ind.: University of Notre Dame Press.

———. (1988). *Whose Justice? Which Rationality?* Notre Dame, Ind.: University of Notre Dame Press.

MacLean, P. (1990). *The Triune Brain in Evolution.* New York: Plenum Press.

MacLusky, N., and Naftolin, F. (1981). Sexual differentiation of the central nervous system. *Science,* 211:1294–1302.

Mahler, M., Pine, F., and Bergmann, A. (1975). *The Psychological Birth of the Human Infant.* New York: Basic Books.

Malinowski, B. (1927). *Sex and Repression in Savage Society.* New York: Harcourt and Brace.

———. (1928). *The Sexual Life of Savages.* New York: Harcourt, Brace and World.

Mandelbrot, B. (1967). How long is the coast of Britain? Statistical self-similarity and fractional dimension. *Science,* 155:636–638.

———. (1977). *The Fractal Geometry of Nature.* New York: W. H. Freeman.

Marsella, A., and Snyder, K. (1981). Stress, social supports, and schizophrenic disorders: Toward an interactional model. *Schiz. Bull.,* 7:152–163.

Marty, P. and de M'Uzan, M. (1963). La pensée operatoire. *Revue Français de psychoanalyse,* 27 (suppl.), 1345–1356.

Marty, P., de M'Uzan, M., and David, C. (1963). *L'Investigation Psychosomatique.* Paris: Presses Universitaires de France.

Mayer, E. (1985). Everybody must be just like me! Observations on female castration anxiety. *Internat. J. Psycho-Anal.,* 66:331–347.

Mazur, A. (1976). Effects of testosterone on status in primate groups. *Folia Primatologica,* 26:214–226.

McCarley, R., Faux, S., Shenton, M., Nestor, P., and Adams, J. (1991). Event-related potentials in schizophrenia: Their biological and clinical correlates and a new model of schizophrenic pathophysiology. *Schiz. Res.,* 4:209–231.

McClintock, M. (1971). Menstrual synchrony and suppression. *Nature,* 229:244–245.

McDougall, J. (1985). *Theatres of the Mind: Illusion and Truth on the Psychoanalytic Stage.* New York: Basic Books.

McEwen, B. (1983). Gonadal steroid influences on brain development and sexual differentiation. In: R. Greep (ed.), *Reproductive Physiology IV, International Review of Physiology*, vol. 27. Baltimore: University Park Press, pp. 99–145.

———. (1991). Sex differences in the brain: What they are and how they arise. In: M. Notman and C. Nadelson (eds.), *Women and Men*. Washington, D.C.: American Psychiatric Press, pp. 35–40.

Mead, M. (1935). *Sex and Temperament in Three Primitive Societies*. New York: William Morrow.

———. (1939). *From the South Seas*. New York: William Morrow.

Mead, M. (1953). National character. In: A. Kroeber (ed.), *Anthropology Today*. Chicago: University of Chicago Press, pp. 642–668.

Meaney, M. (1989). The sexual differentiation of social play. *Psychiat. Devel.*, 3:247–261.

Meaney, M., Dodge, A., and Beatty, W. (1981). Sex dependent effects of amygdaloid lesions on the social play of prepubertal rats. *Physiology of Behavior*, 26:467–472.

Meaney, M., and McEwen, B. (1986). Testosterone implants into the amygdala during the neonatal period masculinize the social play of juvenile female rats. *Brain Res.*, 398:324–328.

Meaney, M., Stewart, J., Poulin, P., et al. (1983). Sexual differentiation of social play in rat pups is mediated by the neonatal androgen receptor system. *Neuroendocrinology*, 37:85–90.

Meyer, A. (1957). *Psychobiology: A Science of Man*. Springfield, Ill: Charles C. Thomas.

Michels, R. (1990). Psychoanalysis: The second century. *Harvard Mental Health Letter*. 7 (6): 5–7.

Miller, J. B. (1976). *Toward a New Psychology of Women*. Boston: Beacon Press.

Miller, J. G. (1984). Culture and the development of everyday social explanation. *J. Personality and Social Psychology*, 46:961–978.

Mitchell, J. (1957). The Sanskrit drama Shakumtala and the Oedipus Complex. *American Imago*, 14:389–405.

Mitchell, S. (1993). Wishes, needs, and interpersonal negotiations. In: *Hope and Dread in Psychoanalysis*. New York: Basic Books, pp. 175–201.

Money, J., and Ehrhardt, A. (1972). *Man and Woman, Boy and Girl*. Baltimore: Johns Hopkins University Press.

Moore, B. E., and Fine, B. D. (eds.). (1990). *Psychoanalytic Terms and Concepts*. New Haven: Yale University Press.

Moran, M. (1991). Chaos and psychoanalysis: the fluidic nature of mind. *Internat. Rev. Psychoanal.*, 18:211–221.

Morris, C. (1972). *The Discovery of the Individual, 1050–1200*. London: Camelot Press.

Moss, H. (1974). Early sex differences and mother-infant interaction. In: R. Friedman, R. Richart, and R. Vande Wiele (eds.), *Sex Differences in Behavior*. New York: John Wiley and Sons, pp. 149–163.

Mumford, L. (1956). *The Transformation of Man*. New York: Harper and Row.

Nakane, C. (1970). *Japanese Society*. Berkeley: University of California Press.

Neki, J. (1976). An examination of the cultural relativism of dependence as a dynamic of social and therapeutic relationships: I. Basic considerations. *British J. Medical Psychology*, 49:1–10.

Nisbet, R. (1969). *Social Change and History*. London: Oxford University Press.

Notman, M., and Nadelson, C. (1991). A review of gender differences in brain and behavior. In: M. Notman and C. Nadelson (eds.), *Women and Men*. Washington, D.C.: American Psychiatric Press, pp. 23–34.

Noy, P. (1977). Metapsychology as a multimodal system. *Internat. Rev. Psycho-Anal.*, 4:1–12.

Nozick, R. (1981). *Philosophical Explanations*. Cambridge, Mass.: Harvard University Press.

Obeyesekere, G. (1990). *The Work of Culture*. Chicago: University of Chicago Press.

Ogden, T. (1989). *The Primitive Edge of Experience*. New York: Jason Aronson.

Okimoto, J., and Settlage, C. (1993). The impact of Japanese separation-individuation experience and later life-cycle stages. *Panel of the American Academy of Psychoanalysis*, San Francisco, May 23rd.

Okonogi, K. (1979). The Ajase complex of the Japanese. *Japan Echo*, 6 (1): 104–118.

Ornitz, E., and Pynoos, R. (1989). Startle modulation in children with posttraumatic stress disorder. *Am. J. Psychiat.*, 146:866–870.

Osgood, C. (1964). Semantic differential technique in the comparative study of cultures. *American Anthropologist*, 66:171–200.

Pardes, H., Kaufman, C., Pincus, H., and West, A. (1989). Genetics and psychiatry: Past discoveries, current dilemmas, and future directions. *Am. J. Psychiat.*, 146:435–443.

Parke, R., and Slaby, R. (1983). The development of aggression. In: P. Mussen (ed.), *Handbook of Child Psychology*, vol. 4. New York: Wiley, pp. 547–642.

Pavenstedt, E. (1965). Observations in Five Japanese Homes. *J. Am. Acad. Child Psychiatry*, 4:413–425.

Perls, F., Hefferune, R., and Goodman, P. (1985). *Gestalt Therapy: Excitement and Growth in the Human Personality*. Bantam, 1977.

Person, E. (1980). Sexuality as the mainstay of identity. *Signs*, 5:605–630.

Person, E., and Ovesey, L. (1983). Psychoanalytic theories of gender identity. *J. Am. Acad. Psychoanal.*, 203:203–226.

Peterfreund, E. (1978). Some critical comments on psychoanalytic conceptualizations of infancy. *Internat. J. Psycho-Anal.*, 61:477–491.

Phoenix, C., Goy, R., Gerall, A., and Young, W. (1959). Organizing action of prenatally administered testosterone propionate on the tissues mediating mating behavior in the female guinea pig. *Endocrinology*, 65:369–382.

Piers, G., and Singer, M. (1953). *Shame and Guilt*. New York: W. W. Norton.

Popp, C., and Taketomo, Y. (1993). The application of core conflictual relationship theme method to Japanese psychoanalytic psychotherapy. *J. Am. Acad. Psychoanal.*, 21:229–252.

Popper, K. (1959). *The Logic of Scientific Discovery*. New York: Basic Books.

———. (1987). Normal science and its dangers. In: I. Lakatos and A. Musgrave (eds.), *Criticism and the Growth of Knowledge*. Cambridge: Cambridge University Press, pp. 51–58.

Prigogine, I., and Stengers, I. (1984). *Order Out of Chaos: Man's New Dialogue with Nature*. New York: Bantam.

Racker, H. (1957). The meanings and uses of countertransference. *Psychoanal. Quart.*, 26:303–357.

Ramanujan, B. (1992). Implications of some psychoanalytic concepts in the Indian context. In: D. Spain (ed.), *Psychoanalytic Anthropology after Freud*. New York: Psyche, pp. 121–135.

Rappaport, D. (1960). *The Structure of Psychoanalytic Theory: A Systematizing Attempt*. New York: International Universities Press.

Read, K. (1955). Morality and the concept of the person among the Gahuku-Gama. *Oceania*, 25:232–282.

Reich, W. (1932). Der masochistiche charakter. *Internat. Zeitschrift f. Psychoanalyse*, 18:303–351.

———. (1933). *Character Analysis*. New York: Farrar, Straus and Giroux, 1972.

———. (1936). *The Sexual Revolution*. New York: Farrar, Straus and Giroux, 1974.

———. (1953). *The Emotional Plague of Mankind: The Murder of Christ*. New York: Farrar, Straus and Giroux.

———. (1967). *Reich Speaks of Freud*. New York: Farrar, Straus and Giroux.

Reichard, S. (1956). A re-examination of "Studies in Hysteria." *Psychoanal. Quart.*, 25:155–177.

Restak, R. (1979). *The Brain: The Last Frontier*. New York: Doubleday.

Ricoeur, P. (1970). *Freud and Philosophy*. New Haven: Yale University Press.

———. (1981). *Hermeneutics and the Human Sciences*. J. Thompson (trans.). New York: Cambridge University Press.

Robbins, M. (1980). Current controversy in object relations theory as outgrowth of a schism between Klein and Fairbairn. *Internat. J. Psycho-Anal.*, 61:477–492.

———. (1981). The symbiosis concept and the commencement of normal and pathological ego functioning and object relations: II. Developments subsequent to infancy and pathological processes. *Internat. Rev. Psycho-Anal.*, 8:379–391.

———. (1982). Narcissistic personality as a symbiotic character disorder. *Internat. J. Psycho-Anal.*, 63:457–474.

———. (1983). Toward a new mind model for the primitive personalities. *Internat. J. Psycho-Anal.*, 64:127–148.

———. (1988). The adaptive significance of destructiveness in primitive personalities. *J. Am. Psychoanal. Assn.*, 36:627–652.

———. (1989). Primitive personality organization as an interpersonally adaptive modification of cognition and affect. *Internat. J. Psycho-Anal.*, 70:443–457.

———. (1992a). Psychoanalytic and biological approaches to mental illness: schizophrenia. *J. Am. Psychoanal. Assn.*, 40:425–454.

———. (1992b). A Fairbairnian object-relations perspective on self-psychology. *Am. J. Psychoanal.*, 52:247–261.

———. (1993a). *Experiences of Schizophrenia: An Integration of the Personal, Scientific and Therapeutic*. New York: Guilford.

———. (1993b). The psychopathological spectrum and the hierarchical model. In: J. Gedo and A. Wilson (eds.), *Hierarchical Conceptions in Psychoanalysis*. New York: Guilford, pp. 284–308.

Roheim, G. (1945). The Eternal Ones of the Dream: A Psychoanalytic Interpretation of Australian Myth and Ritual. New York: International Universities Press.

———. (1950). Psychoanalysis and Anthropology: Culture, Personality, and the Unconscious. New York: International Universities Press.

Rohlen, T. (1974). For Harmony and Strength: Japanese White-Collar Organization in Anthropological Perspective. Berkeley: University of California Press.

Roiphe, H., and Galenson, E. (1981). Infantile Origins of Sexual Identity. New York: International Universities Press.

Roland, A. (1980). Psychoanalytic perspectives on personality development in India. Internat. Rev. Psycho-Anal., 7:73–87.

———. (1982). Toward a psychoanalytical psychology of hierarchical relationships in Hindu India. Ethos, 10:232–253.

———. (1988). In Search of Self in India and Japan: Toward a Cross-Cultural Psychology. Princeton, N.J.: Princeton University Press.

Rose, R., Haladay, J., and Bernstein, J. (1971). Plasma testosterone, dominance rank, and aggressive behavior in rhesus monkeys. Nature, 231:366.

Russell, B. (1945). A History of Western Philosophy. New York: Simon and Schuster.

Sampson, E. (1977). Psychology and the American ideal. J. Personality Social Psychology, 35:767–782.

———. (1985). The decentralization of identity: Toward a revised concept of personal and social order. American Psychologist, 40:1203–1211.

———. (1988). The debate on individualism: Indigenous psychologies of the individual and their role in personal and societal functioning. American Psychologist, 43:15–22.

———. (1989). The challenge of social change for psychology: Globalization and psychology's theory of the person. American Psychologist, 44:914–921.

Sandel, M. (1982). Liberalism and the Limits of Justice. Cambridge: Cambridge University Press.

Sandler, J., with Freud, A. (1983). Discussions in the Hampstead Index of The Ego and The Mechanisms of Defense. J. Am. Psychoanal. Assn., 31 (suppl.): 19–146.

Schafer, R. (1976). A New Language for Psychoanalysis. New Haven: Yale University Press.

Schur, M. (1972). Freud: Living and Dying. New York: International Universities Press.

Schwartz, A. (1988). Reification revisited: Some neurobiologically filtered views of psychic structure and conflicts. J. Am. Psychoanal. Assn., 36 (suppl.): 359–385.

Seeman, M., and Lang, M. (1990). The role of estrogens in schizophrenia gender differences. Schiz. Bull., 16:185–194.

Selby, H. (1974). Zapotec Deviance. Austin: University of Texas Press.

———. (1975). Semantics and causality in the study of deviance. In: M. Sanches and B. G. Blount (eds.), Sociocultural Dimensions of Language. New York: Academic Press.

Selman, R., and Jacquette, D. (1977). Stability and oscillation in interpersonal awareness: A clinical-developmental analysis. Nebraska Symposium on Motivation, 25:261–304.

Selye, H. (1950). The Physiology and Pathology of Exposure to Systemic Stress. Montreal: Acta.

———. (1956). The Stress of Life. New York: McGraw-Hill.

Shapiro, T. (1993). A view from the bridge. J. Am. Psychoanal. Assn., 41:921–928.

Sharaf, M. (1971). Further remarks of Reich: Summer and autumn. J. Orgonomy, 5:101–106.

———. (1983). Fury on Earth. New York: St. Martin's Press/Marek.

Shaw, R. (1981). Strange attractors, chaotic behavior, and information flow. Zeitschrift für Naturforschung, 36A:79–112.

Shaywitz, B., Shaywitz, S., Pugh, K., Constable, R. T., Skudlarski, P., et al. (1995). Sex differences in the functional organization of the brain for language. Nature, 373:607–609.

Sherwin, B. (1988). Affective changes with estrogen and androgen replacement therapy in surgically menopausal women. J. Affective Dis., 14:177–187.

Shweder, R. (1984). Anthropology's romantic rebellion against the enlightenment: Or, there's more to thinking than reason and evidence. In: R. Shweder and R. LeVine (eds.), Culture Theory: Essays on Mind, Self and Emotion. Cambridge: Cambridge University Press, 27–66.

———. (1990). Cultural psychology—what is it? In: J. Stigler, R. Shweder, and G. Herdt (eds.), Cultural Psychology. Cambridge: Cambridge University Press, pp. 1–43.

———. (1991). Thinking Through Cultures. Cambridge, Mass.: Harvard University Press.

Shweder, R., and Bourne, E. (1982). Does the concept of the person vary cross-culturally? In: A. Marsella and G. White (eds.), Cultural Concepts of Mental Health and Therapy. Boston: Reidel, pp. 97–137.

Sifneos, P. (1967). Clinical observations on some patients suffering from a variety of psychosomatic diseases. Acta Medica Psychosomatica, Proceedings of the Seventh European Conference on Psychosomatic Research. Basel: S. Karger, pp. 452–458.

Silvan, M. (1981). Reply to Alan Roland's paper "Psychoanalytic perspectives on personality development in India." Internat. Rev. Psycho-Anal., 8:93–99.

Simon, B. (1978). Mind and Madness in Ancient Greece: The Classical Roots of Modern Psychiatry. Ithaca, N.Y.: Cornell University Press.

Snell, B. (1982). The Discovery of Mind. New York: Dover.

Socarides, C. (1978). Homosexuality. New York: Jason Aronson.

Spain, D. (ed.). (1992). Psychoanalytic Anthropology after Freud. New York: Psyche.

Spelke, E., Zelazo, P., Kagan, J., and Kotelchuck, M. (1973). Developmental Psychology, 9:83–90.

Spence, D. (1982). Narrative Truth and Historical Truth. New York: W. W. Norton.

Spence, J. (1985). Achievement American style: The rewards and costs of individualism. American Psychologist, 40:1285–1295.

Spencer, M. (1984). Black children's race awareness, racial attitudes, and self-concept: A reinterpretation. Journal of Child Psychology and Psychiatry and Allied Disciplines, 25:433–441.

Sperry, R. W. (1969). A modified concept of consciousness. Psychol. Rev., 76:532–536.

Spiegal, L. (1959). The self, the sense of self, and perception. Psychoanal. Study Child, 14:81–109.

Spieler, S. (1986). The gendered self: A lost maternal legacy. In: J. Alpert (ed.), Psychoanalysis and Women: Contemporary Appraisals. Hillsdale, N.J.: Analytic Press, pp. 33–56.

Spiro, M. (1965). *Children of the Kibbutz.* New York: Schocken Books.

———. (1982). *Oedipus in the Trobriands.* Chicago: University of Chicago Press.

———. (1984). Reflections on cultural determinism. In: R. Shweder and R. LeVine (eds.), *Culture Theory: Essays on Mind, Self, and Emotion.* Cambridge: Cambridge University Press, pp. 323–346.

———. (1986). Cultural relativism and the future of anthropology. *Cultural Anthropology,* 1:259–286.

Spruiell, Van (1993). Deterministic chaos and the sciences of complexity: Psychoanalysis in the midst of a scientific revolution. *J. Am. Psychoanal. Assn.,* 41:3–44.

Stern, D. (1983). The early development of schemas of self, of other, and of various experiences of "self with other." In: J. Lichtenberg and S. Kaplan (eds.), *Reflections on Self Psychology.* Hillsdale, N.J.: Analytic Press.

———. (1985). *The Interpersonal World of the Infant: A View from Psychoanalysis and Developmental Psychology.* New York: Basic Books.

Stevens, J. (1982). Neuropathology of schizophrenia. *Arch. Gen. Psychiatry,* 39:1131–1139.

Stewart, I. (1990). *Does God Play Dice? The Mathematics of Chaos.* Cambridge, Mass.: Basil Blackwell.

Stoller, R. (1964). A contribution to the study of gender identity. *Internat. J. Psycho-Anal.,* 45:220–226.

———. (1968). *Sex and Gender.* New York: Jason Aronson.

———. (1968). The sense of femaleness. *Psychoanal. Quart.,* 37:42–55.

———. (1976). Primary femininity. *J. Am. Psychoanal. Assn.,* 24 (suppl.): 59–78.

Stolorow, R., and Atwood, G. (1992). *Contexts of Being.* Hillsdale, N.J.: Analytic Press.

Stolorow, R., Atwood, G., and Ross, J. (1978). The representational world in psychoanalytic therapy. *Internat. Rev. Psycho-Anal.,* 5:247–256.

Sullivan, H. S. (1953). *The Interpersonal Theory of Psychology.* New York: Norton.

Surya, N. (1969). Ego structure in the Hindu joint family: Some considerations. In: W. Caudill and T. Lin (eds.), *Mental Health Research in Asia and the Pacific.* Honolulu: East-West Center Press.

Suzuki, D. (1960). Lectures on Zen Buddhism. In: E. Fromm, D. Suzuki, and R. DeMartino (eds.), *Zen Buddhism and Psychoanalysis.* New York: Harper and Row, pp. 1–76.

———. (1978). *The Lankavatara Sutra.* Boulder, Colo.: Prajna Press.

Swaab, D., and Fliers, E. (1985). A sexually dimorphic nucleus in the human brain. *Science,* 228:1112–1115.

Swaab, D., and Hofman, M. (1990). An enlarged suprachiasmatic nucleus in homosexual men. *Brain Res.,* 537:141–148.

Taketomo, Y. (1986). Toward the discovery of self: A transcultural perspective. *J. Am. Acad. Psychoanal.,* 14:69–84.

Tamminga, A., Thaku, G., Buchanan, R., Kirkpatrick, B., Alphs, L., Chase, N., and Carpenter, W. (1992). Limbic system abnormalities identified in schizophrenia using positron emission tomography with fluorodeoxyglucose and neocortical alterations with deficit syndrome. *Arch. Gen. Psychiatry,* 49:522–530.

Tannen, D. (1990). *You Just Don't Understand: Men and Women in Conversation*. New York: William Morrow.

Tanner, J., and Inhelder, B. (eds.). (1956). *Discussions on Child Development*, vols. 1 and 4. New York: International Universities Press.

Tausk, O. (1919). On the origin of the "influencing machine" in schizophrenia. *Psychoanal. Quart.* (1933), 2:519–556.

Taylor, C. (1988). The moral topography of the self. In: S. Messer, L. Sass, and R. Woolfolk (eds.), *Hermeneutics and Psychological Theory: Interpretive Perspectives on Personality, Psychotherapy, and Psychopathology*. New Brunswick, N.J.: Rutgers University Press, pp. 299–320.

Thompson, C. (1943). Penis envy in women. *Psychiatry*, 6:123–125.

———. (1950). Some effects of the derogatory attitude towards female sexuality. *Psychiatry*, 13:349–354.

Torrey, E. F. (1992). Are we overestimating the genetic contribution to schizophrenia? *Schiz. Bull.*, 18:159–170.

Toulmin, S. (1970). Reasons and causes. In: R. Borger and F. Cioffi (eds.), *Explanation in the Behavioral Sciences*. Cambridge: Cambridge University Press.

Trilling, L. (1971). *Sincerity and Authenticity*. Cambridge, Mass.: Harvard University Press.

Trimble, J. (1991). Ethnic specification, validation prospects, and the future of drug use research. *Internat. J. Addictions*, 25 (2A): 19–170.

Tsui, P., and Schultz, G. (1985). Failure of rapport: Why psychotherapeutic engagement fails in the treatment of Asian clients. *Am. J. Orthopsychiat.*, 55:561–569.

Tuan, Yi-Fu (1982). *Segmented Worlds and Self*. Minneapolis: University of Minnesota Press.

Turiel, E., Edwards, C., and Kohlberg, L. (1978). Moral development in Turkish children, adolescents, and young adults. *Journal of Cross Cultural Psychology*, 9:75–86.

Tyler, L. (1956). *The Psychology of Human Differences*. New York: Appleton-Century-Crofts.

Tylor, E. (1871). *Primitive Cultures*. New York: Harper Torchbooks (1958).

Tyson, P. (1994). Bedrock and beyond: An examination of the clinical utility of contemporary theories of female psychology. *J. Am. Psychoanal. Assn.*, 42:447–467.

Vaillant, G. (1977). *Adaptation to Life*. Boston: Little, Brown.

———. (1993). *The Wisdom of the Ego*. Cambridge, Mass.: Harvard University Press.

Van Praag, H. (1992). Introduction. In: J.-P. Lindenmayer and S. Kay (eds.), *New Biological Vistas in Schizophrenia: Clinical and Experimental Psychiatry Monograph 6*. New York: Brunner-Mazel, pp. xi–xiii.

Vital-Durand, F. (1975). Toward a definition of neural plasticity: Theoretical and practical limitations. In: F. Vital-Durand and M. Jeannerod (eds.), *Aspects of Neural Plasticity*. Paris: Editions INSERM, pp. 251–260.

Vygotsky, L. (1978). *Mind in Society: The Development of Higher Psychological Processes*. Cambridge, Mass.: Harvard University Press.

Waelder, R. (1936). The problem of the genesis of psychical conflict in earliest infancy. In: S. Guttman (ed.), *Psychoanalysis: Observation, Theory, Application*. New York: International Universities Press, 1976, pp. 121–188.

Wallerstein, R. (1988). One psychoanalysis or many? Internat. J. Psycho-Anal., 69:5–21.

———. (1994). The identity of psychoanalysis. Keynote address to the 38th winter meeting of the American Academy of Psychoanalysis, Santa Barbara, Calif.

Watts, A. (1975). Psychotherapy East and West. New York: Vintage Books.

Weiger, W., and Bear, D. (1988). An approach to the neurology of aggression. J. Psych. Res., 22:86–98.

Weinberger, D. (1988). Schizophrenia and the frontal lobes. Trends Neurosci., 11:367–370.

Weiner, H. (1970). The mind-body unity in the light of recent physiological evidence. Psychother. Psychosom., 18:117–122.

Weiss, P. (1959). Animal behavior as system reaction: Orientation toward light and gravity in the resting postures of butterflies (Vanessa). General Systems: Yearbook of the Society for General Systems Research. Vol. IV, pp. 19–44.

———. (1967). The role of systems theory in present-day science, technology and philosophy. In: K. Schaefer, H. Hensel, and R. Brady (eds.), Toward a Man-Centered Medical Science. Mt. Kisco, N.Y.: Futura, pp. 11–16.

———. (1969). The living system: determinism stratified. In: A. Koestler and J. Smythies (eds.), Beyond Reductionism. New York: Macmillan, pp. 3–55.

———. (1977). The system of nature and the nature of systems: Empirical wholism and practical reductionism harmonized. In: K. Schaefer, H. Hensel, and R. Brady (eds.), Toward a Man-Centered Medical Science. Mt. Kisco, N.Y.: Futura, pp. 17–64.

Werner, H. (1926). Comparative Psychology of Mental Development. New York: International Universities Press, 1940.

———. (1940). The concept of development from a comparative and organismic point of view. In: D. Harris (ed.), The Concept of Development. Minneapolis: University of Minnesota Press, pp. 125–147.

———. (1962). Introduction to H. Witkin, R. Dyk, H. Faterson, D. Goodenough, and S. Karp. Psychological Differentiation. New York: John Wiley and Son.

Whitam, F., Diamond, M., and Martin, J. (1993). Homosexual orientation in twins: a report on 61 pairs and three triplet sets. Arch. Sex Behav., 22:187–206.

Whitam, F., and Mathy, R. (1991). Childhood cross-gender behavior of homosexual females in Brazil, Peru, the Philippines, and the United States. Arch. Sex. Behav., 20:151–170.

Whitam, F., and Zent, M. (1984). A cross-cultural assessment of early cross-gender behavior and familiar factors in male homosexuality. Arch. Sex. Behav., 13:427–439.

Whitehead, A. (1967). Science and the Modern World. New York: Macmillan.

Whiting, J. (1959). Sorcery, sin, and the superego. In: C. Ford (ed.), Cross-Cultural Approaches. New Haven: HRAF Press, 1967.

Whiting, J., and Child, I. (1953). Child Training and Personality. New Haven: Yale University Press.

Wilbur, K. (1990). Eye to Eye: The Quest for a New Paradigm. Boston: Shambhala.

Willick, M. (1990). Psychoanalytic concepts of the etiology of severe mental illness. J. Am. Psychoanal. Assn., 38:1049–1081.

Wilson, K. (1983). The renormalization group and critical phenomena. *Review of Modern Physics*, 55:583–600.

Winnicott, D. W. (1951). Transitional objects and transitional phenomena. In: *Collected Papers*. London: Tavistock, 1958, pp. 229–242.

———. (1958). *Collected Papers*. London: Tavistock.

———. (1960). Ego development in terms of true and false self. In: *The Maturational Processes and the Facilitating Environment*. New York: International Universities Press (1965), pp. 140–152.

———. (1971). *Playing and Reality*. London: Tavistock.

Witelson, S. (1976). Sex and the single hemisphere: Right hemisphere specialization for spatial processing. *Science*, 193:425–427.

Witkin, H., and Berry, J. (1975). Psychological differentiation in cross-cultural perspective. *J. Cross-Cultural Psychology*, 6:4–87.

Witkin, H., and Goodenough, D. (1976). Field dependence revisited. *ETS Research Bull.*, 76–39.

Witkin, H., Dyk, R., Faterson, H., Goodenough D., and Karp, S. (1962). *Psychological Differentiation*. New York: John Wiley and Son.

Witryol, S., and Kaess, W. (1957). Sex differences in social memory tasks. *J. Abnormal Social Psychology*, 54:343–346.

Wittgenstein, L. (1980). *Culture and Value*. P. Winch (trans.). G. Von Wright (ed.). Chicago: University of Chicago Press.

Wolff, P. (1960). The developmental psychologies of Jean Piaget and psychoanalysis. *Psychol. Issues*, Mgr. 5. New York: International Universities Press.

Wu, J. (1992). Masochism and fear of success in Asian women: Psychoanalytic mechanisms and problems in therapy. *Am. J. Psychoanal.*, 52:1–12.

Wundt, W. (1916). *Elements of Folk Psychology: Outlines of a Psychological History of the Development of Mankind*. E. Schaub (trans.). London: George Allen and Unwin.

Zubin, J., and Spring, B. (1977). Vulnerability: A new view of schizophrenia. *J. Abnorm. Psychol.*, 86:103–126.

Index